Into the Storm

For Jake,
with all the hope
that tomorrow brings

and

In Memoriam

Capt. James K. Thorp, USMC
Louisville, Ky.
3 February 1990

Sgt. Aaron Pack, USMC
Phoenix, Ariz.
23 February 1990

Semper Fi, Marines

Into the Storm

A U.S. Marine in the Persian Gulf War

by PHILLIP THOMPSON

McFarland & Company, Inc., Publishers
Jefferson, North Carolina, and London

Acknowledgments: Of the dozens of Marines who deserve thanks for making this book happen, first and foremost is Neal Noem, who has served, outstandingly so, as an enlisted Marine, warrant officer and commissioned officer. Neal's leadership and friendship are beyond question. Without him, I wouldn't have made it, and my memory would be even more faulty than it already is. Thanks also to Jeff Speights, who has been there since the beginning, from Twin Towers to the Kuwaiti border, and everywhere in between. He has been like a brother to me, both in and out of the Marine Corps. Lt. Col. Rob Rivers went to bat for me when few others would. A special thanks to him. And finally, special thanks to those Marines of the "Jump FDC" of 1st Battalion, 12th Marines, the original Earthpigs. This book is about them, because of them, and, ultimately, for them.

The author gratefully acknowledges the following people for allowing the use of their names in this book: Bobby Adair (for Aaron Pack), Michael Almanza, Quint Avenetti, Holly Connor, Richard Haddad, Michael Jeffcoat, Pete McCarthy, Joe Molofsky, Steve Morgan, Lynn Nesbit, Neal Noem, Grady Pennell, Rob Rivers, Kyle Schneider, Jeff Speights, William Thorp (for Jim Thorp), and Michael Vontungeln. In some instances pseudonyms have been used to protect the privacy of individuals. Pseudonyms are designated as such where they first appear in text.

Library of Congress Cataloguing-in-Publication Data

Thompson, Phillip.
    Into the storm: A U.S. Marine in the Persian Gulf War / by Phillip Thompson.
        p.   cm.
    Includes index.
    ISBN 0-7864-1013-2 (softcover : 50# alkaline paper) ∞
    1. Thompson, Phillip, 1962– . 2. Operation Desert Shield, 1990–1991 — Personal narratives, American. 3. Persian Gulf War, 1991 — Personal narratives, American. I. Title.
DS79.74 Txx   2001
959.7044'24 — dc21   2001031274

British Library cataloguing data are available

Manufactured in the United States of America

On the cover: A gutted T-62 Iraqui tank destroyed by Marines with a burning oil well in the background *(Capt. Neal Noem, USMC)*

McFarland & Company, Inc., Publishers
  Box 611, Jefferson, North Carolina 28640
    www.mcfarlandpub.com

· C O N T E N T S ·

Acknowledgments   iv

List of Abbreviations   vi

   Introduction   1

Book I: Operation Desert Shield   7

   Part One: Settling In   9

   Part Two: Gearing Up   75

Book II: Operation Desert Storm   119

   Part One: Air War   121

   Part Two: Ground War   157

   Epilogue   184

Military History of Phillip Thompson   187

Index   189

· A B B R E V I A T I O N S ·

AAFES: Army/Air Force Exchange System

AAV: Amphibious assault vehicle

ACR: Armored cavalry regiment

AFRTS: Armed Forces Radio & Television Service

Amtrack: Amphibious assault vehicle

ANGLICO: Air-Naval Gunfire Liaison Company

AO: Area of operations

AOA: Avenue of Approach

APC: Armored personnel carrier

ARCENT: Army Central Command

BCT: Battlefield computer terminal

BDA: Bomb damage assessment

BMP: Soviet-made infantry fighting vehicle

Bn: Battalion

Btry: Battery

CAS: Close-air support

CBR: Counterbattery radar

CG: Commanding general

CINCCENT: Commander in Chief, U.S. Central Command

CMC: Commandant of the Marine Corps

CO: Commanding officer

COC: Combat Operations Center, sometimes called "Center of Confusion"

CP: Command post

CPX: Command post exercise

Div: Division

DF: Direction-Finding Apparatus

DMZ: Demilitarized zone

DPICM: Dual-Purpose Improved Conventional Munitions, the artillery version of a cluster bomb.

EA: Engagement area, the area, usually a terrain feature, in which an enemy formation is taken under fire.

FDC: Fire direction center

FDO: Fire direction officer, sometimes called "Fido"

FFG: Naval designation for guided-missile frigates

FIRECAP: Fire capable; denotes an artillery battery or battalion which is fully capable of firing a mission

FIREX: Firing exercise

vi

FLB: Forward Logistics Base

FO: Forward observer

Frag O: Fragmentary order, an abbreviated version of an operations order (see "op order")

FROG: Free Rocket, Over Ground

FSCC: Fire support coordination center

FSCL: Fire support coordination line

FSSG Force Service Support Group

Fwd: Forward

gun line: An artillery battery's howitzers when emplaced in tactical position, usually in a staggered line.

HARM: High-speed antiradiation missile

HE: High explosive, a type of artillery round

Helo: Helicopter

HMM: Designation for Marine Medium Helicopter Squadron, i.e., HMM-161

HMMWV High-Mobility, Multi-Wheeled Vehicle, also known as a humvee or "hummer."

Intel: Intelligence, as in military intelligence

KIA Killed in action

LAI Light Armored Infantry (now termed Light Armored Reconnaissance)

LAV: Light armored vehicle

LZ: Landing zone

MAGTF: Marine Air-Ground Task Force; pronounced "MAG-taff"

Mar: Marines; refers to a Marine regiment, i.e., "3rd Mar."

MARCENT: Marine Central Command

MARDET: Marine detachment

MARDIV: Marine division

MEB: Marine Expeditionary Brigade

Mech: Mechanized, as in mechanized brigade

Medevac: Medical evacuation

MEF: Marine Expeditionary Force

MIA: Missing in action

MOPP: Mission-oriented protective posture, of which there are four levels as means of chemical-biological defense.

MPF: Maritime Prepositioning Force

MRE: Meal, ready-to-eat; also known as "Meals Rarely Eaten"

MRL: Multiple rocket launcher

Msn: Mission, as in fire mission

MSR: Main supply route

MVV: Muzzle velocity variance, an element of determining a howitzer's accuracy

NBC: Nuclear, biological, chemical report

NGFS: Naval gunfire support

NLT: No later than

op: operation

OP: Observation post

op order: Operations order, a lengthy document describing a unit's plan of attack or defense.

OPP: Offload Preparation Party

POL: Petroleum, oil, and lubricants

PTA: Pohakaloa Training Area, a firing range on the Big Island of Hawaii.

PX: Post exchange

RAP: Rocket-assisted projectile. RAP increases the range of the M198 155mm howitzer from 14.7 kilometers to 30 kilometers.

Regt.: Regiment

REMF: Rear echelon motherfucker

RGFC: Iraq's elite troops, the Republican Guards

ROE: Rules of Engagement
RPV: Remotely piloted vehicle
RSOP: Reconnaissance, selection
            and occupation of posi-
            tion; a method by which
            artillery units select posi-
            tions for the emplacement
            of howitzers.
S-1:   Administration
            Office/Adjutant
S-2:   Intelligence Officer
S-3:   Operations Officer
S-4:   Logistics Officer
SANG: Saudi Arabian National
            Guard
SIMCAS: Simulated close-air sup-
            port
SNCO: Staff Noncommissioned
            Officer
Stress ex: Stress exercise; derisive
            term for an event that
            causes a high level of

stress among the planners
and/or the participants
TAOR: Tactical area of responsi-
            bility
TEWT: Tactical exercise without
            troops
TF: Task force
TOT: Time on target, a sched-
            uled artillery fire mission
TOW: Tube-launched, optically
            tracked, wire-guided;
            anti-tank missile
WIA: Wounded in action
WM: Woman Marine
WO: Warrant officer
WP: White phosphorous, a type
            of incendiary artillery
            round. Also called "Willy
            Peter."
XO: Executive officer, the sec-
            ond-in-command

· INTRODUCTION ·

In the spring of 1990, I could not have been happier with my life.

At twenty-eight, I was a newly promoted Marine Corps captain. I was in outstanding physical condition and at the threshold of a professional military career. I had just completed the Army's Artillery Officers' Advanced Course at Fort Sill, Oklahoma, and had secured the orders of my dreams—an assignment with an artillery battalion in Hawaii.

I had received my commission in 1984 upon graduation from the University of Mississippi, known in the South as "Ole Miss." Following The Basic School, the Marine Corps version of a finishing school for lieutenants, I attended the Artillery Officers' Basic Course, also at Fort Sill.

After graduating from Fort Sill in May 1985, I reported to my first Fleet Marine Forces station, the Marine Corps Air Ground Combat Center MCAGCC at Twentynine Palms, California, a dusty, remote outpost in the Mojave Desert, three hours east of Los Angeles. The Combat Center, as it is known, is the largest Marine Corps base in the world, comprised of 932 square miles, most of which is live-fire impact area. It is the only base where Marines can maneuver while firing every weapon in their arsenal. Quite an impressive place to be for a twenty-two-year-old artillery officer. During that tour, I served as a forward observer with "G" Battery, 3rd Battalion, 12th Marines and eventually became the executive officer of "N" Battery, 5th Battalion, 12th Marines.

The mid and late 1980s were wonderful times for young officers. The Reagan Administration and the Cold War ensured an abundance of ammunition, equipment, money, and an "Evil Empire" for an enemy.

1

We trained incessantly in the desert, taking pride in our lean frames and leathery skin. The training hardened us and gave us confidence. Under the guidance of two battalion commanders, Lt. Cols. Leslie M. Palm and "Nick" Carlucci, we were allowed to push our men, our equipment and ourselves to the limit. We trained at night. We slept during the day. We fired our howitzers under the worst conditions and by every method taught at Fort Sill. We found ways to communicate when communication was impossible. Our units bonded, we loved our jobs, and I loved my men. In 1986, my battery—"N" 5/11—spent more than six and a half months in the field, more than any other battery in the battalion. We were the baddest of the bad, and we loved it.

Because the units at MCAGCC were part of the 7th Marine Amphibious Brigade (MAB)—later the 7th Marine Expeditionary Brigade (MEB)—we trained constantly for a possible "mount-out" to the Middle East. In those days, the obvious enemy was Iran, and we trained accordingly, preparing to fight a highly mobile mechanized enemy in mountainous desert terrain, an enemy armed with Soviet weapons and the skill to use them. I had no idea how valuable this experience would be a few years later.

Being young, and full of war stories from the Vietnam era, I longed for combat. Or at least my romanticized version of combat. The Cold War, however, was in full swing, which precluded the possibility of the 7th MAB being involved in full-scale land combat. We were a deterrent and we knew it—the down side of peacetime warrior training. We conducted so many exercises that we called ourselves "1st Marine Division's largest training aid."

In 1987, I received a set of orders that thrilled me. I was to report to the mighty dreadnought USS *Missouri* for duties as Marine Detachment Executive Officer. I could hardly contain my joy—both at leaving the desert and serving aboard the most famous battleship in the world. As fun as it was, two years in the rugged Mojave was enough for my wife Angie and me.

After a ten-week aerial observer's course at Marine Corps Air Station, New River, N.C., I reported aboard the "Mighty Mo" off the coast of Oman after a breakneck drive from the East Coast to Los Angeles, then to Tokyo, Manila, Diego Garcia, and finally Masirah, Oman, where I hopped aboard a Navy helicopter for a quick ride out to sea.

While I had been learning the intricacies of the OV-10 "Bronco" in North Carolina, the *Missouri* had been ordered from her homeport of Long Beach, California, to the Gulf of Oman in support of Operation Earnest Will, the escorting of reflagged Kuwaiti tankers through the Strait of Hormuz during the Iran-Iraq war in late 1987.

This was the first time I would have to deploy to the region on account of the Kuwaiti government.

During the six-month cruise, we waited tensely for an Iranian attack, which, fortunately, never came. However, it was the closest to combat I had been so far in my short career, and the experience was both exhilarating and frightening. Our job was to be the "big stick" and provide cover for the "small boys"—frigates and destroyers—doing the actual escorting. We spent many hours at General Quarters, straining our eyes in the dark toward the Iranian coast, looking for a boat attack that always seemed imminent but never came.

Professionally, sea duty was very satisfying. Personally, however, it took a toll on my marriage. Angie grew tired of the constant absences as I steamed to Hawaii, Canada, and Australia. When I wasn't overseas, I was at sea off the coast of California for days or weeks at a time. In port, I stood duty every six days.

After a two-year tour at Twentynine Palms in which I spent at least a year in the field, I spent almost a year and a half of my two-year sea duty tour away from home. In our four and a half years of marriage, I'd been gone for more than two. This strain compelled me to resign my commission and return to civilian life. But at the last minute, I had a change of heart and petitioned Headquarters Marine Corps to have my resignation rescinded. After many serious discussions with Angie, I realized that I still wanted to be around Marines doing Marine things.

So, in August 1989, less than three weeks after my being promoted to captain, Angie and I moved back to Fort Sill, this time for my attendance at the Artillery Officers' Advanced Course (OAC).

I loved it. The student officers were completely immersed in the technical art of artillery and warfare. We wrote countless operations orders, war-gamed numerous scenarios, briefed a platoon's worth of field-grade officers on our make-believe war plans, and generally inundated ourselves with all things military. We also blew off a lot of steam after hours and formed friendships that lasted for years.

On the home front, Angie and I rediscovered our marriage. For the first time since our wedding in December 1984, I came home every night for nearly six months. Although I studied for hours, plenty of time remained for us to go to movies, take day trips to Dallas, or go on hikes and bike rides at a nearby state park. This time would serve us well in a few months. Our enjoyment was interrupted only by two events: the invasion of Panama in late 1989, which, as a harbinger of things to come, we watched via satellite from our living room; and the collapse of the Berlin Wall. We watched these overwhelmingly emotional events, which I never expected to see in my lifetime, from our living room television.

We left Fort Sill in May 1990, overjoyed with my permanent change of station orders to Marine Corps Air Station, Kaneohe Bay, Hawaii, home of the 1st Marine Expeditionary Brigade. With these orders, I had managed to get myself assigned to the Corps' only standing brigades, the 1st and the 7th. After a long vacation and a leisurely trip to California, I reported to 1st Battalion, 12th Marines (Reinforced), the MEB's artillery battalion, in June.

I was assigned duties as the battalion operations officer, or the "S-3." Normally a senior captain or a major holds this billet, but the Marine Corps frequently must fill positions with whatever manpower is available. As I had been promoted to captain the previous August, the S-3 job was quite a task for me, the junior captain in the battalion. Luckily, I had the confidence and "book knowledge" gained at the Officers' Advanced Course. I threw myself into the job, enjoying the hectic pace, happy to be with artillery Marines again, and loving the beauty of Hawaii.

My assistant operations officer, or S-3A, was a first lieutenant who also served as the fire direction officer for the battalion. Jack Marshall [*pseudonym*] was extremely proficient at gunnery and brought me back up to speed. He and I also enjoyed discussions on global politics and current affairs in the office. Our lunch hours were often spent at the on-base beach, surfing on our "boogie boards" or playing volleyball on the court behind the battalion headquarters.

That summer, the battalion, based on the windward side of Oahu, flew to the Big Island's Pohakaloa Training Area, a large tract of lava flows and scrub brush nestled between the volcanic peaks of Mauna Loa and Mauna Kea. We planned to train there for a month. As the S-3, I arrived on the Big Island with the battalion's advance party in late July. We would not stay long.

On August 2, we received word about the Iraqi invasion of Kuwait. Our regimental commander, Col. John Admire, informed the commanders and staff officers of the invasion in a clapboard building in PTA's base camp. One look at his face told us that this was far more serious than we realized.

Sometime during the ensuing week, I began my journal.

I had kept a journal for years, from the time I was in college until I attended OAC, when the demands of school precluded daily journal writing. But the Iraqi invasion and our impending deployment reignited my desire to keep track of the events unfolding before me. As the months passed, I kept a small, green, military-issue notebook with me twenty-four hours a day. I wrote down everything I could, drew maps, and listed as much information as I had. I wanted to capture every scrap of information possible. I also used the journal to try to explain my emotions and, some-times, to vent my anger. The journal became my escape, my solace, my friend. When I returned home from Saudi Arabia in April 1991, I had filled three notebooks.

Angie and I read through several passages in an effort to explain and understand the previous months' events and how they had affected us. Eventually, I stowed the notebooks with the rest of my gear from that deployment, happy to put it aside.

Books about the Persian Gulf War are few, and most discuss the war from the strategic standpoint. As I saw these books appear and new dis-cussions about the war unfold, I realized there were few if any books that discussed the war from the standpoint of the "guy on the ground." I found this fact interesting — even more so when stories of sick Gulf veterans began to appear in the media. Not many Americans had heard from these men on the ground.

This book, then, is one man's perception of Desert Shield and Desert Storm. It is not intended to be a historical narrative of the war. Indeed, some of the information quoted here from my journals later turned out to be completely wrong. It was not my intent, however, to write a history of the war — that is the work of historians. My intent was to show the reader what I thought and felt at any particular moment, along with the people around me.

Troops in the field seldom receive the most accurate information. They live off rumors and garbled radio messages; they yearn for mail and treat it as gospel. While Americans at home saw the war live on television (if Vietnam was the first televised war, then Desert Storm was the Super Bowl of televised wars), most of us who fought the war knew nothing of truck-chasing Tomahawks or flak-dodging F/A-18s. All we knew was what we saw in front of us.

But although the American people thought they were seeing all of the war, actually they saw only what the media showed them — which was only what the military let them show. Lost among the four-stars and the daily briefs and the stealth fighters and Tomahawks and yellow ribbons were thousands of troops just trying to survive another day in a godforsaken wasteland.

The following pages are intended to give just one insight into that life. Some of the entries quoted from my journal are indicative of my emo-tions, which ranged from boredom to fear to outright rage. Sometimes I directed that anger towards people named in this book. I do not hold grudges, and that anger is forgotten.

Above all, this account is about a group of people who came to be very important to me. The men in the following stories aren't superheroes. They are as common, and as real, as any man in any neighborhood in America. The only thing that makes them special is the fact that they are all Marines. Most of the Marines in this book are enlisted men, kids really. But, like the countless thousands of Marines who went before them, these kids bore the weight of a nation on their shoulders and put in a good account of themselves. I have many memories of the Persian Gulf, many unpleasant. But my best memories revolve around the Marines I worked with day after day for nearly eight months. I'll never forget them.

Between the journal entries that appear in this book I have attempted to explain settings and contexts and to correct any erroneous information. But it is the entries themselves that show the war from an unvarnished, sometimes marred, but always immediate and honest point of view.

BOOK I

OPERATION DESERT SHIELD

Part One

Settling In

· C H A P T E R O N E ·
---

4 Aug 1990

Started writing again because this may be the biggest thing of my life. Correction, is. Last week we learned, while in the field at PTA, that Iraq invaded Kuwait. Iraq accused Kuwait of overproducing oil, driving prices down, thus "robbing" Iraq. They attacked with 8 divisions plus 2 brigades and an 800-tank column. The 20,000-man army of Kuwait stood no chance.

Currently, an Iraqi government is in place in Kuwait.

7 Aug 90

Our part is getting bigger. After Iraq conquered Kuwait, Saddam Hussein began massing his troops on the Saudi-Arabian border. Amid sweeping embargoes by virtually all of Europe—and even the USSR—Pres. Bush drew the line. The U.S. stand is that if Saudi Arabia is invaded, we will retaliate.

Since that statement, much has happened inside the military. Too much to really detail here, much still classified, but the bottom line is that 1st MEB is going. This morning, Col. Admire, 3rd Marine Regiment Commanding Officer, held an emergency meeting to fill us in.

As for me, I'm skeptical about us going, along with other emotions. I find it incredible that after all the posturing we've done for so many years in the face of what I consider more serious crises, we are suddenly ready to send an entire MEF.

The plan Col. Admire outlined calls for the 7th and 1st MEBs (MPE brigades) to form I MEF and land in Saudi Arabia. There, we would all marry up with the gear brought in on ships from Diego Garcia and Guam. But I'm skeptical. I don't think Hussein would fuck with the U.S. or the West. He has too much to lose.

Another scary factor is chemical weapons. Hussein has been gassing his own people for 10 years. And that scares the shit out of all of us. They use mustard, phosgene, and nerve gas. We can survive it, but that's just plain dirty pool. Right now, I've just finished listening to Lt. Col. Rivers (C.O., 1/12) brief the staff. He's convinced — more than I am — that we are going. He's authorized battery commanders to start planning to go back to Kaneohe. So far, it looks like we go back to Oahu early.

I haven't even called Angie about this. I don't want to lie to her and I can't tell her anything.

Wed., 8 Aug 90

Much confusion, rumors rampant, not enough time to get ready.

We have to redeploy from PTA *to K'Bay by Fri. a.m. I'm working as hard as I can to run the battalion's training and reorganize the redeployment. It's a madhouse. We got word today to get to Kaneohe today.*

Iraq is moving chemical arty rounds to the front, uploading chem on planes, massing troops, etc. Looks like a preinvasion move.

Also, the 82nd Airborne dropped a brigade into Saudi Arabia today. The Egyptians are sending armored units; the Germans are dropping paratroopers; 2 naval battle groups are moving (Independence and Wisconsin). The 82nd is light and can't last long. They are there presumably to prep a port for our arrival. The "C-Day," or the day the operation commences, was 2 days ago. C+17 is supposed to be the day we hit the beach, which is 23 Aug. However, Lt. Col. Rivers said today that we would be in Saudi Arabia by 15 Aug.

Right now we are trying to get rid of ammo, figure out what is on the MPF *ships, what we have to take, etc. Everybody's excited to the point of being fucking stupid. Three years ago I was a lot closer to combat than this on the* Missouri. *This is the easy part. Lieutenants and troops are being idiotic — luckily it's only from overexcitement and not incompetence.*

In today's post–Cold War superpower vacuum and crisis-response mentality, it's hard to imagine the time, only a few years ago, when the U.S. military trained for one major threat — a showdown with the Soviet Union.

The 1980s, in which I spent half my Marine Corps time, were great for training, but they certainly were not the good old days. The nuclear tension between the United States and the Soviet Union was real, and it was frightening. But that superpower Mexican standoff did offer a certain, if perverted, comfort zone — the balance of power kept a lid on many of the world's flash points and petty tyrants. Unlike the 1990s, in which the Corps was flung across the globe to Haiti, Sierra Leone, Somalia, Liberia, and Bosnia — none of which had any direct impact on the national security of the United States—the Corps of the '80s did its scheduled deployments and training exercises without worrying about a midnight "911" call that would have them waking up ten thousand miles away in a country most Marines couldn't pronounce, much less find on a map.

Until August 1990.

Sure, we trained for such an eventuality, but now we were suddenly doing it for real, and against an adversary few of us had ever heard of. Once we got our men and equipment off the Big Island and back to Oahu, we saw just how difficult our task was. Kaneohe Marine Corps Air Station was a scene of bedlam. My own operations shop alternated between pandemonium and chaos as we struggled to get equipment, clothing, ammunition, and last-minute training for the battalion. The "word" came down from brigade and regimental headquarters several times a day; orders were issued, and then countermanded. By mid-August, 1/12 had launched its Offload Preparation Party—the OPP, an advance party designed to fly to Saudi Arabia and prepare for our arrival—only to have it turned back.

In the midst of the frustration, there were moments of hilarity, if only from that dark sense of humor for which Marines are famous. The threat of chemical warfare sent units into a sort of "Gas Mask Frenzy" as they donned protective gear in an attempt to become "acclimatized." Seeing a gas mask–wearing Marine pedaling a bicycle in to work, puffing all the way through the restrictive air filters, became a common, and humorous, occurrence. I lost track of how many times I saw a Marine in a gas mask clomping down the street wheezing in the tropical humidity.

Already working up to seventeen hours a day, I worked most of the first weekend back on Oahu to develop a training schedule for the battalion—rifle ranges; desert briefings; nuclear, biological, and chemical warfare classes; spouse's briefings, and dozens more events. And, amazingly, the threat of war caused the typical military bureaucracy to crumble like the walls of Jericho. I couldn't believe my good fortune as nearly every training request was approved in record time. Only a month earlier, I swam through a sea of red tape just to complete the most mundane of tasks. Now, nearly everything I asked was approved before my startled eyes.

Of course, that caused its own problems. Battery commanders, eager to train their men, sometimes circumvented the operations shop and scheduled their own training, which caused a fair amount of duplication.

For example, I might have scheduled "A" Battery for the rifle range on Monday morning without knowing that the "A" Battery commander also had scheduled the range for Monday afternoon. Snafus such as these only added to our growing anxiety and frustration. By August 14, we had received a "window" of opportunity for our flight to Saudi Arabia via chartered 747: August 25–27. That date changed so many times that I began to think we would never leave.

A week after our return to Oahu, Capt. Richard Matthews [*pseudonym*] reported to the battalion. By virtue of his seniority, he was named operations officer for the battalion, while I was relegated to the training officer role, a move I didn't initially resent, given the circumstances and my inexperience.

While we played "hurry up and wait" in Hawaii, stories began to trickle back from the Saudi port of Al-Jubayl, and they were not comforting. The chaos being reported there reminded me of accounts I had read of Korea in 1950. Our enthusiasm began to wane.

We also took our first casualty, or at least a casualty of sorts. Our battalion chaplain, a Navy lieutenant, struggled for days with his moral convictions, his fear, and his self-confidence, as he contemplated what we all thought would be a Dante's inferno of chemical warfare and bloody fighting. Ultimately, he asked for reassignment and was transferred to Pearl Harbor.

The loss of the chaplain was particularly difficult for me. He and I had served together just two years earlier, aboard the *Missouri*, where we had become good friends, the Irish Catholic priest and the Scot-Irish Protestant. He'd even shanghaied me on St. Patrick's Day, 1988, while we were on liberty in Vancouver, Canada. He dragged me to an Irish bar, where suddenly I became Phillip McThompson.

But now he, like the rest of us, faced the most ominous journey of his life. We had several conversations in his cramped, humid office in the battalion headquarters. He marveled at the spirit of the Marines around him and their ability to be so enthusiastic to face what he was convinced was a sure death. I tried to explain to him that we weren't necessarily thrilled with the prospect of being drenched in Saddam's chemicals, but that this deployment, this throwing down of the gauntlet, was something we had all trained for. It was the ultimate challenge, in the macho world of the Marine Corps, and we were eager to prove ourselves up to the challenge. Arrogant in my ignorance, I had no idea just how much of a challenge to my "macho" world this expedition would be.

By the last week of August, the operations shop had done all it could do and passed the reins of the battalion to the S-4 shop — the logisticians. They took on the unenviable task of physically moving a battalion of artillery halfway around the world. Added to the S-4 shop's already difficult task was the fact that our frustration had reached a crescendo. Our fly-out date had been changed so many times that we didn't believe in any date anymore, and I noticed that there was little mention of the Hawaii brigade on CNN's nearly continuous coverage of the deployment. Most of the coverage was devoted to the Army's 82nd Airborne, already in-country, and the 24th Mechanized Division, which clawed its way aboard shipping in Savannah, Georgia. In California, the 7th Marine Expeditionary Brigade — my old Twentynine Palms unit — loaded its desert camouflage-painted equipment and began moving troops to Saudi Arabia.

We began to feel like a sideshow, a feeling that would return again and again.

Wed., 29 Aug 90

I'm on my way to Saudi Arabia, somewhere over the Indian Ocean, aboard a C-5A. Got the word Monday morning (actually it was yesterday, but we've crossed the International Dateline) that I would fly at 1930 with the advance party. So I went from not knowing when — or if — I would go to leaping through my ass to get ready on a few hours' notice.

Angie took it well, all things considered. We had the afternoon together, and it was idyllic. Already I feel the pain of having left her behind. And I think it's more intense, and deeper, than 3 years ago. The last 12 months have been good to us. We have had a lot of time together — well-spent time. We've recovered our marriage and even grown much, much closer. So, we parted with that optimistic note in mind. Still, I feel as if a part of my soul has been ripped away.

Even after anticipating my departure for nearly a month, getting the word to leave was like a blow to the chest. I had driven into work and, over coffee, Lt. Col. Rivers informed me that I'd be leaving for Saudi Arabia with the advance party that evening.

I went home right away and told Angie, who had resigned herself to the fact that her husband was about to go to the Persian Gulf for the second time in less than three years. We spent a very subdued, almost surreal, afternoon together, trying to focus on each other and not the seabags that stood by the door.

We didn't talk much that afternoon, mainly because neither of us wanted to say out loud what was on our minds: unlike any other deployment I'd ever made, this time I was going to war, and the possibility of not coming home was very real. It was an unspoken fear, one just below the surface of our relationship. It was a fear that had shown itself from time to time during the weeks of August, but because we didn't really know how to deal with it, we stifled it and concentrated on each other.

And even though we'd been through this before, it wasn't any easier the second time around. We had finally salvaged and strengthened a marriage that had been terribly eroded by too many absences. We had grown closer during my stint at Fort Sill, and had found a deep well of joy in our relationship. We had come to Hawaii only a few weeks earlier with high hopes, a renewed romance, and a sense of adventure. And now all that was being put on hold before we could even enjoy it.

Late in the afternoon of August 29, Angie drove me to the battalion's staging area, a parade deck near the 3rd Marines headquarters building. The Marines I would join on the long flight sat under a metal awning, their gear piled high behind a set of aluminum bleachers.

Angie and I talked for a few minutes, but not about anything in particular. Then we held each other for a long, sad moment before I hoisted my seabag and joined the rest of the Marines. My last image of my wife was of her standing quietly — and alone — as tears coursed down her face. I made a silent vow that I would never put her through this kind of pain again.

· C H A P T E R   T W O   ·

My first stop on the way to war was the other side of Oahu.

The runway at Kaneohe was not long enough to accommodate the massive C-5 cargo plane loaded with equipment and troops. The crew had to sacrifice fuel for lower weight to get airborne. So rather than have us transported by bus to Hickam Air Force Base near Honolulu — which would have allowed us a little more time with our families — we waited hours for a plane, only to climb off the bird ten minutes later and wait in the Hickam terminal for additional hours while the plane's fuel tanks were topped off.

We left at 0200 for U-Tapao, Thailand, an airport near Bangkok. We arrived early on a steamy morning to a hospitable group of Thais who provided us with coffee, water, Cokes, and sandwiches at rows of tables on the tarmac near a huge open hangar. They had even set up a television set on one of the tables, and we passed the time watching a Madonna concert and munching sandwiches in the already sweltering Asian heat.

I stretched my legs and had a cup of coffee with Marshall and Joe Molofsky, an infantry captain I'd met on the flight. We noticed an English-language newspaper carrying a front-page headline denying that U-Tapao was being used as a staging area for U.S. forces en route to the Persian Gulf. Amused, we took turns having our pictures made holding the paper.

Americans used the U-Tapao base during the Vietnam War, and it still had the look and feel of an Air America hangout, with its rusted barbed-wire fence along portions of the perimeter and ancient commercial

Top: Marines enjoy a chance to stretch their legs in U-Tapao, Thailand, en route to the Persian Gulf. The Thai government denied the fact that Americans were using the base as a stopover for the Gulf. At center, Capt. Joe Molofsky, facing camera, relaxes with other Marines. *Bottom:* The runway at U-Tapao, Thailand, our first introduction to the type of heat that awaited us in Saudi Arabia.

airplanes scattered across the apron. The newspaper denials only added to the clandestine feel about the place.

After a couple of hours, we climbed back into the stratosphere, jammed our yellow-foam earplugs in our already itchy ears, and resumed the brain-numbing monotony of flying in a military aircraft. The boredom ebbed only when we refueled in flight, a bumpy, nauseating affair that turned at least one Marine green.

I tried to imagine the port city of Al-Jubayl as we flew, and pictured a huge gaggle of people and utter chaos. We had been told that we'd spend some time in a "cantonment" area, a fancy word for "tent city." We'd already heard that most units were clustered around Al-Jubayl in tents, rather than in tactical defensive positions. I'd soon find out that that assessment was only half right.

Before leaving Hawaii, I'd learned that Saddam had "shielded" himself with Americans and westerners by placing them in likely target cities, evoking a "hostage crisis" syndrome in the U.S. media. But, as he would do many times throughout the months ahead, President George Bush was able to keep the American public focused on the goal: getting the Iraqi Army out of Kuwait.

Wed., 30 Aug 90, Al-Jubayl, Saudi Arabia

Arrived in-country last night at the port of Al-Jubayl. Strangely enough, there was a minimum of jerking around. We were driven from the airport to the port and billeted immediately in a large warehouse on the pier adjacent to our MPF ships. Got my cot, took a quick shower and hit the rack.

Jet lag caused me to wake up at 0430. Hot chow was brought in at 0700, and after I ate I hooked up with Joe Molofsky and Pete McCarthy, both of Regt S-3. We got a vehicle and did some recon south and north of here.

This is a fascinating place. Arabs in traditional dress and headgear, camels, and an unbelievably BARREN landscape. And it's HOT. Strangely, though, it's also very humid, here especially, as we are on the coast. Today 113 degrees/50% humidity. Drank water all day. We have bottled water here, and I drank at least five 1.5-liter bottles today. The heat and humidity don't bother me — Mississippi is good training — but what does is the rapid dehydration of the body. You have to constantly replenish.

It's a strange feeling driving through a foreign country's city streets with a weapon strapped to you. The Arabs (Saudis) we've seen so far have all been friendly — unlike the raghead terrorist image our media projects. Still, I wonder if we are considered the invaders or the protectors.

As serious as this is, there's a lot of bullshit. There is an extremely high terrorist threat, yet security, as in Beirut in '83, is a joke. The Rules of Engagement (ROE) are verbose and ambiguous, a lack of balls from the top down. We did manage to draw small-arms ammo today, though.

The first thing most people recall about Saudi Arabia is the heat.

Stepping off the C-5 in Jubayl was an experience similar to opening an oven door. A blast of searing evening heat slammed into us as we descended the ladder to the scorching runway. It was almost as if this heat was a living organism. You didn't just feel the Saudi heat; it assaulted you, as if it were invading your nose and mouth to scorch your lungs. Indeed, some days were so hot it was difficult to breathe.

We were greeted, not by the hordes of supply pogues I'd anticipated, but by a lone lance corporal in desert utilities and a mangled desert cover, a "bush hat." As we piled off the plane and staggered in the late-afternoon heat, blinking like moles and shielding our eyes from the brilliant orange glow of the Middle East sun, the Marine barked out orders to us, making it clear that this was his runway and he didn't give a tinker's damn about rank.

I was fascinated with this Marine. The entire Marine Corps was in near panic and scrambling to deploy to potentially the biggest war since Vietnam. Hundreds of troops, scores of aircraft, and tons of equipment were passing through this airport daily. Yet we were not met by some space-age, computer-wielding platoon of logisticians. Instead, a single scruffy Marine had, apparently, taken charge of this airport armed with only a clipboard and a loud voice. It's possible that he was the only person in the country who knew what the hell was going on.

As he hurried us along, we scooped up our gear and headed for the terminal, where, for the first time in my entire Marine Corps career, I didn't wait long for transportation.

We rode on a school bus—complete with wire mesh over the windows for protection against rockets, grenades, or other such missiles—to the port of Jubayl. It was a modern port with seemingly endless piers, cranes, and the usual debris found in a crowded port. The place looked like a kicked-over anthill. Men and equipment teemed. We rode past a row of enormous warehouses, which would serve as our quarters. I caught glimpses of the huge Maritime Prepositioning Force ships through the vast, open interiors of the warehouses, some of which were already filling up with Marines, cots and gear.

Already, working parties were disgorging the equipment of war from the mammoth ships. For years, I'd heard about these vessels—and even seen them swing at anchor at Diego Garcia in the Indian Ocean in 1987. Now, through jet-lagged eyes, I saw the MPF fleet fulfill its purpose of providing combat equipment to a brigade of Marines in a far-off port.

The idea was to sail the gear in and fly the troops in, and it seemed to be working. Each squadron of ships was designed to fully equip a Marine

Expeditionary Brigade for combat, with the exception of small arms. How-itzers, light armored vehicles, humvees, trucks, and the like were crammed into the holds and "preserved," or protected from the elements. Occasionally, a civilian crew would unload the equipment, check the seals and gaskets, give everything a test drive, then reload the ships. Now, Marines were doing that, minus reloading the ships. This equipment was coming off the ships for good — or at least until the end of the war, a time we couldn't even comprehend.

Somewhere along the line, someone shoved a liter bottle of water into my hand, thus starting a habit that would continue for most of the next eight months.

A person could dehydrate in his sleep in that heat, especially with the incredible humidity along the coast. I quickly got in the habit of keeping a bottle of water in my hand at all times. As soon as I finished one, I opened another. To this day, if I open a bottle of water, I gulp it down in nearly one drink.

We learned quickly that drinking 130-degree water from a plastic bottle is practically impossible, so foul is the taste. To keep the water somewhat cool, we soaked a cotton rag, pilfered from a first-aid kit, wrapped it around the plastic bottle, and held it in place with a boot lace or one of the elastic boot bands Marines use to "blouse" their trouser cuffs. The evaporation of the water from the rag sufficiently cooled the water for drinking. We also spiked the water with "bug juice" from our MREs — the powdered drink mixes. Any flavor was better than none, even MRE flavoring. In time, Marines would write home begging for powdered Gatorade to add to the water.

The "strange feeling" of being in Saudi Arabia and wearing a weapon would soon pass, but it was something of a shock the first few days, especially as I rode through the city in a humvee, stopping at traffic lights between Jaguars and Mercedes-Benzes. On those forays into town — my only contact with the Saudi people during the entire deployment — I noticed kids flashing the two-finger "V" sign, what Americans know as the "V for Victory" sign or a peace sign, depending on their generation. I took it to mean the former, and I returned the gesture every time I saw a smiling child — until someone explained to me that what the kids really were doing was showing their support of the Palestinian intifada, the uprising against Israel. Palestinians in the West Bank used the same symbol as a sign of unity. There was a significant Palestinian population in Saudi Arabia and Kuwait. It dampened my enthusiasm for the children.

Rules of Engagement, or ROE, are designed, supposedly, to allow a Marine to fire his weapon to defend himself while minimizing "collateral

damage" to noncombatants. In other words, ROE make sure the right people get shot in situations short of all-out combat. In practice, however,
ROE usually do exactly the opposite. Rather than make it crystal clear when
and whom a Marine can shoot, the ROE, usually written by senior staff
officers, are often wordy and confusing. This confusion can result in
Marines being so unsure as to when they can fire that they don't fire at all,
even when their lives are threatened. I, along with several other company-
grade officers, groused about the ROE every time someone mentioned them.
I still consider it a minor miracle no one got killed.

Almost as soon as I hit the ground, I heard dozens of theories of what
Saddam might do. Most of these rumors spun circles around whatever
group of Marines happened to be discussing them: Saddam will attack us,
we will attack him, no one will attack, etc. There was even what some,
myself included, derisively called the "Howling at the Moon Theory." That
supposition revolved around the dates of September 2–5. According to his
past war record, Saddam moved his assault waves into position under a
full moon, then attacked at dawn. Our next full-moon dates were September 2–5. Most worrisome about that theory, no matter how ridiculous
it may have seemed, was the fact that the U.S. defensive posture in those
very early days of Desert Shield was not what the media would have their
audiences believe.

My plane brought in the remainder of the 3rd Marine Regiment's
staff. Since the only way a staff can measure its progress is in the frequency
and length of its meetings, a staff meeting schedule was immediately and
ruthlessly enforced — every day at 1800.

Mon., 3 Sept 90

Saw Bill Sanders, [pseudonym] formerly of 5/11 w/me, yesterday. He
is now with 3/11 and in the field. They have taken up defensive positions, but have not done any type of RSOP. No alternate or supple-
mentary positions. Disturbing. Guess they plan to die in place. Was
in the desert all day yesterday with 11th Mar Survey, looking for survey control points and testing trafficability. It's wide-open tank country to the west of the USMC sector. 24th ID will be there, when they
get there. The 101st is here, best news about that is they have tank-
killing Apache helos.

Other than that, and a few brigades of Saudi Arabian National
Guard (SANG), the only thing facing the Iraqi border is one regiment
of USMC infantry (7th), one battalion of USMC LAI, and one battalion
of USMC artillery (3/11). For all the ballyhoo in the U.S. about the
number of forces we have here, hardly any are combat troops, and
less are in the field. There is a disgusting amount of REMFs, staff, and
generals here.

Saddam has been doing things that are indicators of pre-offensive ops. Moving arty forward, repositioning units, overflights, etc. That, coupled with the fact that we're within easy range of his Scud missiles, is not a nice thought.

The second—and far more unsettling—note is that we were informed 2 nights ago that there has been possible surveillance by terrorist groups of the MEB CP (located on the pier where, incidentally, thousands of marines sleep packed in warehouses, myself included) and that there is an extremely good chance of a terrorist attack "in the next 48 hours." That period has almost elapsed, but nobody is relaxing. Guess the memory of Beirut is still fresh. Hope so. Security around the pier has been really beefed up—real security, not cosmetic. Entrances to the warehouses have been blocked and are guarded by armed sentries. All weapons are loaded—mine has been since issued ammo on the 29th. It's still too easy for an Arab to get on this base, though. We can't tell one from the other. That really worries me.

This is going to be a long expedition, I can feel it. And I think it will involve a lot of sitting on our asses in meetings. Go to 2 nightly, 3rd Mar at 1800, 11th Mar at 2000.

11th Mar takes control of 1/12 on 6 September. Their meetings aren't bad—calm and orderly. Mainly run by S-3, Lt. Col. Stuart, who, I assume, is acting XO. Col. Howard, C.O., is soft-spoken, courtly, and I imagine iron-willed.

Capt. Bill Sanders and I had served as lieutenants in "N" Battery, 5th Battalion, 11th Marines, in 1986. We'd also been classmates at The Basic School in Quantico, Virginia, in 1984.

At the time, he was the battery's fire direction officer—in charge of computing firing data for the howitzers—and I was the battery XO. We were a classic study in opposites, he a northerner from Rochester, New York, and I a southerner from Columbus, Mississippi. But we had similar temperaments. We were both outspoken, gregarious and, at times, hotheaded. Our clashes were many, so much so that we actually left Twentynine Palms without ever really becoming very close. We crossed paths again at the Officers Advanced Course at Fort Sill. Like me, Bill came to Oklahoma after a two-year sea-duty tour, aboard the aircraft carrier USS *Constellation*.

By that time, both of us had matured, and, over drinks at a Marine mess night—a formal dinner party of officers—we put our differences aside for good.

When I saw Bill in the field, I was shocked. He was obviously uncomfortable in his exposed position, a bald patch of blistering sand north of Jubayl and just a few hundred meters off the ribbon of highway that traced the north-south coastline. When I questioned him about it, he shrugged philosophically, as if to say, "What can you do?"

One of the most common misconceptions about Desert Shield is that the United States had a considerable force in the field immediately. A great deal of air time was given to the 82nd Airborne, which was scattered across the northern desert, and the 24th Infantry Division (Mechanized), most of which was still in Georgia. Perhaps this was good old military sleight of hand, misinforming the media to keep the enemy from knowing our real dispositions. But whatever the cause, the reality is that there were very few combat troops in the field at the time. I was shocked to learn that only the advance party of the 24th Infantry Division was in-country in early September.

In the three weeks before I left Hawaii, I had seen countless CNN reports from Fort Stewart, Georgia. Footage of long lines of vehicles being loaded aboard ships dominated the news, along with reports from Jubayl that the division was already up and running.

This is simply not true, although it wasn't the Army's fault. Moving an entire mechanized division from one continent to another is a Herculean task to say the least, especially when it involves a division not necessarily designed to deploy on short notice.

Marine divisions, by their very nature and organization, are more expeditionary, and we were having enough problems of our own. 1st MEB's gear wasn't completely off-loaded and the main body hadn't even left Hawaii. Much of 7th MEB was ashore, but by no means all of the brigade. The American defense consisted primarily of the 7th MEB's 7th Marine Regiment and a light brigade of the 82nd Airborne. I heard a report that one battalion of Marines had been trucked far to the north to straddle the coastal highway that ran from Kuwait City to Jubayl. Supposedly, this battalion had been given a "die in place" mission to defend the road at all costs. I thought the mission ridiculous, considering the battalion potentially faced several armored or mechanized divisions of Iraqi troops. But, at the time, there were few alternatives for the nascent MEF being organized in Jubayl.

I could only imagine the chaos of the 24th Division's deployment. If Saddam had had the wherewithal to attack then, it would have put us in the hurt locker.

The REMFs were always a favorite target for the men in the field. Rear Echelon Motherfuckers. The guys who hung out back in the rear in luxury, living like fat cats with all the amenities they could find while the real trigger-pullers, the warriors, suffered in misery. It's a fairly general, and relative, term. A REMF is usually anybody behind you, regardless of distance.

In Jubayl, the REMFs were very easy to spot. They wore desert utilities, while the combat troops wore stateside green cammies. That's because the REMFs know how to wheedle the supply system, we complained. Also, they were always freshly showered and well-rested, because they were usually billeted in a concrete, air-conditioned building with showers and real toilets, while we were sentenced to the huge, humid warehouses—the "Swelterdomes" as I called them —with porta-potties. A shower was a nozzle over a wooden pallet, a tepid dousing of water after standing in line for nearly half an hour.

The 11th Marines staff was ensconced in an air-conditioned migrant workers' camp a few miles away and carried on the business of a regimental staff, which consisted of, as far as I could tell, holding meetings and griping about the ice machines, which weren't working properly. The only units I knew to be in the field were Bill Sanders' 3rd Battalion, 11th Marines, and a battalion of light armored infantry, or LAI. Several Marine task forces—tank/infantry mixtures—were forming up and heading to the desert north of Jubayl as well.

When I wasn't traveling from the pier to 11th Marines or doing reconnaissance in the field, I was picking my way through the rat maze of vehicles pouring out of the cargo ships. I'd never seen so many vehicles. What seemed to be a never-ending stream of humvees, trucks, and howitzers rolled down the ramps into a chain-link enclosure on the pier.

One afternoon, as I was checking out our humvees, I spied a row of M109A3 self-propelled 155mm howitzers, the same type I had trained on in Twentynine Palms. Unable to resist the lure of the "hogs," I walked over to get a closer look.

From one howitzer came a cacophony of swearing and clanging. The cursing voice sounded oddly familiar, so I stuck my head into the dark interior of the howitzer. Hunched over the partially disassembled breechblock was SSgt. Michael Almanza, sweating and cursing at what seemed to be a stubborn piece of howitzer.

I laughed. Almanza had been my platoon sergeant three years earlier, when I had been the executive officer of Battery "N," 5th Battalion, 12th Marines. Almanza and I had been through countless days and nights together, training in the Mojave Desert, and we had become as close as a lieutenant and a staff noncommissioned officer could.

Irreverent and experienced, Almanza had become my "go-to guy" in the field when we had a problem with a howitzer — or a crew. He had gotten to know me so well that seldom a morning passed when he wasn't the first to greet me with a steaming cup of coffee.

Now, though, he had a problem on his hands.

"Hey, Almanza," I called. "Are you finished breaking that howitzer yet?"

Without turning or missing a beat, he replied, "Almost, sir! How you doin' Lt. Thompson?"

"That's *Captain* Thompson to you," I joked as he climbed out of the howitzer.

We played the catch-up game common among Marines who haven't seen each other in a while: Have you seen so-and-so? What ever happened to him? Where's the CO these days?

He told me how the battalion — 5/11 — had been reorganized and that he was now a member of the newly formed Battery "S" of 5/11, the only M109A3 battery left in the battalion. Almanza showed me the problem with the breechblock, and I promised not tell anyone he was conducting unauthorized maintenance on the howitzer. We shook hands a final time.

I didn't see him again during the deployment, but a few months later, I heard about him.

Thurs., 6 Sept 90

Today last day of the so-called "howling at the moon" theory, the 2–6 Sept invasion window. 0625 now and preparing to go out on a recon, or what is becoming more and more known as a "recce." We seem to be catching on to a lot of British and Afrika Korps phrases. Silly, but I guess it gives one the idea of what kind of mindset everyone is in.

I've seen more high-speed gunslinger pistol rigs than I knew existed. Mostly SNCO/officers, definitely the REMFs. As usual. We've had 13 accidental discharges, mostly SNCO/officers. Any relationship here? One major was responsible for two of them; he had his pistol taken away.

Finally saw Jeff yesterday, and it was great to see him. He's been here two weeks. He talked to Tammy on the 3rd, their anniversary. We talked for an hour, mostly shop, but it didn't matter. I was in a funk already, and it felt good to talk to him.

The main body — or the first part of it, at least — arrived w/CO, XO, and others.

Went to 11th Marines, where everyone was discussing how long we're going to be here. Depressing and irritating. They were speculating a year — or more. I don't want to be here a year.

Also disagree with their opinions that (1) Saddam will attack, and (2) we will attack Saddam. I think we're only here as part of a power play on two levels. The first is the Commandant's, the political move. To show the Army, Pentagon, and Congress that we can be the first with the most. That will keep us in the budget and in existence (much to the dismay of the XVIII Airborne Corps).

The second is more cynical, and I hope untrue. We're here to protect some greedy oil barons' interests. That's what really put me in a bad mood — the realization that that might be the case. Jeff and I talked about it. Officially, we're here because Iraq illegally invaded Kuwait (is there such a thing as "legal" invasion?) and we want to see the Kuwaiti gov't restored. But, I wonder. People say that Pres. Bush has the guts to kick Saddam out of Kuwait. He should, it's our guts. All he's doing is issuing orders from the White House. We'll see.

In 1/12, I was effectively out of a job, as most of the battalion had finally made it in-country.

No longer the S-3 for the battalion, and with hardly any training to conduct in my capacity as training officer, I was relegated to basically a "staff officer" status. Already, I had begun to feel like extra baggage, especially when Rivers announced that 11th Marines was short two officers and that "one of the battalions" would have to give up an officer temporarily. And we had one "extra" officer — me.

Besides that, the novelty of being in Saudi Arabia — or the very limited view of Saudi Arabia we were allowed to have — had worn off. Rumors were flying, our living conditions were atrocious, and our actions bordered on the ludicrous. The number of accidental discharges is an example.

Nearly every day, we heard a new story, sometimes true, of a Marine — usually an officer — who had accidentally fired his weapon. That didn't surprise me, since for many, it was the first time they had been required to walk around with a loaded weapon. The most common cause of accidental discharges was unfamiliarity with the 9mm pistol.

"Clearing barrels" had been set up outside each building in the area. The 55-gallon drums were usually cut in half, and then filled with sand. The top of the half-drum had a top that looked like a doughnut — the hole in the middle was the aiming area. Before entering a building, Marines were required to unload their weapons and dry-fire their weapons by pointing it into the hole and squeezing the trigger, thus "clearing the weapon."

The proper sequence for clearing a pistol is to remove the magazine, then "rack," or pull and release, the slide to eject a round that may be chambered. The weapon is then empty and ready to be aimed into the clearing barrel and dry-fired.

However, several Marines reversed the sequence. They pulled the slide to the rear and let it go home, thus chambering a round, then removed the magazine. They then pointed what they thought was an empty weapon into the clearing barrel, squeezed the trigger, and fired a round into the sand, an embarrassing and stupid error.

It was a miracle nobody got killed. Many of the stories were unsubstantiated, and probably not true, but they made good grist for the rumor mill. Still, there were enough accidental discharges to compel commanders to clamp down on pistol wearers and enforce strict rules about when a magazine could be inserted in a weapon. However, I must admit, I never paid attention to those rules and always kept a magazine in my weapon.

Jeff Speights was the son of a Marine officer who followed his father's career path and became a Hawk missile officer. I met Jeff in the fall of 1980 at Ole Miss, and we became nearly inseparable through our college years, until Jeff graduated two semesters ahead of me. We went to Officers Candidates School together, and I was a groomsman in Jeff's wedding in 1983. A little more than a year later, he returned the favor in my wedding.

During the previous five years or so, Angie and I had stayed in close contact with Jeff and his wife, Tammy, so I knew that he'd left Marine Corps Air Station, Yuma, Arizona, for Saudi Arabia before me. In fact, he telephoned me in Hawaii just hours before he left Arizona.

I had searched for him in the field several times since landing in-country, only to come up empty-handed each time. But I had managed to find the Hawk battalion headquarters, where I left word that I was in Jubayl.

He surprised me in the Swelterdome, but it lifted my spirits to see him. We hunkered on cots facing each other in the dank heat and marveled at our presence in the Middle East. We had been rushed overseas so quickly that the expedition still had a dreamlike quality to it, and we shook our heads repeatedly as we chatted. As we did so, rivers of sweat poured off us into dark pools on the concrete floor.

The more we talked, though, the more we questioned our government's motives, a conversation that unsettled both of us. The question of fighting for oil would come up again and again. Even today, I am sometimes visited by the thought that the American military was—and maybe still is—a Saudi mercenary force, a sort of Saudi Foreign Legion called out whenever Saddam Hussein decides to start acting up.

Months later, when I would stand in the streets of Kuwait City surveying the work of the Iraqi army, the reasons why we came to the Middle East would be made forever clear. But the thoughts I discussed with Jeff that September were the very beginning of a change in me that I couldn't recognize at the time.

With most of the MEF's units in-country by Labor Day, we had received defensive orders from 1st Marine Division. The plan called for 1/12 to move north into the field and support 3rd Marines. When the division's two tank battalions combined to form Task Force Ripper, we were to move farther north to support Ripper. Seventh and 3rd Marine regiments were to be in defensive positions south of Task Force Ripper, forming a kill zone, or "fire sac," northwest of the division's zone of operation.

The kill zone took advantage of a major highway that angled southeast toward Jubayl from the town of An Nahriyah, just south of the

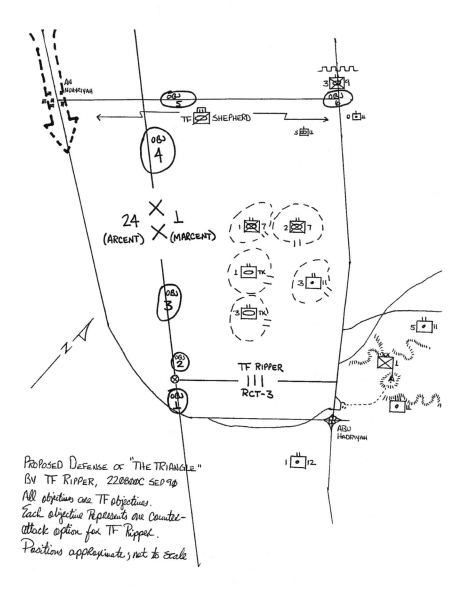

1st Marine Division's proposed defense of the "Triangle" in October 1990. The plan took advantage of a mobile defense and open terrain. I drew this map from the 11th Marines situation map. Not to scale.

border. The north-south coastal road formed the eastern boundary of this kill zone, which consisted of miles of open desert. To the north, where an LAV battalion patrolled, an east-west road formed the third leg of what we had dubbed "the Triangle." Along with 1/12, the division's other two artillery battalions— 3/11 and 5/11— were oriented toward the kill zone.

The plan was to conduct a simple delay-and-defend action. The artillery regiment's job was to knock out as much Iraqi armor as possible, then channel them into the kill zone and pour it on them. If necessary, Task Force Ripper would attack to destroy the Iraqis, supported by a furious barrage of Dual-Purpose Improved Conventional Munitions, an artillery form of the cluster bomb, and a very effective one.

Each ninety-five-pound DPICM projectile carries eighty-eight bomblets, each about the size of a tennis ball. When fired, the projectile releases the bomblets from its base. The shaped-charge bomblets then sprinkle over the target area and are capable of taking out personnel or armor.

When each gun from a battery fires— known as a "Battery One" in artillery circles— 704 bomblets rain down over the target. That number can be added for each battery firing at any given target. For example, had every gun in 1/12, 3/11, and 5/11 fired one round at a target, about 2,100 DPICM bomblets would have fallen on it. In short, DPICM is a very nasty killing tool.

We had two fallback positions, the last being the "die in place" line a little north of Al-Jubayl. It was a plan with many merits. All units were mutually supported, and all had access to the hard-surface roads in the area. Task Force Ripper had plenty of room to maneuver and was supported by up to three battalions of artillery, plus air support. My only hope was that we would be able to kill enough of the estimated 1,500–2,000 Iraqi tanks.

1600, Fri., 7 Sept 90

96 more people from 1/12 arrived today, just moments ago. Almost 200 in-country now. Troops are getting bored, hot. Gear is steadily being drawn, our (battalion) defensive op order is being written.

Our daily routine consists of breakfast, sweat all day, meetings at night, showers, and then the rack. Not much else to do except drive out into the desert and look at the terrain.

Actually, that's better than here. The temp out there is about 130, but I like it better than this warehouse. This place is a sweltering hole. It takes only a few minutes — lying absolutely still — to be soaked to the skin in your own sweat.

We're supposed to do a shoot next week to test all of our brand-new M198 howitzers. We managed to twist the Saudis' arms to let us. Going to try and shoot about 350 rounds. Units are slowly getting into position all over the desert for the long stalemate that I'm sure is coming.

I really don't think Saddam will attack. He has to know what he's facing, and every day he waits, we get stronger. The 24th Infantry Division (Mech) is trickling in, we have an incredible amount of air power, and the USMC is finally getting unfucked.

If he does attack, however, it won't be the "splendid little war" everyone seems to think it will. It'll be dirty and bloody. We will take untold casualties that will shock the American public. We can win, of that I'm confident. But it will be a nasty fight. The current belief is that the 2 or 3 Saudi mech brigades up north will fight to the death, attritting Saddam as he moves south. Let's hope so. Even w/his inept logistics, extended supply route, and our air pounding him, we'll be facing a lot of tanks. We'll be some busy boys.

Of course, we could attack him. Don't think that will happen, either. That plays right into Iraq's hands for a jihad against the Great Satan. He can't lose either way. I think that the quickest way for us to get the hell out of here is to attack. "Liberate" Kuwait and go home. But, in the eyes of the world, I don't think we can risk that politically. Thus, a stalemate.

Meanwhile, we sweat. I'm really concerned about the marines' state of mind in 6 mos. Here they are, 13,000 miles away from home in the most desolate region on earth. Suffering in brutal heat, no outlet for frustration, no indication of how long they must endure this. No liberty, no beer, no women — hell, they can't even look at a picture of a naked woman!! (No pornography is allowed in-country, not even Playboy.)

Another worry is the WMs, although they shouldn't even be here. Fucking Congress. Pat Schroeder won't be happy until she gets a woman in a body bag. I predict either a lot of rapes in a few months or a lot of WMs making tons of money.

Part of the reason for the troops' boredom was the conditions in which they lived. Because, I suppose, the MEF headquarters was located in the port and the off-load was under way, we were housed on the pier adjacent to the massive Maritime Prepositioning Force vessels.

There were about five warehouses on the pier, huge, cavernous structures made of steel. Designed to store large quantities of cargo containers, the buildings were perfect for cramming hundreds of Marines side-by-side. One could almost walk from one end of the warehouse to the other across the cots without ever touching the concrete floor. The temperature inside was unbearable, compounded by the incredibly high humidity, which surprised all of us. We expected a dry desert heat.

Luckily, I could escape the torture of the warehouse and ride into the desert on reconnaissance trips. Most of the troops, however, had no such mobility and spent much of their time battling boredom and trying, vainly, to find a cool spot.

The heat made even menial things difficult tasks, as evidenced by my earlier entry about my conversation with Jeff Speights. Meals were no longer a relaxing interlude for conversation. When chow was delivered to the warehouse, Marines gritted their teeth and stood in the blazing heat just long enough to get through the chow line, then hunkered on their cots to silently choke down the meal. It didn't matter what was being served or that the food was barely edible; it was too hot to enjoy it anyway.

Sleep was nearly impossible, especially in the daytime, when temperatures inside the warehouse could reach 140 degrees. The nights were slightly cooler but just as humid as the days.

Even if I was able to drift off to sleep, I would be jarred out of my cot by, of all things, a forklift operating inside the warehouse. I presume the reason for driving a roaring forklift in and out of a building full of sleeping Marines was that it was too hot to work in the daytime. Nonetheless, I heard several Marines muttering about taking out the evil forklift operator.

Our only relief from the heat came from the portable showers provided by 1st Force Service Support Group. 1st FSSG could purify its own water and had generators to pump the water to the prefabricated shower units. We had to stand in line for twenty minutes to get a shower, but it didn't matter. We soon began dreaming each day of the shower we would take each night. It made no sense to even think about taking a shower in the daytime. Of course, the relief was short-lived. In the time it took to walk the 200 or so yards back to the warehouse, I'd be drenched in sweat again, already dreaming of the next day's shower.

Speculation about the Iraqis was constant in the early days of Desert Shield. We received hardly any news or mail. Instead we operated on information we received from briefings or meetings, rumors, overheard conversations, and everyone's favorite source, "so-and-so's driver." High-ranking officers' drivers were considered to be the guys with all the inside scoop. A rumor attributed to a driver was given considerable weight. Rumors, however, can undermine morale, especially when nothing is done, or can be done, to quell them.

The issue of female Marines—WMs, or women Marines—in the theater was an emotional one for me, and still is. Simply put, I didn't think that the female Marines should be there, because of the nature of our existence. Though all Marines are trained for combat and realize that regardless of military occupational specialty they could find themselves in a combat zone, during Desert Shield that included just about every position occupied by the Marines, given Saddam's missile capability. I am opposed to women serving in ground combat, and I felt that this situation violated the law preventing women from doing so. But I no longer hold that opinion with the vehemence displayed in the journal entry above.

Before the deployment was over, however, I'd work with two female Marines and would be impressed by their abilities and their toughness. And in the years after the war, I had many opportunities to work with women, and was equally impressed by many of them, some of whom I'd gladly serve alongside in combat.

Still, I believe that the issue of women in combat revolves around strength and ability. For the most part, women are incapable of handling the duties of being on an artillery gun line. It takes a lot of brawn and stamina to handle ninety-five-pound projectiles, known as "joes" to cannon-cockers. Cannoneers "hump joes" all day, and sometimes all night, even when they're exhausted and hungry. Imagine carrying a bag of concrete mix around from 5 A.M. to midnight. That's an approximation of working on a gun line.

As a lieutenant, I served as the XO of a 155mm self-propelled artillery battery. Several of my cannoneers were small in stature. One in particular was only about 5' 5" tall and weighed no more than 110 pounds. But like the biggest cannoneer on the gun line, he humped joes with the best of them, thus he wasn't a liability.

Few women of similar stature could muster the same brute strength, and regardless of what the social scientists claim, strength is still important in combat. Equally important is endurance. It's one thing to pick up a projectile once, but cannoneers may do it hundreds of times a day for days on end. Any Marine who cannot perform the physical demands of the job is useless and endangers the lives of the Marines around him. As a gunny who had done two tours in Vietnam once explained to me, "Try walking 25 miles with wet feet and no socks with 80 pounds on your back after you've been awake for three days and eaten twice." That's the life of a combat Marine, and there are many strong men who would quail at that prospect.

Certainly, there are women that can perform the job of an artilleryman, or an infantryman for that manner. Indeed, one of the best, if not the best, sergeants I ever worked with was a woman who could do dead-hang pull-ups, and she ran sometimes twelve miles a day. Sgt. Holly Connor could run the 3-mile men's physical fitness test course and score higher than most men. In the workplace, she was a thorough professional and could do her job better than nearly every other Marine with whom she worked.

But, Sgt. Connor was the exception, not the rule—for both men and women. Would I be willing to fight alongside her? Absolutely.

But, should all women be allowed to serve in ground combat? My answer is no, but that's a question the American public needs to decide, after carefully deciding if America is ready for such an eventuality as its women coming home in body bags.

If an individual woman is up to the physical demands of the job, it is difficult to deny her the right to choose whatever job she wants—female fighter pilots being a case in point. But serving as the only woman in a squadron of male fighter pilots is a bit different from serving as the only woman on an all-male artillery line in the field. For one, the living conditions preclude any semblance of privacy whatsoever. And regardless of what the so-called sociological experts and politically correct pundits say, putting men and women together under those conditions for long periods—and under immense stress in some cases—will affect a unit's cohesion.

All the social engineering in the world won't erase the biological and psychological differences in men and women. And when young, healthy, fit men and women are forced to live that closely with equal amounts of sexual deprivation, it's only natural to assume that nature will run its course, as the saying goes. And when it does, it begins to distract people. And on the battlefield, distraction can result in destruction.

It's fashionable today to say, "Oh, today's men and women are far too sophisticated to let petty sexual urges get in the way of their jobs."

Then what explains the seemingly endless sex scandals in the military today, scandals that occur in boot camp and in generals' offices? Or the pregnancy rates aboard Navy ships?

Thankfully, the Marine Corps has stuck to its guns by continuing its practice of segregating men and women in boot camp, a policy that works. It allows both men and women to focus on their jobs—becoming Marines—without such "petty" distractions as the opposite sex.

Besides the issue of women in combat, the rumors, heat, and boredom caused me great concern for the Marines, as I noted in this entry. But, for the most part, the concern was unnecessary. We adapted to the heat, began to ignore most—but certainly not all—of the rumors. And we were soon busy enough.

Mon., 10 Sept 90

Finally out of that godforsaken warehouse! Moved north a few miles to a migrant workers' camp built by the Saudis two years ago. Never been occupied. It's plush compared to the desert and the warehouse. A full compound w/rec rooms—half is now the Bn CP—that has Ping-Pong, pool tables, and air-conditioned, three-man rooms; full showers and head; mess hall. After 2 weeks of sweltering heat, I'm freezing my ass off and the a/c is on low.

Rumor is that we are going to the field tomorrow, which would piss off the troops, as they just got into their rooms today. Plus, the battery commanders say they aren't quite ready (I agree) and we have no ammo yet. Staff is trying to convince the CO to wait until our scheduled MVV shoot on the 14th. We meet at 2100, so maybe we will have some luck. I'd like to get my wind back.

Already I feel rejuvenated; my temper has lengthened greatly in only a few hours. Same for whole battalion. Out in that heat, tempers flared constantly, nothing got done, and the CO stayed pissed. Not surprising. This heat really fucks with your head. It puts a zap on you that you aren't aware of, and suddenly you're sullen, furious, and hostile to everything around you. Already tonight, productivity is increasing because of the vastly improved conditions. I feel like a human again. Finally unpacked my seabag, after 2½ weeks. I'm actually in a real rack. Even a bookcase. It's nice.

We were overjoyed with our new digs. The Saudis had spent enormous amounts of money on building several camps for the thousands of migrant workers imported from other nations. Inside the concrete walls of our camp, known as "Haii 3," we found all the makings of a modern suburban neighborhood, or at least a modern trailer park.

Lining the paved roads were permanent buildings: a communications center, dispensary, cafeteria, laundry rooms, and administrative buildings. Laid out in a grid across most the camp were dozens of trailers, each of which held about half a dozen rooms, including bathrooms. The rooms comfortably housed three people with a closet, bed, lamp, and bookshelf for each. Every room had its own air-conditioning unit as well.

There were also several trailers designed to be recreation rooms, complete with billiard tables. These became the battalion command posts, where the battalion CO and XO conducted business with the administrative section. The CP also became our mail distribution point.

There was even a small PX. Humble though it was, Marines lined up for hours to buy tea, coffee, tobacco, or "pogey bait"—candy. Usually it didn't matter what you bought, just as long as you were able to satisfy your American consumer instinct.

Surrounding the camp was a high concrete wall. We could never decide if the Saudis built it to protect the workers or to protect themselves. But, compared to the warehouse, Haii 3 was Paradise, even if the rooms were coated in a thick layer of fine dust, had a musty smell, and needed hours of air conditioning before being habitable. We were finally living like humans again, and our morale immediately registered that fact. It wouldn't last long—in keeping with Marine Corps tradition, almost as soon as we moved in, rumors started flying that we'd move to the field "tomorrow"—but we made the best of it while it lasted.

The cafeteria was a great place to run into old friends, which happened often. Several times a week, I shared a meal or a cup of coffee with a Marine with whom I had served at Twentynine Palms, or a friend from The Basic School or the Fleet Marine Force.

An "MVV shoot" was nothing more than a "break-in" period for our new howitzers that had just come off the MPF ships. Artillery pieces have "muzzle velocity variances"—MVV. These variances fluctuate from round to round and can affect a howitzer's accuracy. A precision instrument, the M90 chronometer, which is mounted on the piece, measures the variations. After firing a series of several rounds, the muzzle velocity data is input into the computer used to compute firing data—the Battery Computer System, or BCS. The data, which are stored and averaged, enable the computer to compensate for each howitzer's variance in muzzle velocity, which makes the howitzer more accurate. It is a small detail, but one that pays huge dividends in combat.

In 1/12, Marshall and I kept after the battery fire direction officers to make sure that they constantly updated their MVV files. It didn't make us any friends in the batteries, but a few months later, our accuracy in combat would get the attention of the division commander.

11 Sept 90, Haii 3

As of today, I work for 11th Marines Regimental Staff. Lt. Col. Rivers fought against losing 2 officers, and won, in a way. He had to give up one captain — me — instead of two. There was simply no other choice. It wounded me at first when he told me in last night's meeting, like a kick to the belly. But I got over it. After all, I have no choice, really.

I'll be in the S-3 shop, w/Capt. Mitch Jones [pseudonym], Maj. Scott Dean [pseudonym], and Lt. Col. Lynn A. Stuart, the actual S-3. CO of 11th Mar is Col. P.G. Howard, and I like him. Seems pretty straight up.

My job, as one of the watch officers, will be to act as one of the regimental FDOs, which means I need to hit the books again w/Jones to get up to speed. I haven't been in the FDO mode for a long time.

I tried to put a good face on my abrupt transfer to 11th Marines, in an attempt to convince myself that I wasn't considered "excess baggage" in 1/12. Besides, I rationalized, it was only supposed to be for ninety days.

After a warm welcome by the officers at 11th Marines, I was able to relax and orient myself to my new job, which proved exciting. Capt. Mitch Jones and I had completed the Officers' Advanced Course at Fort Sill together, and we enjoyed a cordial relationship, especially as we broke out the manuals in the regimental headquarters and focused on how to employ a regiment's worth of artillery in combat, then how to write the artillery plan.

In official military gobbledygook that plan was known as Tab B (Artillery Fire Plan) to Appendix 12 (Fire Support) to Annex C (Operations) to MarDiv Frag Order 10-90 to Operation Desert Shield. Jones and I shared the research, and I did most of the actual writing—"wordsmithing," we called it. We had written several such documents at Fort Sill, but this was the first "real world" fire plan we'd ever attempted. When Stuart accepted it with only minor changes, Jones and I felt a huge sense of accomplishment.

Dean would provide much hilarity in the weeks to come. Alternately cynical and thoughtful, sometimes caustic, other times quiet, he worked primarily as Stuart's assistant. I quickly learned the idioms of his speech and was able to do an impersonation that amused my fellow captains.

Stuart was a professional, through and through. I spent many nights with him in the combat operations center, or COC, discussing tactics, the Civil War, current events, or college football; he could discuss each subject with equal enthusiasm. The only disadvantage I felt in working for him was that I was something of an interloper, coming from a battalion outside the regiment, which was based in California. As a result, I never really felt as if I had his full confidence.

Col. Patrick G. Howard was a breath of fresh air. Tall and quiet, he reminded me of a Virginian general in the Confederate Army. He praised his officers and troops often, and—most importantly, to me—he kept meetings on track, cheerful, and free of most of the self-important bullshit that always seems to be present at staff meetings. Howard was never too busy to stop and talk to a radio operator, or the battery first sergeant, or a captain on watch. Unlike many colonels, he didn't scare the hell out of you when he showed up on your watch. And he didn't think he had all the answers. He welcomed input from his staff and gave each man an opportunity to state his case. It was a thriving command climate, and the Corps noticed it. Howard was eventually promoted to major general.

But, even without the mind-numbing minutiae that I endured in most of the 1/12 daily meetings, I still spent more than two hours in meetings my first full day with the regiment. Plus, all the meetings started after 2000. It seemed as if we sat around all day and went to meetings all night. It was a pattern that had begun on the pier, and, unfortunately, it continued when we moved to Haii 3.

At 11th Marines, I got an introduction to the rarefied air of the division headquarters, a world I had scrupulously avoided until this point in my career. Stuart hauled me along to a daily briefing—a routine with which I would become very familiar in the next few weeks—at 1st Marine Division's COC, which was in the field north of us, near Abu Hadriyah. I was not impressed. To me, it was a bunch of field-grade officers standing in a cluster under a camouflage net not doing very much to further the war effort. They did, however, manage to have their vehicles parked in a neat row outside the net. I saw only one sentry in the entire area, and nowhere did I see fighting holes or protection from shrapnel. I also noticed the unnerving oddity of Marines saluting officers in the field. To me, the whole command post stunk of complacency and laziness. In the next few weeks, when I attended the meetings alone, I did notice the place becoming more shipshape, but that first impression was shocking.

And when it came to security in the camps, a current of anger rippled through the Marines when an edict came down from on high that weapons were to be unloaded inside the camps. That was probably a wise decision, given the number of accidental discharges. But it served only to infuriate us, and make us feel that we were being stripped of any means of defending ourselves—even though we were ensconced behind concrete walls and protected by Marines manning machine guns at every entrance.

In retrospect, the lack of security in those very early days was more a result of intelligence gathered on Saddam than on our own laziness. Though we all felt vulnerable, as if we could be overrun by the Republican Guard at any moment, the reality was quite the opposite. Threat assessments at this point, I learned later, showed that not only was Saddam no longer interested in attacking to the south, he seemed to be settling in for the duration.

We all suspected as much as the days went on, but that did little to allay our fears of being attacked by terrorists or being hit by a Scud missile.

· C H A P T E R   T H R E E ·

I moved to the field with 11th Marines on a blistering Wednesday morning, Sept. 19. Our first position was about an hour's drive up the four-lane highway from Al Jubayl, just south of the division headquarters.

We settled into deep sand east of what we called the "Abu Hadriyah cloverleaf." Rising out of the desert, and inexplicably leading nowhere, the cloverleaf interchange knotted the north-south coastal road. But the ramps didn't lead to any other roads. The cloverleaf just sat there useless, a concrete anachronism — a sort of Saudi Stonehenge — leaving us scratching our heads and wondering why it had been built in the first place.

Abu Hadriyah was one of the points of the "Triangle" where the bulk of the 1st Marine Division's forces, including the newly attached Hawaii units, waited for the unlikely Iraqi attack. As a town, it didn't amount to much, a couple of off-limits gas stations — all civilian locales were forbidden — and an oil pumping station.

We set up our headquarters against an escarpment that ran east and west, perpendicular to our ostensible route into Kuwait. As soon as we established communication with the battalions and division, we set up a watch schedule. I recorded my first on-watch diary entry at 0435 the next day. The ungodly hour had its rewards. It was cool and quiet, a rarity. And the solitude allowed me the time to write, something I began to do more and more, as I tried to organize my thoughts and emotions so that I could make sense of what was happening around me — and to me.

11th Marine Regiment moved to the field in September 1990. As the headquarters for all the artillery in 1st Marine Division, we set up along a line of barren dunes between Abu Hadriyah to the south and 1st Marine Division headquarters to the north.

Sat., 22 Sept 90

In the rear now for my two days "R and R," and it's a good thing. Caught a cold, and it's kicking my ass. Sweating all day, going to bed damp, then cooling off quickly did me in. Hope to get well while I'm here. Got a card from Angie today.

NEWS: We are now receiving "imminent danger pay," as I did 3 years ago, retroactive to 1 Sept; the Saudis are getting pissed about booze being smuggled into the country (mostly through the mail); Customs discovered a bottle of Jack Daniel's in a package going to a Marine, so they searched the next 96 packages. Supposedly, the Marine is in the brig w/a $10,000 fine slapped on him.

Rumors about booze being smuggled in were common, and usually they bordered on the outrageous. Nobody I knew was stupid enough to try and have alcohol mailed to them, but I'm sure there were some Marines out there trying to do just that.

The whole issue of alcohol struck me as hypocritical, and not only because we were being told that while we were good enough to do the fighting and dying for the Saudi government, we weren't good enough to have a drink to break the monotony of that godforsaken desert.

Adding to this mentality was the fact that American employees of Aramco, a huge oil company in Saudi Arabia, were housed to the south of us in compounds similar to ours. Like military bases in the United States, these compounds had all the amenities of a small, walled city. Including what some employees called the "still room."

Each house had a small anteroom, not much bigger than a laundry room, with all the makings of a whiskey still. Since you can't buy alcohol in the country, you have to make your own, and that's exactly what some people were doing in their homes. But there had been some injuries caused by exploding stills, so the Saudis made it a little easier — and safer. In each house, they installed the still rooms including directions— so the operator wouldn't blow himself up in the process of distilling sour-mash whiskey.

One employee, on a visit to 11th Marines at Abu Hadriyah to distribute ice and Cokes, even gave us his recipe for converting nonalcoholic beer, which was legal, into alcoholic brew. With a little sugar and yeast, and some patience, he said, we could have all the beer we wanted. In fact, I heard stories about Marines and soldiers writing their wives for yeast and sugar to do that. I never tried it, even though we received mountains of nonalcoholic beer. But that beer was canned, and the "conversion beer" required bottles.

The nonalcoholic beer became something of a focus of derision. Major American distributors flew tons of "near beer" over to thirsty troops, and the unleaded brew was passed out freely. Not that anybody wanted any. I'm sure whoever came up with the idea had his heart in the right place, but for most Marines, it added insult to injury. Cases of faux beer piled up in our positions, unwanted. It got so bad that we started drinking it with meals—sometimes breakfast—just to get rid of it. We made a game out of it, since each can actually contained a minuscule amount of alcohol. Some Marines took turns seeing how many beers it would take before they felt a buzz. Most gave up after a twelve-pack.

0217, 24 Sept 90, Haii 3

I've had a lot of time to think about combat. I used to think that I wanted to experience it, not at all for "glory," but just to experience it, but now I don't know. This one would be bloody—and there's the chemical threat.

The only thing combat would do for us would be to give us one little ribbon and a whole lot of casualties. I don't dwell on it, though. Better off not thinking, just doing the day-to-day jobs, taking it as it comes. I know that I'm ready for it, mentally and physically, although I don't necessarily want it. Not here. There are a lot of unknowns out there, and if the American public learns of them, I don't think they'll support a war.

Like most Americans, I grew up with visions of combat romanticized by Hollywood. For my generation, the images were from Vietnam and, occasionally, World War II. As a young boy, I watched *The Dirty Dozen*, *The Longest Day*, *A Bridge Too Far*, and *Kelly's Heroes*. As I got older, though, the genre shifted its focus to the Vietnam War.

Generally, movies on Vietnam were edgier, and uglier, and attempted to portray combat more realistically than the war flicks of the previous generation, which produced romanticized versions of war like *The Bridge at Remagen* and the *Sands of Iwo Jima*.

Likewise, books on Vietnam were harsher in their depictions of war, especially individual combat. Where Richard Tregaskis's classic *Guadalcanal Diary* brilliantly described the privations of war from an observer's point of view, James Webb's wrenching *Fields of Fire* was written by a participant of the Vietnam War—Webb was one of the Corps' most decorated officers in that conflict. Webb's book had a huge impact on me during my first year of college.

I had already read Philip Caputo's *A Rumor of War*, but his tale left me confused and uninspired. But Webb hit me right between the eyes with the brutality of war, and it was a lesson I never forgot. That was important, because it began the long process of stripping away all the veneer that surrounds the mythical "glory of war." *Fields of Fire* scared me, caused me to doubt myself, made me ask myself if I could take the rigors and death and fear of war. I reasoned that I could — from the safe cocoon of a dorm room. Now, those questions seeped back into my mind. The circumstances in which I found myself weren't in the script. There were no war movies about fighting an enemy determined to soak you up to your earlobes in nerve gas.

It's one thing to convince yourself that you can hack it when you are lounging around a college campus with a cold beer in your hand and your mind full of images of medals and valor. But when the reality of going into combat and killing the enemy stares you in the face, the question takes on a different gravity. It's the ultimate gut check.

During these boring, hot days of Desert Shield, I spent many hours rolling these questions over in my mind, not realizing that the process was turning me into a new person. My doubts as to our mission and my fear that the American public wouldn't support us were evidence of that. I couldn't escape the thought that we were hired guns, and it made me very uncomfortable.

At the time, our news of the support of the American public — gleaned daily from whatever newspapers we could find — gave us the perception that the home front had finally woken up to the fact that Saddam's chemical threat was serious enough to cause an untold number of casualties.

And that, we reasoned, would force President Bush to try to conduct a "limited war." That, I felt, was a huge mistake. Out in the desert, we were almost unanimous in our belief that the only way to win the war was to unleash the U.S. military machine and let it utterly destroy the Iraqi military. Anything short of that would hamstring our ability to fight, and it would get people killed.

Luckily, Gen. Colin Powell felt the same way.

Thurs., 27 Sept 90

Left U.S. one month ago today. Very bizarre — and uncomfortable — turn in the weather. Woke up in what I thought was fog. Turned out it was haze/mist from incredible humidity. Has to be 95% or higher. Thoroughly soaked now. Not helping the remnants of my cold.

Hussein has started his rhetoric again. Last couple of days have not been very encouraging by either side. UN air embargo could spell trouble. Arabs say chance for peace looks slim, more troops arriving, etc. Hussein starting to move divisions back into Kuwait. Who knows what will happen. I think three months from now I'll still be sitting in this same pos.

Everybody likes to talk about how combat is imminent, and how we've got to do something, but I think it's just self-delusion. If anything, we're trying to provoke Iraq. The battleship Wisconsin *and*

> *carrier* Independence *are cruising north for "exercises" and the* USAF
> *is doing same. That, w/Hussein's blustering, could be fatal. From*
> *what I've read, if the quotations are accurate, Hussein seems to be*
> *losing his grip.*
>
> *Haii 3 has had a couple of terrorist-related incidents — someone*
> *climbing the fence at night, and people in cars, scoping us out. In the*
> *field, 1/12 chased off someone in front of the gun line night before last,*
> *and last night we had someone sneaking around the* FLB *(Forward*
> *Logistics Base). Activity increase usually means target selection; we're*
> *going to get hit, I can feel it.*
>
> *It's screwed up, though, because we can't even detain people, thanks*
> *to the damn Saudis. So how do we protect ourselves? Good question.*
> *That bothers me more than the thought of war.*

My prediction about being in the same position for the next three months wasn't far off the mark. As it turned out, nobody began moving north until December.

We did manage to try to train, though. We set up several "comm-exes"—communication exercises—during which we essentially fought a scripted war without firing any rounds. It was more a test of our ability to communicate across various radio networks, more than anything.

The results were frustrating and discouraging. Frustrating because the exercises seldom went as planned and discouraging because, at this early stage of Desert Shield, we were still gripped by a peacetime mentality that we had to have perfect communications to train. Rather than train with the units we were able to talk to, and allow the others to catch up when they unsnarled their own communications, we stalled until all our units—down to the battery level—could talk to us. At times, the entire division sat around waiting for a company- or battery-sized unit to come up on the network.

It was, I thought, ridiculous. In combat, we wouldn't be afforded the luxury of waiting until conditions were perfect to conduct battle. We would have to make-do. Part of our training should have to do just that — adapt and improvise. But our habit of having perfect comm to do anything was as hard to break as drug addiction in those days.

1754

> *Did something wild today. About 1230, I called Angie — from my*
> *tent. Maj. Dean just started playing with the field telephone in our*
> *tent and suddenly he was talking to his wife — on the first try. I called*
> *division switchboard, asked for the* MEF *switchboard, then asked for*
> *a Hawaii* AUTOVON *line. Told AV operator I wanted to make a*
> *commercial call. The connection was atrocious — I could hardly*
> *understand a word she said — but it was great. We talked for about*

3 min., and it was worth every second, because the lack of mail, the boredom, and frustration are slowly putting me into a deep, silent belligerence.

It's hard to overstate the value of mail to a deployed Marine. Our very survival depended on that tenuous link to the outside world. "Mail call" were two of the most important words we could hope to hear.

Marines—and sailors, for that matter—are accustomed to long, lonely deployments at sea, relying on a helicopter to ferry in the bright-orange bags of mail: word from home, pictures of the family, magazines and newspapers. But in Saudi Arabia, where our deprivations were so plentiful that our desires were intensified exponentially, mail took on an almost mystical quality. A man who didn't get mail from his wife for three days running might think he was headed for a divorce. The amount of mail a Marine received was as good as a barometer to his mental well-being as anything else. The good leaders learned to pay attention to little things like mail as a way to take care of their Marines.

My own personal mail drought affected me just as it would any other Marine, and in my desperation to hear something—anything—from my wife, I tried Dean's method of communication. The connection was choked with static and we had to wait through long pauses for our voices to bounce off satellites, but it worked. And although we talked for only a few minutes, the phone call had the rejuvenating effect of the two weeks worth of mail I hadn't received.

Fri., 28 Sept 90
Two incidents last night. 5/11 had some boys caught out in town on liberty (strictly verboten; we are allowed NO contact w/the Saudis) by none other than BGen. Hopkins, Ass't MEF CG. They'll fry. 2nd time for them. Within a week of my arrival here, 5/11 had 8 people, including a gunny, caught at the Dairy Queen in Al-Jubayl.

Second incident much more serious. USAF airman was shot last night by a terrorist at King Fahd Airport, near Riyadh (about 800 miles from here). He was driving, when a white sedan got behind him, started flashing its headlights. Unbelievably, he pulled over, walked back to the car. Got hit w/a 9mm bullet; terrorist fled. No other witnesses, but doctors say it was definitely not self-inflicted. He'll live, but I can't believe that he was either that stupid or that naive. Wonder what the reaction back home will be. Read yesterday that there have been many acts of violence against Arab-Americans in U.S.—typical American narrow-mindedness. Most probably don't even know where Saudi Arabia is.

Most of the supposed terrorist incidents and attacks were never substantiated, but the accounts of such attacks were passed around every circle, from the "third shitter on the left" all the way up to the division headquarters. Nearly every day, we heard a frightening new story about a terrorist attack or one about Marines doing something stupid.

These stories are great examples. I recorded them as if they were facts, when actually they were just rumors passed on during a staff meeting. We never verified either story, but we talked about them for days as if they were true.

2030, Sun., 30 Sept 90

Ate supper with Bill Sanders. He related the third part of the comedy trilogy of the last few days, what I hereby name the "Three Blind Mice Incidents."

Last night Haii 3 was in utter turmoil when, in the darkness, shots were fired inside the compound. Sentries reported an intruder in the compound, firing a weapon. Terrorist attack.

The react force, about a squad of heavily armed Marines, responded. Machine gunners got behind their .50 cals, ready to blast the raghead bastard into smithereens. People ran to and fro dousing lights, loading weapons, taking cover, etc. The situation was tense as Marines yelled and scurried — mostly into each other. No more shots were heard. After a while, things calmed down. The culprit had been captured. The "terrorist" was one undoubtedly grossly embarrassed Marine, w/an armload of freshly laundered utilities, who had accidentally fired his rifle into the ground as he left the laundry room!

Unbelievable. If I wasn't pissed at the injuries caused by something like that and the danger of accidental discharges, it would be absolutely ridiculous.

Sanders and I laughed long and hard about this incident days after it happened, but, as I wrote, it angered me, too. Especially since it was the third such incident in which Marines overreacted, both in the field and in Haii 3.

The first two had involved similar reports of gunfire in the compound, followed by a response by the camp's reaction force. In all three cases, however, Marines were chasing shadows.

Mon., 1 Oct 90

The two Germanys reunited today. Wonder how long it will take to build the Fourth Reich. German reunification bothers me. I'm a little leery of a huge, powerful Germany in Europe. But I bet it'll be a hell of an Oktoberfest.

We have been descended upon by flies. They are always bad out here, but yesterday and today have been absolutely repulsive. Our tent was sprayed two days ago. I guess they feed off the pesticide. They come in hundreds, on the food, always around my face, esp. my mouth. God only knows what kinds of diseases we're going to come down with. I hate the fuckers.

The issue of a reunited Germany was surprising, because I still had not fully recovered from the shock of watching the Berlin Wall come down. I had watched the Cold War end from my living room at Fort Sill, astounded as young Germans, from the East and the West, pulverized the most emblematic symbol of that era. I cheered them on, thrilled that they had at last done what so many had wanted to do for so many years.

But like a bad hangover on New Year's Day, the reality of that moment set in months later, as I realized that the collapse of the Soviet Union and the destruction of the Berlin Wall only meant that life suddenly had become more uncertain and more complicated. It also meant that an entire way of life, on both sides of the Atlantic, had come to an end. We could no longer rely on the Tom Clancy scenarios of the Red Menace to get us through when it came to defense budgets. The disintegration of the USSR meant the potential loss of control of thousands of nuclear warheads, and the inevitable rise of nationalism throughout the underbelly of Europe. The monster that became Bosnia began the day the Berlin Wall collapsed.

The specter of nationalistic genocide scared me. Had I been smarter, or more aware of history, I might have been scared for Sarajevo. Instead, I worried about Germany.

The flies of the desert are one of the most powerful, and most repugnant, memories of my time in Saudi Arabia. At times, I could sweep my hand across a table and scoop up a handful of squirming flies.

Any food left uncovered was plundered, any bottle of water left uncapped soon became a swimming pool for half a dozen flies. There was no escape from them, and we learned the peculiar habit of constantly waving your hand over your food — even while raising a spoonful to your mouth — to keep the bastards away. The flies turned chow time into a challenge.

We had pesticides everywhere, but nothing seemed to come close to even putting a dent in the fly population, which was reminiscent of a plague in the book of Exodus. We spent hours swatting flies, spraying our gear, our tents, and our racks.

I still wonder about the diseases or other damages to our immune systems the flies may have caused. With such heavy concentrations of pesticide, and the normal filth distributed by flies, I wouldn't be surprised if the insects are responsible for some of the maladies of Gulf War Syndrome today.

2250, Thurs., 4 Oct 90

LONG meeting this a.m. w/Col. Howard and others. Some notes from that:

1. Division hasn't paid much attention to a barrier plan for the proposed defense of the "Triangle." It's needed because there is NO restrictive terrain to canalize the enemy into the designated EA. The EA is nothing but grid squares on the ground. There is nothing to make the enemy go into it.

2. Div steadfastly believes the main avenue of approach is the coastal road, rather than the road through An Nahriyah. Nobody here believes that. The inland road offers too many advantages. Besides, if the main AOA is the coastal road, why is the division oriented away from it?

3. Div estimates it would take Iraq 96 hours to reach Dhahran.

4. The Iraqi 2nd echelon is estimated to have 1,200 tanks/300 howitzers, presumably Republican Guards. Much ado about how to defeat this at division.

5. Division assumes chem weapons will be used by Iraq (don't we all?).

6. 11th Mar very successful in initial liaison w/24th ID (Mech) arty honchos.

7. Priority of fires in the covering force battle to 101st AB (Air Assault). Unclear if this is Army, or theater-wide.

8. 212th Brigade will be on our left flank. 3rd ACR may be tying in there after covering force battle.

9. Long discussion over the fix the Iraqis will be in. If they attack USMC, 24th ID has a beautiful flank shot as Iraq moves SE from An Nahriyah. If they attack USA, they will run into a real shit sandwich.

10. Targeting Objectives of XVIII Airborne Corps are to create a 24- to 36-hour gap between 1st and 2nd echelon of Iraqis.

11. 24th ID is totally in-country, but not in tactical defensive positions. The division is in a tactical assembly area, w/1st Brigade up near An Nahriyah.

12. There is no unified (i.e., combined SANG/US) ground commander. Has anyone at the "echelons above reality" level ever heard of the Principles of War?

13. USS Wisconsin is either in port in Bahrain or just off the coast.

Throughout my meetings at division headquarters, I marveled at how things that seemed so obvious at our level — the regiment or battalion — seemed so elusive to the great minds at "higher headquarters."

I'm sure Saddam would have loved to read the notes I took from this particular meeting. If he had, he probably would have attacked immediately, because at times it sure seemed like we didn't have any idea what the hell we were doing.

But that's an easy attitude to take when you have only one side of the picture. After the war, I served on a staff at "higher headquarters," Fleet

Marine Forces Pacific, the highest Marine headquarters in the Pacific theater. From my perch in the stratosphere of "echelons above reality" I had access to an enormous amount of information. I truly saw the big picture. It was so big, in fact, that I lost sight of the details, part of the problem with any headquarters staff. But seeing the big picture made me realize that, more often than not, there are reasons for doing or — in the case of the barrier plan in the Triangle — not doing things.

We, the little people, were damn near convinced that we would stand off Saddam's hordes at Abu Hadriyah. After all, we'd been tasked to come up with a defensive plan to do just that. We'd targeted every grain of sand and every painted stripe on the asphalt roads.

The "EA" — engagement area — was a feature of our rapidly becoming outdated Cold War doctrine. Though that was more the case for the Army — tasked with defending Europe in Germany's Fulda Gap — than the Marine Corps; we too had been trained in tactics that would counter either the Soviet Army or one of its surrogates.

That was one good thing about the Evil Empire: When it exported its philosophy it went all the way, right down to equipping satellite nations with its own equipment, ammunition, and doctrine. We didn't fight the Soviet Union in Saudi Arabia, but we did face Soviet gear and tactics.

And we knew how to fight both, after training for years to face T-72 tanks or D-30 howitzers. Our defensive tactics called for us to lie back in positions that would allow U.S. mechanized or motorized infantry to pounce on the lead elements of the attack after artillery and attack aircraft had pounded them. The goal was to start hitting the enemy with artillery at the maximum range — for 11th Marines about thirty kilometers if we were using rocket-assisted projectiles, or RAP rounds. The RAP rounds had tiny booster rockets that fired shortly after the round left the muzzle.

The disorder caused by the artillery fire would be useful in "canalizing" the enemy — forcing him to move down a predetermined route into our engagement area, called a "fire sac" by the Soviets. Aiding in that canalization would be man-made barriers, such as trenches, minefields, concertina wire or other barriers, all part of our "barrier plan." Saddam used the same "barrier plan" idea with his minefields and trench lines in Kuwait.

Once in the EA, the armor-mech task forces would launch an all-out attack, supported by heavy doses of artillery and air support. Ideally, the engagement area would be a clearly defined terrain feature, such as a valley or mountain gap.

If facing superior numbers, our doctrine called for a vicious but brief attack, then a "fighting withdrawal," also known as hauling ass backwards to another position, from which the entire process would be repeated, until the enemy's supply lines were hopelessly extended and his numbers were depleted from the constant attacks. That left his rear areas and logistics trains vulnerable to attack by motorized infantry or cavalry and air attacks.

Thus, the lack of a plan to install barriers to force the Iraqis into the engagement area was, to me, a huge omission, an act that bordered on criminal. But perhaps division knew more than a lowly captain, and knew there was only a snowball's chance in hell that Saddam would attack us. Still, that's a hell of a gamble. More evidence that division was blowing smoke came from the staff's pronouncement regarding the coastal road. Every bit of preparation we conducted had been to blunt an attack coming from our northwest, not from the north, the direction of an attack that would have come down the coastal road from the border town of Khafji.

Oddly enough, the Iraqis' attack of Khafji months later bore out the division's belief, but at the time we didn't know who or what to believe.

The road from An Nahriyah caused more confusion. The most northern portion of the road, from the Iraqi border to a few miles south of An Nahriyah, belonged to the Army's zone of action. As such, the Army's 24th Infantry Division (Mechanized) carried the responsibility of defending that portion of the American position. But, the road entered the Marine Corps' zone south of the town and continued all the way to Abu Hadriyah, where the 1st Marine Division waited for an attack.

That created a potentially massive problem. Tanks moving on an asphalt road can travel about 35-40 mph, an incredible speed when two division-sized units each have responsibility for the same area. If 1st Marine Division didn't coordinate properly — and seamlessly — with the Army, there would be a "gap" in which the Iraqi Army could conceivably advance without receiving any fire whatsoever from either the Army or the Marine Corps.

This potentiality was recognized very early, and the result was one of the most professional and efficient relationships I have ever seen. At 11th Marines, we worked almost daily with our counterparts at "divarty" — the 24th artillery gurus — to make sure that, come hell or high water, the Iraqis would have more than their share of artillery fire if they attacked down that road. Planners at the 24th also prepared for the chance to slam into the Iraqi flank, should Saddam be so bold, and brash, as to attack us.

My comment regarding no unified commander is a bit skewed. There was, in fact, a unified commander, General Norman Schwarzkopf. The comment likely refers to the struggle within the Marine Corps, which was dealing for the first time with the issue of "componency," another layer of military bureaucracy best described as the layer of command between the operational level — the U.S. Central Command — and the tactical level, in this case the MEF. That layer was known in the Army as "ARCENT"— U.S. Army Central Command. Its commander, usually a three-star, and his staff report directly to CINCCENT, the four-star commander in chief of the Central Command — Schwarzkopf, during the war.

ARCENT's job was not to fight the war, but to ensure that all the Army units under its aegis were able to do so. Thus, ARCENT developed the Army scheme of maneuver and provided the logistical, administrative, and manpower support to get the job done.

The Marine Corps had no such animal before Desert Shield. The closest parallel was the commander of the Fleet Marine forces, three-stars. But neither the Pacific or Atlantic commanders reported directly to a CINC. What was needed in Desert Shield was a Marine "component commander" who was the link between the MEF and CINCCENT.

That eventually became the job of Lt. Gen. Walt Boomer, the I MEF commander, who had started the expedition as the 1st Marine Division commander. Boomer, however retained his "hat" as MEF commander and became a "dual-hatted" component commander. Ironically, as the MEF commander he was responsible for following his own orders— those of MARCENT.

One of the lessons learned from Desert Shield/Storm was that the Corps needed commanders above the MEF level that could act as component commanders. Thus, the Atlantic and Pacific commanders have since been redesignated Marine Forces Pacific and Marine Forces Atlantic.

CHAPTER FOUR

On October 5, Saudi Arabia finally caught up to me and ambushed me.

I finished up a routine watch in the COC at 0600. As I turned the watch over to my relief, I didn't feel well, so I skipped breakfast and hit the rack in Dean's cramped, hot tent. But I couldn't sleep, as I was overcome with nausea. I was also sweating profusely.

I ate an MRE, which only made things worse. In half an hour, I was throwing up in the aid station while a corpsman took my temperature and jammed an IV needle into my arm, just as I collapsed in his arms. My temperature climbed up over 101 degrees in the 104-degree air of the tent, and with the sudden loss of body fluid, I was becoming dangerously dehydrated. The corpsman put two liters of fluid into me even before I was medevacked.

By this time, people were starting to notice I was missing. The headquarters commandant, Capt. Rich Huenfeld, discovered me and reported my condition to Dean, who immediately ordered me to the rear.

The trip back to Jubayl was memorable. I was thrown on the first vehicle available, a five-ton being piloted by two NCOs that, together, were about as bright as a ten-watt bulb. The bone-jarring, teeth-rattling ride across the open desert and down the coastal highway was almost as excruciating as the illness itself.

When I checked into the Regimental Aid Station, the doctors there seemed puzzled by my condition. The initial diagnosis was gastroenteritis because of the vomiting and abdominal cramps, but the doctors disagreed when they saw my temperature, which they thought was more indicative of appendicitis.

Whatever it was, it was never fully diagnosed. The doctors and I eventually passed it off as a reaction to something I ate. Probably the flies. But the bout cost me a few pounds and a lot of strength, so I was ordered to bed for at least two days.

While in the rear, I hit the mail jackpot, which buoyed me through the next week. Another morale booster was the installation of AT&T's free 3-minute overseas calls for Desert Shield participants. I walked gingerly to the 11th Marines command post and was rewarded with a 20-minute — I said to hell with three minutes—conversation with Angie.

I, like nearly every other Marine in theater, came to rely on those international phone calls. Unlike my first trip to the Gulf in 1987 aboard USS *Missouri*, this time I had access to instant communication with my wife, and I planned to take advantage of it. For as long as we had them, I planned to use those phone calls to keep my grip on sanity. Those calls probably did more to keep me going, and to cement my marriage, than anything else during the months of Desert Shield and Desert Storm.

I returned to the field on October 10, rejuvenated and ready to get to work. And the first order of business was to get out of the tent I was sharing with four other officers. It was designed to house two at the most, but we were short tents, so most of the captains piled into Dean's tent. It was cramped, smelly and uncomfortable, which in the Marine Corps is quite normal.

But I had become friends with the regimental intelligence officer, Captain Rich Haddad, a tall, boisterous graduate of the Naval Academy. His claim to fame was being the recipient of a pair of perfumed panties from a stateside girlfriend. But he was also known as the man who unofficially started the U.S. invasion of Panama about a year earlier. Haddad was the officer wounded by Manuel Noriega's goons as he sped through a roadblock thrown up by the Panamanian military. That event, and the detention of an American couple, gave the American government the excuse it needed to go after Noriega.

Haddad, the driver of the car, was shot in the foot. His passenger, a friend of his, was killed by a shot to the head. U.S. forces invaded as Haddad recuperated in a Panamanian hospital. He promptly checked himself out of the hospital and spent most of Operation Just Cause hobbling through the streets on his one good foot looking for a Marine unit.

Haddad and I had decided to build our own hooch, one that would be free of the flies that plagued us. So we went to work digging an eighteen-inch deep foundation, around which we built a two-foot wall of

Be it ever so humble ... the fly-proof summer quarters Capt. Rich Haddad and I constructed out of mosquito netting in October 1990.

sandbags. We tied our mosquito nets together, then fastened them to the overhead camouflage net. We anchored the sides of the netting under the sandbags.

The result of this all-day construction project was a fly-proof mosquito-net tent that looked a lot like the canvas-and-aluminum-tube models popular with campers. The hooch was tall enough for us to stand in, and we had room to stow our gear. Best of all, it was a place to eat our meals without worrying about flies. And the netting allowed air to flow through, which gave us a relatively cool place to sleep when we weren't on watch, especially since the nights and early mornings had started to cool off. Most of the 120-degree days were past, but it was still much too hot to sleep inside a canvas tent during the daylight hours.

By this time, we had settled into something of a routine at 11th Marines. We knew we weren't going to be moving anytime soon, so we all got used to our surroundings and tried our best to block out the boredom and uncertainty.

I still stood watches from midnight or 0200 to 0600, thankful for the peace and quiet and a chance to read, write, or get to know the enlisted Marines manning the radios, which by now included two women, both of whom quickly proved they were more than capable of "packing the gear" right alongside the men.

The afternoons, when it was hot, were spent either in the COC or wrestling with a homemade set of weights Haddad and I had rigged up. Haddad was a huge, muscular rugby player. Disgusted with watching himself turn soft, as was I, we took a few of the poles used to hold up camouflage nets and lashed sandbags to the ends to make barbells. It was crude and terribly unbalanced, but it allowed us a chance to work out and vent some frustration at the same time. Soon, others began to show up at our "iron pile" to work out and pass the time. Pretty soon, we had a small, regular crew of weightlifters who stopped by nearly every evening.

I marveled at our ability to adjust to our surroundings. We'd all learned ways to stay occupied and busy, and we found that we could pass time quite easily this way. It was a lot better than sitting around bitching about how long we'd be there.

The evenings were spent watching the troops play volleyball or reading until the chow trucks arrived with the evening meal — and the term "meal" is a loose interpretation of the rice dishes shoveled out by the cooks.

The food was horrible during Desert Shield. There were times when, no matter how hungry I was, I couldn't stomach the chow. We ate so much rice and "chili mac" — chili and macaroni — that I still have a hard time eating either.

The bad food couldn't be blamed on the cooks, though. They did the best they could with what they had and fed thousands of Marines a day. And to their credit, as the months passed, the food coming out of their chow halls got better and better — and not just because I was getting used to it. The foodstuffs — vegetables, meat, bread, and milk — they were issued got better.

At first, the U.S. military bought foodstuffs from local distributors, which created some very suspicious-looking "mystery meat" meals, but as time passed, the cooks were able to get better quality food, either flown in from the States or from better distributors. We were also fortunate enough to get canned bread and "UHT" milk, which comes in boxes and requires no refrigeration. It tastes strange, but it's a taste easily acquired. I always kept a case of UHT milk near my rack or in my hole because I knew it wouldn't spoil. Some days, when the food was particularly bad, I'd live off UHT and the cereal Angie sent me in the mail.

After evening chow, a small group of officers, usually Huenfeld, Haddad, and a few others, would gather around for coffee.

Our routine served to boost our spirits, and most of us were happy, or at least relieved, to be living with something resembling normalcy.

Plus, there was the added excitement of our first Scud missile alert.

0018, Thurs., 11 Oct 90

In COC. *Just received word from division via radio that there is a possibility that Iraq could fire 1 Scud missile tonight. This is from "what is termed as an unreliable source."* MOPP *Level 0; no additional alert increases. No amplification on source of info.*

Called Lt. Col. Stuart, told him I'd handle it. Div trying to raise all units on division intel nets now, without much success. Now we wait.

0803, Fri., 12 Oct 90

Nothing at all came of the Scud alert, although at Camp 3, panic once again prevailed. The word got scrambled into "the missile is inbound." Marines were tumbled out of their racks and into MOPP *suits. Another good lesson in who cracks up under pressure.*

Arabs are going through garbage and taking return addresses off mail. Two potential problems: (1) people sending letters to the States saying "your son is dead" or (2) letter bombs. Other problems, too, I'm sure. We've been instructed to burn any envelopes we throw out. I save mine anyway.

Wish we were doing something a little more constructive. Or destructive.

Still don't see any way out of this except to destroy Iraq, economically and militarily. That is the only way to guarantee peace and stability in the region for the next 20 years. If Saddam pulls out of Kuwait w/o us attacking, and leaves his army intact — along w/his chem and bio capability — we're screwed. Then we can't attack and hope to survive the barrage of world criticism that would surely follow. If we roll into Kuwait and "liberate" it, the American public would support it. But Saddam would probably sacrifice the National Guard divisions to cover the withdrawal of his Republican Guard divisions, and cede Kuwait to us. After all, he's stripped the country bare. And the bulk of his army would still be intact, leaving him 2 options: (1) stay in Iraq until we leave; then he'd have a free rein in the region, or (2) counterattack us w/an armor-heavy force. If he goes w/#1, I don't think the U.S. would support a drive into Iraq. That's not what our stated mission was. So we'd wind up setting up a DMZ, *as in Korea.*

We misstated our objective: the release of Kuwait and reestablishment of the government. We should have said that our objective was to destroy Iraq's military capability completely, thereby ensuring stability in the region for the future. As usual, we went for the instant gratification. Too late now. If we attack, we're screwed politically. All we'll be able to do is fight a "limited war" of "containment." I despise the phrases. Limited wars accomplish nothing except killing people for no real, tangible purpose. Fighting for the status quo ante — especially in this case — is ridiculous. It won't solve anything.

Nobody wanted to really admit it at the time, but we were more than a little nervous the night I assumed the watch, waiting for a Scud launch.

I comforted myself with the knowledge that even the division headquarters had not given much credence to the word. Luckily, I completed my watch with no incidents, except for the Keystone Kops routine in Haii 3, an incident that, once again, underscored the need for leaders to get the word out correctly the first time.

No one ever verified the story of Arabs going through the garbage for our addresses, but this rumor created quite a stir in the 11th Marines CP for a day or two.

When I wrote that the U.S. misstated its objectives, I was unaware that General Colin Powell, chairman of the Joint Chiefs of Staff, was planning to do just what I wanted to do: destroy as much of the Iraqi army as possible. It was gratifying in January to hear his remark about cutting off the Iraqi army and "killing it." One of my fears was that the U.S. military, à la Vietnam, would not be allowed to bring all its might to bear on the enemy, or that it would be restricted in one way or another. I knew that such restrictions ultimately cost American lives. The same restrictions also would have allowed Saddam to escape with most of his army intact, a future menace to the region.

I also continued to fret over the reason for Operation Desert Shield. Were we simply protecting someone's oil interest? At the time, that thought was repulsive to me. Still young and fairly idealistic, I preferred to think that we were in Saudi Arabia for the nobler cause of restoring the country of Kuwait to its rightful citizens.

In the final analysis, we were there for both. Like it or not, oil is a U.S. national interest, and that national interest was threatened when Saddam ordered his divisions into Kuwait. I am firmly convinced, and there is some evidence to support this, that Saddam would have invaded Saudi Arabia had the United States not responded so quickly and forcefully.

Still, the United States failed in one respect, and that was another concern for me through the long nights on watch. We smashed the Iraqi war machine in Desert Storm, but we didn't smash enough of it, and we didn't cripple Saddam's regime. And we're still paying for that today. Regardless of how much we destroyed, and it was plenty, the remnants of that shattered army were all Saddam needed to rebuild and strengthen his hold on power. By not annihilating the Iraqi military and severely crippling the infrastructure, we allowed Saddam to consolidate his power.

The bitter years of confrontation with Saddam since the end of the war are the result of that failure. I once commented in a meeting that we should kill every single tank and every single rifleman in his army, because I didn't want my son, if I ever had one, to have to go to the Middle East to finish the job.

My son, born after the war, is five as of this writing, and the United States is still grappling with Saddam, with no end in sight.

There are now Gulf War vets still on active duty that could conceivably have sons in the Persian Gulf today.

0830, Sat., 13 Oct 90

Lots of mail yesterday, including a very touching letter from Angie. She was worried that her words sounded awkward, but I found them right on the mark. Great letter w/an extremely funny card. Read the letter several times. She said the "newfound peace" and security of our marriage made her miss me more than ever.

I feel exactly the same way. We grew so close over the last year; we not only salvaged our marriage, we made it better. And it's an indescribably good feeling being consumed w/love for her. That's about the only thing these separations are good for — making me realize how much I love and miss her — and how much I need her.

2 "incidents" yesterday. Outside our pos, guards reported that a fuel truck approached at a high rate of speed, stopped abruptly, and 2 Arabs (why is it always 2?) jumped out and ran away. A cordon was quickly established and Marines hunkered behind vehicles waiting for the bomb to blow. Turned out to be one Bedouin who drove his water truck up to feed his sheep. The Marines looked pretty silly watching those sheep drink water. Passed them on my way to division.

Last night, approx. 1900, "A" 1/12 reported jets low and fast over their pos. They said a plane dropped something about 2000m N of them, which struck the ground and exploded. How they could see the plane pickle something in the dark with 0% illumination remains a mystery. I called division, who confirmed 2 A-6s in the area doing SIMCAS. Planes reported no drops, no explosions. Dave Head, "A" CO, went forward to check for damage and casualties. Nothing.

Marines are crying wolf much too often and the effect will soon be exactly as in that old fable. They are inventing bad guys and boogy monsters.

Angie was my anchor throughout the deployment, and I'm sure many Marines felt the same way about their families. Our families were more than our loved ones. They were symbols of the "real world" and of the lives we had stateside. They were the living proof that there was a reason to put up with all the petty bullshit, the boredom, and the fear. They gave us reasons to live. And reasons to get the war over with and get home.

The story of our Arab shepherd-bomber made the usual rounds and kept us in stitches for days. The sight of a Marine fire team crouching behind rocks and gesturing wildly as sheep passively lapped water spewing from the truck is one that still makes me smile.

The case of the mad midnight bomber in front of "A" Battery was a different matter, however. Rumors like that wasted an enormous amount of time and energy, which only contributed to the "crying wolf" mentality. When the battery called 11th Marines, we had to go through all the motions of verifying the story. I was in the COC when the call came in, and it took at least two hours of radio calls and reconnaissance to learn that somebody had mistaken the A-6s for an enemy bomber.

It took a great deal of discipline to treat each rumor with the same weight and not say, "To hell with it, it's just a rumor."

1514, Wed., 17 Oct 90

Angie said in a letter that she was concerned about the effects of the stress here, which I've written her about. Wrote her a letter telling her not to worry about it. Then I really began to zero in on my state of mind, so I'm going to reproduce portions of the letter here.

Stress has been replaced by boredom. Everybody now realizes that we are here to sit on our asses until the politicians make oil safe for democracy. Unfortunately, it has made us complacent and lethargic. We've lost our edge. We've been lying around for so long that we don't want to do anything. Even a simple task like filling up a water can seems to take a huge amount of effort. Quite frankly, this has turned into another bullshit exercise. This isn't gratuitous griping; my morale is OK, considering. I'm used to the desert now, and quite comfortable in it, except for the chow that keeps tearing up my insides.

But, we're out here "just fucking around" in the field. The field-grade officers, who hate to see anybody not doing something (even if there is nothing to do) come up with all kinds of Mickey Mouse shit. It's amazing what people w/idle minds will come up with; they invent things to do.

Nobody is really in a wartime mentality. It's hard to be. We all rushed out to the field and set up little camps all over the desert, which get more and more permanent every day. Every day it gets a little more like PTA, 29 Palms, etc. We aren't moving to avoid detection, we chatter incessantly on the radio, we don't train, we don't do much of anything except draw on maps and spread wild rumors. Rumors are still our biggest enemy.

The ennui that settled over us was a constant enemy. Haddad and I tried to stay busy, either building our hooch, improving our fighting holes, visiting units, or trying to stay in shape with our homemade weights.

There were also the command post-exercises, but this training seemed only half-hearted. It was half-assed training and we all knew it, and many times we found ourselves simply going through the motions. Our minds were numb and our bodies, not used to week upon week of inactivity, were growing soft.

Added to that was the fact that though rumors raced throughout the division, nobody knew how long we would be in Saudi Arabia. We had figured six months, the normal length of a peacetime Marine Corps deployment. But, this wasn't peacetime, technically, and when it became apparent that we were settling in for the long haul, we began to ask, "Now what?" The answer was silence or, worse, conjecture. Nobody seemed to have any idea how long we would stay in the desert, and higher headquarters wasn't talking.

It was hard to divine from the meager clippings exactly what the mood was at home, but it didn't appear encouraging. I began to wonder if we'd been forgotten about, flung into a wasteland until the politicians found a solution. Only after I returned home did I learn just how wrong I was on this point.

I also learned how wrong I was on the inactivity of the America military. We didn't attack in the early days of Desert Shield because we couldn't. We simply didn't have the combat power ashore to oust Saddam. It would take us until January to build up that power. So, while it seemed we were growing weaker as individuals by the day, the American military machine was actually growing stronger.

0818, Sat., 20 Oct 90

Long meeting last night to discuss the new division frag order reflecting our new northern boundary. The Saudis finally agreed to extend it into what was previously their AO.

So now, TF Shepherd is going to move north, be in place by Monday. 3/9, manning their strongpoint w/a "die in place" mission, has extended their Tactical Area of Responsibility — it resembles a fist w/the index finger pointing at Kuwait. They plan to move forward into battle positions, then delay and defend back to the strongpoint. They'll have their work cut out for them; they'll probably be facing an armored brigade that is the advance guard.

Lots of discussion last night about battle handover between us and Saudis, passage of lines, etc. USMC doesn't practice either often or well. It's going to be a clusterfuck. The plan is for TF Shepherd to dash forward when the shooting starts and "escort" the Saudis thru the USMC zone, aided by ANGLICO units attached to the SANG.

Much discussion also on FSCLs and other fire support coordinating measures; current FSCLs don't follow terrain. They were determined on lat/long lines, ostensibly to allow the pilots to "find" them on instruments. That's great, but the grunts can't see lat/longs! Really stupid. We talked about the minimal role NGFS will play, because the deep-draft ships can't get in close enough.

Don't know if all this is based on new info of Saddam's supposed attack, but if he does attack, we better get our shit together quickly.

There's too much confusion now, and bullets aren't even flying. Every-
body wants to be a maneuver warfare guru, but they are actually
acting like a bunch of self-deluded cowboys.

Col. Howard said that, in his heart of hearts, he doesn't think Sad-
dam will attack, and neither do I. Hope not. Our list of priorities for
a 12-hr notice of an attack has revealed some serious deficiencies.
We've been in this position a month, and we still don't have every-
thing ready. No overhead cover for the COC, *crumbling fighting holes,*
no rehearsals for defense against ground attack, we're not wired into
the battalions so we can talk when the radios go to shit. S-4 argued
that point adamantly this a.m. at meeting.

Comm O whined and said it can't be done. I say bullshit. We need
the wire. I had brought that up before, and again last night to Lt.
Col. Stuart. Also, we don't have any real counterbattery plan for the
reg't.

1st MARDIV *is simply not ready to fight a war. We can't get our heads*
out of our asses. We talk and talk of what needs to be done, but don't
DO anything about it.

A great deal of political and military negotiating went into convinc-
ing the Saudis to allow the Marine Corps, and the Army on our left flank,
to extend our tactical area of responsibility or TAOR, northward to the
vicinity of the coastal border town of Khafji. The Saudi National Guard
would still man the border itself, but from this point on, Marines would
be working with the Saudis more closely than ever.

The move, which gave the division much more flexibility when it
came to devising a defense of eastern Saudi Arabia in the "Triangle," didn't
really improve the lot of Task Force Shepherd, the battalion of LAV-
mounted infantry to our immediate north. Shepherd was performing
essentially a cavalry mission, screening and patrolling the desert near the
border. As such, Task Force Shepherd was in direct contact with our Saudi
allies.

Shepherd wasn't equipped to deal with an armored brigade, the predicted size of the Iraqi force if the Iraqis attacked. Light and mobile, Task
Force Shepherd performed best in the cavalry mode — although Corps preferred the less-Army-sounding "reconnaissance and scouting" mode — or
as a sort of "dragoon" battalion, where the infantry would dismount to
fight as infantry, then load up and speed away.

But facing an armored brigade, packed with T-72 tanks, Shepherd
would have resembled a piece of toilet paper trying to stop a .22-cal. bullet. The hope was that Shepherd could slow, if not stop, the Iraqi advance
long enough to allow the rest of the division to deliver a killing blow.

Battle handovers and passages of lines can be the most difficult task
in all of modern maneuver warfare. It requires an enormous amount of

coordination, concentration, and communication. Under ideal conditions, a unit that is falling back does so through the unit to its immediate rear. As it passes through the lines of this rearward unit, it hands over the responsibility for the conduct of the battle, to ensure that the enemy remains engaged and under fire. I'd practiced it enough at Twentynine Palms, during combined-arms exercises, to know the Marine Corps didn't do it enough to be good at it. It was one area where the Army, the majority of which is mechanized forces, had a leg up on us.

The problem is exacerbated when the battle handover is being conducted across a language barrier, which accounted for Task Force Shepherd's "escort" role, along with Marines from the Air, Naval Gunfire Liaison Company, a collection of parachute-qualified artillery forward observers (both officer and enlisted), radio operators, Naval officers and Marine naval gunfire spotters. The ANGLICO had the sometimes difficult but very important job of working with other services or other nations to conduct liaison for naval gunfire, artillery, and other fire support to make sure the right people got hit by supporting arms on the battlefield.

With ANGLICO talking on the radios, and Task Force Shepherd escorting the Saudis with clearly identifiable Marine LAVs, the unspoken reason for all the hand-holding was that this was the best way to keep Marines from firing up the first Arabs they saw heading south in unfamiliar vehicles.

As an artillery officer, fire support coordination was my bread and butter, and I thought it was ridiculous to go against doctrine to placate a bunch of pilots when it came to deciding fire support coordination lines, or FSCLs.

The lines should be drawn along terrain features that can be recognized quickly and easily — from the ground and the air. The FSCLs act as trip wires to keep falling bombs and artillery rounds at a safe distance in front of friendly troops. A mechanized infantry battalion, for example, may have several FSCLs in front of it as it moves toward the enemy. As it crosses each line, that "trips" the next FSCL, which causes most supporting-arms fire to shift beyond the FSCL, to avoid friendly-fire incidents.

It's up to the ground unit to report when it crosses the FSCLs, so it only makes sense for the FSCL to be an identifiable piece of terrain — a highway or a wadi or a tree line. Instead, to accommodate pilots who were having trouble identifying anything on the flat, brown, Saudi desert, the FSCLs were arbitrarily drawn. Once the latitude and longitude of each line was determined, the information was distributed to the air wing to input into the planes' computers. As I mentioned in my journal, though, that didn't help the grunts.

I was wrong about deep-draft ships being able to work in close for naval gunfire support, or NGFS. Both the *Missouri* and the *Wisconsin,* each with a draft of 37 feet, were able to maneuver into the Gulf close enough to fire their 16-inch guns at the Iraqis— several times and with great effect.

Our "12-hour" list had been compiled after an order from Col. Howard. It contained all our priorities in the event that we got a 12-hour notice that the Iraqis were headed our way. The work that went to that list revealed one thing quite clearly: complacency. We'd gotten lazy with the heat and inactivity. And it had become too easy to say, "It's too hard." I'd harped for weeks about the need to run communications wire to the battalions in the inevitable event that our radios didn't work in battle. Slowly, I'd begun to convince others, and now this became a near-constant topic during our long meetings.

1221, Sun., 21 Oct 90

Feeling really irascible. It's not the lack of mail, it's not the desert. Think it's the inaction, plus I tried to write Angie this a.m. and got frustrated. Was trying to explain some of the results of all the soul-searching I've done lately, but either I couldn't get it down on paper, or if I did, it didn't sound right.

I have done a lot of thinking, about how I've lived, my attitudes, opinions, etc. Part of it was the situation (and still is), part was watching some of the people here in action. Bothered me — in those people, and bothered me more to think that people could have perceived me as being like some of the bullshit artists I've seen here.

Since then, I've been attempting the hardest of all tasks, behavior modification. I've just realized that I don't have to announce my opinions at every given opportunity; it's not my job to expose all the fools on the earth; and I don't have to bluster about w/tough talk the whole day long.

That's about as in-depth as I can get. Maybe that's all I need to say, but I feel there's more. There is a need within me to fully explain it, but I can't get the explanation out coherently. I've discovered something I don't quite understand, I guess. Strange feeling.

Could this be a form of stress? I doubt it. I'm not stressed. In fact, I have quite a bit of peace of mind. The most difficult thing I do is combat boredom, which I suppose is better than being shot at. But I long for activity. Anything to make the time go faster, even though I must admit I can't believe 56 days have passed already. This time 3 years ago, I was just over a month away from leaving the Persian Gulf on the Missouri. *That time seemed to move much more slowly.*

Tactically, there is zero going on. Saddam has not made any major changes to his tactical deployments, as he would if preparing for an offensive. About the only thing he's done is move a 122mm self-propelled battalion north and replace it w/a 122mm towed battalion. That isn't too significant. Other than that, no change. Sitzkrieg.

For the first time in my life, I'd come face-to-face with myself, and I wasn't very happy with what I saw.

I'd joined an organization of swaggering Type A personalities, arrogant males with a penchant for perfectionism. And like many, I'd bought into the culture of the Corps, lock, stock, and barrel. I was just as swaggering, arrogant, and boastful as anyone. But two months into this deployment, I realized that, whether I liked it or not, I had to change my behavior. This entry is indicative of that, and it was another step along the path of self-discovery that, in the end, was the biggest thing I took away from Desert Storm.

I have always had a deep need to explain the things that happen around me and to me. That's why I am a writer. It's my way of trying to find some sense, to organize and explain my experiences. What I saw every day in the desert challenged that need as never before.

During the time I'd already spent in the desert, I'd seen my share of trash-talking, macho men. Bullshit artists faking it. But I had been unable to see that they were faking it because I was, too. But a funny thing happened to me on the way to a war. I ran into reality, and it scared the hell out of me. Slowly, I began to realize that this was no place for macho men, no place for bullshitters and braggarts.

And then there's the elephant.

During the War between the States, soldiers on both sides referred to "seeing the elephant," a euphemism for experiencing combat. A quirky saying, it held more depth than the simple experience of a combat situation. To see the elephant was to undergo a metamorphosis, a life-changing experience. Men who "saw the elephant" were never the same.

Everyone who goes to war, regardless of its length or intensity must learn about the elephant, and learn that war is not a great dream of adventure, glory, and glamour, but loneliness, death, anger, despair, and sadness. And short though the Persian Gulf War was, there was plenty of each.

Curiously, I thought the war's brevity would mean that veterans of other, bloodier, conflicts would dismiss the combat experiences of the Persian Gulf. But in 1993, I found out differently. I had the pleasure of attending the fiftieth anniversary of the battle of Tarawa in the Pacific Island nation of Kiribati. During the course of the commemoration, I spoke with dozens of Marine veterans who had somehow managed to survive the slaughterhouse that was Tarawa.

When they learned I had served in the Persian Gulf, they were eager to hear of my experiences. Feeling utterly foolish in the company of such men, I tried to change the subject, but they would have none of it.

"Look, don't try to tell us it was nothing," said one former Marine mortarman as we sipped drinks in a hotel bar. "At least back then we knew what we'd be facing. Thousands of dug-in Japanese. You faced being gassed, or germ warfare; who knows what else. The weapons today are a hell of a lot scarier than ours were."

That surprised me, and, in a way, vindicated my experience.

In the desert, I was beginning to see the elephant, though I didn't know it at the time and wouldn't fully understand what the Persian Gulf did to me until years later, when I began to write about it. For the moment, I was embarrassed when I realized that I had been exactly like the men I now began to despise, and vowed to change that. Cowboys were only going to get Marines killed, and I was determined to not let that happen to the Marines around me.

Years later, I can see that what was really happening was that I was finally growing up. This self-examination was part of maturation, and a part of the process of shedding my youth.

1238, Fri., 2 Nov 90

At long last, there is some quasi-official word on rotations.

Talked to 11th Mar S-1. There was a powwow at division yesterday. Apparently CMC left the rotation plan w/MEF on his visit last week. Our replacements will be here in February, and it looks like we'll be leaving in March. There is still some work to be done on dates and signing over gear. I'd imagine that 1/12's advance party will be out of here sometime in February, and I aim to be on it. If I'm going to be a staff puke, I'm going all the way. Besides, I came over here on the advance party.

The number one topic of discussion for most of Desert Shield: rotations. Specifically, when — or if — we'd rotate back home.

Not everybody believed that we were in Saudi Arabia to attack the Iraqi army, and depending on my mood and the day of the week, I was in this school of thought. Many of us believed, as we were led to believe, that our mission was to provide a shield against any further incursions by Saddam, similar to the situation on the Korean Peninsula. And if that were, in fact, the case, we all wanted to know when we were going to get out of that miserable desert.

The problem was that we were getting nothing in the way of information from higher headquarters, and that led to a huge amount of frustration among the troops. Every time I came back from a division meeting, at least one Marine would sidle up to me and quietly ask if I had any word on rotations. And, of course, I had my own contacts at various administrative shops, but those officers were in the dark, too.

I didn't care how long I was going to be there, but I wanted to know something. It would have given all of us something to point to, something to focus on.

Marines are accustomed to long deployments, at sea and abroad, and usually adjust without complaining. Morale is seldom a pervasive problem. But the one thing Marines always know — or did before Desert Shield — was when they would rotate back home.

But that wasn't the case during Desert Shield. We had no idea how long we'd be there. We didn't seem to be accomplishing much, although we were all aware that a massive military buildup was taking place behind us and to the west of us. We saw hundreds of low-boy trucks hauling Army tanks to the desert every day. You didn't have to be a genius to figure out that the reason we weren't going home was because we were preparing to strike, but, again, nobody was saying much about that, either.

So we sat around, bored stiff. The boredom was like a form of madness. I could hold it at bay for a few days; it always crept back not to ambush me, but to invade me, taking over my entire being, making even the simplest task seem difficult.

Years later, I discussed this with one of my best friends, Neal Noem. I'd met Neal, a warrant officer who joined 1/12 as the battalion communications officer just days before our deployment. We became close after my eventual return to 1/12. Neal remarked that one of his most vivid memories of the war is how tired we always were.

I agreed. We stood watch and slept in holes or under hooches, usually in extreme temperatures. We probably averaged four or five hours of sleep a night during Desert Shield — and less during Desert Storm. But even that wasn't enough. It always felt as if you never slept at all. Standing watches or being called away to long meetings at division or regiment usually broke up what sleep we did get. Occasionally, we conducted commexes at night. Sleep became a luxury.

And in the midst of this atmosphere of near-despair, boredom, and exhaustion, nobody told the troops anything. And in that information vacuum, Marines began pouring out rumors and speculation — and their frustration with the whole deployment. The excruciating inaction left us with little to do except wonder when we were going to make it home. Or attack Saddam. And our attitudes, as we became increasingly hostile and restless, turned more and more to a philosophy of "Somebody's going to have to pay for this."

Perhaps that was the psychology behind the reticence of the "higher headquarters." Maybe they wanted us to reach the point where we would gladly attack into the teeth of the Iraqi defenses just to have something to do. I've always thought a similar psychology works aboard Navy ships: Put the Marines in such miserable living conditions in troop berthing that they will be happy to charge across a beach laced with machine-gun fire just to be free of the ship.

So we welcomed the news on rotations with glad hearts and sighs of relief. But we only knew half of the story. The units coming to Kuwait in February wouldn't be coming to replace us; they would come to *reinforce* us. And, the planners expected to have us out by March, not to rotate, but for good, after an offensive. There was no way we could have known that then, though.

1107, Sun., 4 Nov 90

Had breakfast w/Morgan, who was visited by Lt. Gen. Boomer yesterday. Boomer said that we will continue to use diplomacy, but unfortunately it ain't working, and we're almost out of options. Then again, Morgan has been the Prophet of Doom ever since we got here.

Morgan said Gen. Boomer implied a January op. We also discussed the length of the war, if there is to be one. Morgan said 1-2 months, meaning to push Saddam out of Kuwait. If we do that, I'll be severely disappointed. That's fighting for nothing in my eyes. If we do that, Saddam will still have the bulk of his army— and NBC capability— intact to use the next time he gets a wild hair. The only way to guarantee any kind of real peace in the next 20 years is to destroy Saddam and his army. Period. Like in The Heart of Darkness: "kill them all."

But, we'll probably fight a "limited war," let Saddam conduct a fighting withdrawal, salvaging his regular RGFC divisions while sacrificing his National Guard. Then we'll leave, and Saddam will smirk smugly. And try it again someday.

Saddam did try it again ... and again. Today, my worst fears in 1990 are displayed annually. It's hard to believe that I wrote those words before Desert Storm even began, years before the never-ending "Desert"-named operations, before the no-fly zones and the ignored air war against Iraq.

Generals Powell and Schwarzkopf were actually planning a combination of the options Capt. Steve Morgan and I discussed over coffee. Their goal was to eject the Iraqis from Kuwait while inflicting as much damage as possible on the army and Saddam's war-fighting capability.

And to a large degree, the United States succeeded. Even with the post-war analysis that showed that we didn't inflict as much damage from the air as originally advertised, we hammered the Iraqi army, from both the air and the ground. I certainly saw enough evidence of the destruction we handed out. But, like a football team that blows a fourth-quarter lead, we failed to put the other team away. President Bush, quite simply, ended the war too soon, when the horrific images of the "Highway of Death" bounced into American living rooms via satellite.

We had the Iraqis on the run, but they weren't knocked out. One of the most important aspects of modern warfare is pursuit, something at which the American military doesn't typically excel. Perhaps it is our nature to be viewed as a good sport, or to go easy on the underdog.

Pursuit is more than just chasing the enemy off the battlefield, which we did beyond all doubt. Pursuit is relentless, dogged, and does not stop until the enemy is shattered, either physically or emotionally.

No American commander defined it better than Confederate Lt. Gen. Nathan Bedford Forrest, who once pursued a beaten enemy nearly a hundred miles after a victory, chasing the Yankees into the night until he fell from his saddle from exhaustion. And Union Gen. George Meade passed up an opportunity to end the war quickly when he chose not to pursue a thoroughly whipped Confederate Army out of Pennsylvania after Gettysburg.

I do not believe we should have rolled into Baghdad, but I do believe we should have hounded the Iraqi army into oblivion. We had the wherewithal and the motivation to do it in 1991. Had we done so, the United States would not still be dealing with a despot like Saddam.

1738, Thurs., 8 Nov 90

Busy day today! First Haddad and I tore down our hooch for better "winter" quarters, a CP tent formerly used by the regimental XO. We turned it into a palace, complete w/large dining table, shaving table, pantry, and solar shower under the net. Wooden floors and electricity inside the tent. It's really a blast.

Went to a CG's meeting the other night and the 15-21 November Division TEWT was discussed. Think division is trying to start a war. We're moving north; USAF is flying lots of night sorties near the border; 4th MEB is doing an amphib landing at Mishab, way north of here; USN is putting 3 cruisers and an FFG extremely close-in and close to the border. G-2 all worried about Iraqi reaction. No shit, boss, so am I.

Actually, worried is a bad word. Rather, he was cavalier. Very flippant. He said, "Worst case scenario ... he could throw a couple of Scuds our way." As if he welcomed the missiles. Greatly disturbed by such a devil-may-care attitude. Felt like saying, "What the fuck do you mean, 'throw a couple of Scuds our way'?" Looked at the battalion commanders who were there. Several shook their heads, whether in dismay or disbelief, I don't know. It's as if the staff really, really wants a war. Or that the division staff is looking for some glory and ribbons.

The weather had begun to change, and Haddad and I knew we couldn't stay in our open-air hooch much longer. The nights had already gotten cool enough to require a sleeping bag, especially since we had become accustomed to the blistering heat.

We turned our move into a grand event, just to break up the boredom. When the regimental XO moved out, we pounced on the opportunity to upgrade our mosquito-net hovel into something resembling real quarters. We turned to the task with gusto, and we were amazed at what we could build with sandbags and wooden ammunition pallets.

The table was essential, given Haddad's enormous appetite and the endless supply of "care packages" he received in the mail. Angie kept me well stocked, also, sending heaps of peanut butter, chocolate, trail mix, and powdered drink mixes. With all the food we had between the two of us, Haddad and I could have opened a restaurant.

Haddad also owned a priceless luxury item — a portable camping shower. Essentially a plastic bag with a tube and a spigot, we filled it each morning and let the sun heat it until evening. Once we installed a wooden ammo pallet as the floor and dug a sluice around it, we were able to enjoy a hot shower in the field every evening, a sure-fire morale booster.

The "winter quarters" I shared with Capt. Rich Haddad. Note wooden pallets scattered throughout.

Civilians may chuckle at the excitement over something as simple as a shower, but when you are deprived of nearly every creature comfort, every sign of civilization, the value of a hot shower skyrockets. Haddad and I even opened the shower to the general public. Soon we had a group of regulars soaping up and singing daily. If we'd charged a fee, we'd be millionaires by now.

The intelligence officer's comment shocked me, as I recorded the day it happened. And it wasn't just me. Several field-grade officers muttered derisive comments after the meeting.

It really rattled me to see officers treating our situation as if it were a game or a movie. Some of that attitude is typical on a staff, especially a high-level one. But to refer to the possible deaths of Marines as cavalierly as "throwing a couple of Scuds our way" disgusted me.

Apparently, Maj. Gen. Mike Myatt, the division commander, was none too pleased with the officer, either. We heard a few days later that he had been transferred to Riyadh.

· C H A P T E R   F I V E ·

Saturday, 10 Nov 90

Well, the USMC *birthday celebration was marred by the comments of Maj. Gen. Myatt, although it really wasn't his fault.*

He informed us today that the Secretary of Defense issued a message calling for more troops to be sent here — not to replace us, but to reinforce us. As I was the narrator for the birthday celebration, I was in front of the formation, and could see the reaction. The whole battery literally sagged when he said, "All talk of rotations at this point is just that — talk." He all but said we're going to be here a long time.

I couldn't believe it. Still hasn't really sunk in. What timing. At the Birthday Ball.

We're going to stay here when 2nd MARDIV *gets here. I've already written home about the supposed February rotation w/10th Marines. Wrote again tonight w/this news. I am deeply angered w/the mind-fuck we have all been through since Aug., whether it's been intentional or not. It just isn't right to put people through what we've gone through physically and emotionally. This was a real cruel blow. I'm trying to figure out the process going on in Washington. It seems awful screwy. If we're going to fight Saddam, then let's fucking do it, and quit dicking around, talking tough. I read just the other day that the Secretary of Defense was going to sign off on his rotation policy. What a joke that was. We were all hoping for that one. Nobody has said anything yet about leaving, now because nobody knows.*

Actually, I'm just angry and railing at the ubiquitous "they." I'm prepared to do what I have to do, be patient, and wait for the word. But I am getting frustrated at the inaction. Something has to give. I don't necessarily want a war, but I want to do SOMETHING, fight, go home, whatever. Anything besides sitting on my ass for months.

Once my temper cooled, I was grateful for Myatt's straightforward-ness. His words shocked us, but at the same time provided a catalyst for us to shake off the ennui that had engulfed us. My own complacency and inaction had caused me to become shortsighted and angry. But about a week after I wrote about my frustration with our lack of activity, Myatt jolted us all awake. We began to get our "game faces" on.

When I wrote that inbound units had to be operational by 15 January 1991, I had no way of knowing that date would become — or already had at echelons far above my pay grade — Saddam's deadline for getting out of Kuwait.

1936, Mon., 12 Nov 90

All talk of rotations ceased. Still some dazed looks. Col. Howard said that the news has already stated that the troops inbound are rein-forcements, rather than replacements, so the wives already know what's going on. Wrote Angie a long letter, which exhausted me, explaining what I could.

Angie's letters were a fountain of support and strength during this difficult period. I found myself taking an hour or so each day to write her a letter from the solitude of my tent. Sometimes I felt her presence so strongly it was as if she was sitting across the table, and my written words were a conversation. In my mind, I could hear her responses.

Similarly, I read her letters as if she was talking to me, and I concentrated on the memory of her voice in my head. Still, there were times when I recalled her tears in August. Those teardrops were like acid on my soul, but even the negative seemed to draw us closer together.

13 Nov 90

Thanksgiving card from Angie today. Front was a cartoon of a girl eating a TV dinner. The caption read, "We won't be together at all this Thanksgiving." Kind of depressed me. Also got a letter; she's feel-ing the holiday blues. I miss her very badly.

We both hated the separation, but we shared a feeling of "we're in this together." Whenever one of us was down, the other responded with a let-ter of support. Sometimes, it seemed as if we were reading each other's minds. Several times, I received a letter in which Angie knew what I was thinking even before I did.

Our misery in the desert now had a tangible objective, not some altru-istic goal that meant nothing to warriors. Having that objective gave us something to prepare for, something to work toward. We had our focus back, and it showed in the faces and actions of all the Marines. We began to resharpen the edge.

Part of that preparation was a huge, division-size exercise, Imminent Thunder. Part CPX— radio wars— and part TEWT— tactical exercise without troops— Imminent Thunder raised more than a few eyebrows. With so much radio traffic and a division's worth of Marines and vehicles moving to and fro across northern Saudi Arabia — not to mention the air and sea forces involved — some intelligence people and civilian analysts feared Saddam might mistake the exercise for the real thing and attack. Division claimed the whole exercise was classified, but when Angie asked me in a letter if I were participating in Imminent Thunder, I had to chuckle at our "opsec"— operational security. Apparently, we weren't fooling anyone.

The exercise kicked off on the evening of November 18 I had the first watch and grew bored waiting for things to start happening. Within hours, however, I was up to my ears in the first real training I'd done in months, and I was loving it. Once the "war" got into full swing, the controlled chaos of the fire direction center got my blood pumping.

Life in an artillery FDC is a frenzied atmosphere not designed for the faint of heart, a cacophony of shouted orders, crackling radios, and Marines rushing back and forth, conducting fire missions, receiving and transmitting radio messages, and scribbling on maps. It's an adrenaline-fueled, stress-filled ride. Loads of fun.

2025, Wed., 21 Nov 90

TEWT debrief at division today was usual soft soap BS — we kicked ass, we never lose. Air wing general took up most of the time going on and on. Why do aviators always have to be the center of attention?

Gen. Myatt not pleased w/fire support coordination and took it out on Col. Howard, unfortunately. Hey, we're displeased too! But that is a function of the fire support coordination center. Problem is, most maneuver units, and especially the air wing, don't give a shit about fire support coordination, nor do they know much about it. There was hardly any artillery play in the TEWT— yet they "killed" 250 tanks.

Pres. Bush visits tomorrow. HUGE stress ex going on at division. Media, Secret Service, etc. Bush will eat w/the troops, then make a speech on live TV. Word is that this is his last good shot at getting back the public support, which has apparently dropped sharply lately.

Maj. Gen. Myatt had a fearsome reputation as a no-bullshit officer who could really chew some ass when he wanted to. Most of the time, he was amiable and easy to talk to.

In fact, one of his drivers, a corporal, had served with me aboard the *Missouri*. When we bumped into each other during a meeting, he introduced me to Myatt, whom I found very down-to-earth. Years later, I met him again in Korea, and before I could introduce myself, he asked, "Didn't you serve in my division in Saudi Arabia?" I was impressed.

A tough-looking leathery Texan, Myatt looked like a cowboy in a Marine uniform. In his meetings, he usually sat hunched in a director's chair, arms folded, a bush hat — or a watch cap, in cold weather — pulled low over his eyes. It gave him a serene, almost sleepy, appearance.

Until a staff officer or briefer screwed up, or until Myatt heard something he didn't like. Then he would lash out at the unfortunate one. It was like watching a snake strike.

Unfortunately, Col. Howard became a victim of a Myatt strike over fire support coordination — or the lack of it — during Imminent Blunder, as we had taken to calling it. Fire support coordination is an all-hands responsibility, but artillerymen are generally considered the "resident experts," probably because they do so much of it as part of their everyday jobs. It's part science, part dogma and part art, and it requires study and practice to get it right. Artillery officers get hours of training on fire support coordination at Fort Sill, unlike most other combat-arms fields.

Coordination is accomplished at nearly every level of command on a battlefield, mainly by use of graphic elements on a map — lines, boxes, and circles on either a computer or an acetate-covered tactical map. Direct- and indirect-fire systems, from rifles to artillery to B-52 strikes, are coordinated using boundaries, "minimum range lines," "no-fire areas," and various other means to prevent friendly-fire accidents.

That coordination is done by the fire support coordinator, an officer who works in the fire support coordination center, or FSCC. Actually, since the fire support coordinator for an infantry regiment is the artillery battalion commander, the assistant fire support coordinator, usually an artillery major, often runs the FSCC.

If done correctly, fire support coordination is seamless in the flow of the battle. If done the usual way, however, the resulting confusion is similar to throwing gasoline on a fire. It's one of the most difficult functions on the battlefield — both in training and in war. The number of friendly-fire casualties in the Persian Gulf War is a grim testament to that.

Besides our need for more practice at fire support coordination, I don't remember if we learned many lessons during Imminent Thunder, other than employing a modern Marine division on a desert battlefield is a real pain in the ass.

President Bush's visit was the talk of the division, and most Marines were impressed that he would visit 1st Marine Division. It vindicated our long stay in Saudi Arabia and legitimized our self-proclaimed "first with the most" status.

1831, 22 Nov 90

Thanksgiving. Good meal tonight, after a day of "holiday routine," courtesy of Col. Howard. Someone put up a volleyball net and we played all afternoon.

Holidays under these circumstances are quite depressing and lonely. Said a prayer of thanks a few minutes ago. Actually felt as if God was indeed watching over me. Made me feel a lot better.

Have been thinking about war a lot — too much. Asking the taboo question of "what if?" Not a good question to linger on. Better to have faith that you'll get through it, God willing. I know this much, though. Should I die, the pain of not being around my wife, to not ever see her or be with her ever again is far worse than the pain of simply dying. I don't even like to think about not ever seeing her again. It hurts too much. Part of it is because of the pain it would put her through, and I can't bear to think of her in so much pain. That is truly too much.

So, I pray every night that this will end soon, and that we are together again. I have enough faith in God that, whether war comes or not, I'll return to her. That faith is all the assurance I have, but I think that's all I really need. I know of nothing else that can give me that assurance. It chases away depression, loneliness, doubt, and fear.

The president has come and gone. Tried to pick up his speech on AFRTS, *but couldn't. Tomorrow I'll have to ask. Not expecting any earth-shattering revelations, though.*

My Desert Shield Thanksgiving was one of the most memorable in my life. It was the day that, in the cradle of Islam, I rediscovered the key element of Christianity — faith.

I'd been raised in the Southern Baptist church in Mississippi. I'd grown up knowing about the Father, Son, and Holy Spirit. The Calvinist-influenced Baptists teach that God's will prevails and that Christians should have enough faith to allow God's will to work in their lives. I believed in God and Christ, considered myself a Christian — albeit not a very good one — but I'd never had my faith tested. I'd never had to analyze my faith and what I believed, to see if those beliefs held up.

After joining the Marine Corps, I drifted away from the church. Part of the reason was that, as a Marine in the Fleet Marine Force, I deployed or went to the field often, making it difficult to worship in the manner to which I was accustomed. I'd also become disenchanted with the Baptist denomination, which I'd begun to view as judgmental, inflexible, and sanctimonious. Another reason: Angie is Methodist, so finding a church we both liked was nearly impossible.

I'd begun to pray again during Desert Shield — out of fear and frustration mostly — as the uncertainty of the future loomed before me. On Thanksgiving Day, after a delicious Marine Corps meal and an exhausting afternoon of volleyball, I felt the need to be alone.

For the first time, I fully realized my own mortality. Another thought caused me anguish — Angie and I had no children. We'd never seriously considered kids — we were young and didn't want them and that's all there was to it. And then I went to Saudi Arabia. I began to reconsider.

Emotions I'd never felt before, and couldn't even begin to understand, roiled within me. I prayed for nearly half an hour. For the first time in my life, I truly felt as if I was talking directly to God, and it gave me great comfort. A calm settled over me and I decided then and there that I would make it on faith alone and try not to worry about the rest.

I failed in that, numerous times, but it never shook my faith. And it still hasn't today.

Part Two

Gearing Up

· C H A P T E R   S I X ·

By the end of November, the division had shifted to a war footing, both physically and emotionally. Where two weeks earlier we thought of ways to improve the volleyball court, now we lightened our loads and tried to get our hands on more ammo or went out on recons for new positions.

As proof of the new attitude, on November 23, we were informed that the division would change its task organization — the way it was organized for combat — on December 1.

Since our arrival, the division's regiments and battalions had been formed into task forces, combined-arms teams built around infantry units to maximize speed, firepower, and maneuverability. In fact, we had transformed the division from a collection of regiments and battalions into a collection of task forces.

Task Force Shepherd, the LAV task force skirting the border north of us, remained in the division, but was beefed up with tanks and mechanized infantry. The added punch allowed it to take over the area manned by 3rd Battalion, 9th Marines, near the coast, along the highway.

3/9 would return to Task Force Ripper, which had been built around 7th Marines. Ripper would lose a battalion of tanks and some amphibious assault vehicles, or AAVs, to Shepherd.

3rd Marines was to become Task Force Taro, a name that, while certainly identifying us as a Hawaii task force, infuriated Col. Admire, our CO Taro is a Hawaiian root, like a yam, used to make poi, a starchy, gluelike substance that is a staple of the Hawaiian diet. Almost immediately,

3rd Marines were known as "Task Force Poi." Whatever the name, the regiment was to be mounted in AAVs or serve as the helicopter-borne reserve.

Task Force Cunningham would be an air maneuver element comprised of division air assets, which caused many of us to scratch our heads wondering what the division would do for close-air support.

For the cannon cockers, the artillery organization stayed the same. The mission of 1/12 depended on the fate of 3rd Marines. If the regiment became the heliborne reserve, 1/12 would have possibly been designated as a general-support battalion — a "catch-all" battalion which normally supports a division-sized unit.

Finally, the British 7th Armour Division would move in behind us and occupy 3rd Marines' position south of Abu Hadriyah.

We also spent several days playing stop-and-go games over Haii 3. Several times we were told to move out, then ordered to sit tight. By now this back-and-forth routine became known as a "jerk-ex," a term for repeatedly jerking the troops around. The problem with a jerk-ex is that, left unchecked, it could turn into a full-blown "clusterfuck."

Meanwhile, my time with 11th Marines was running out. I was closing in on my three-month mark, and I was eager to return to my battalion, especially when new officers reported to 11th Marines, filling out the regimental headquarters quota on captains. Once again, I was an extra captain. My frustration level had begun to grow, but not because of anyone at the regiment. I truly enjoyed working for Lt. Col. Stuart and especially Col. Howard, but I always felt like an interloper. I was a Hawaii Marine in a California outfit, and I just didn't belong. I mentioned this to my battalion XO, Maj. Mike Von Tungeln, and he promised to talk to Stuart. He did, and by the first week of December, I was back in 1/12.

My first reaction to returning to the battalion was shock. My first impression of the battalion FDC, as recorded in my November 29 entry was that they were " ... *demoralized, and have an 'I just do my job' attitude.*"

I didn't quite know what to make of it, but I decided on the spot to do something about it. That decision was well timed, because on Dec. 1, Capt. Steve Morgan brought his battery back to 1/12. Morgan had been on loan to 3/11 for about as long as I had been an indentured servant to 11th Marines.

Steve Morgan was, and is, quite a character. An admitted Anglophile, he had the quirky habit in the field of stopping daily at 4 P.M. for tea. Sometimes he invited me, and that's how I got to know him.

The day he came back, Steve said he would be giving no quarter to anyone. Apparently, he came to the conclusion that he had been too

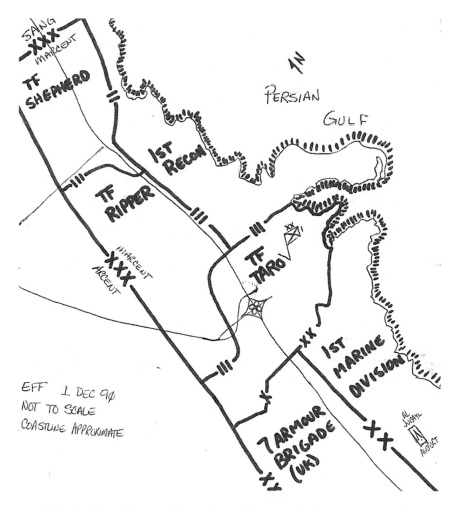

I Marine Expeditionary Force dispositions as of 1 Dec 90. Not to scale.

compromising in the past, which I thought hilarious. I'd never thought of him as compromising, just irascible. His temper and tongue could hit the afterburners in the blink of an eye and reduce a person to ashes before he could open his mouth. That's what I liked about him. No bullshit, just a right-between-the-eyes attitude.

During that first week back in the battalion, I was lucky enough to hear the most moving speech I've heard in my life. By now, it's famous, but when Brig. Gen. Tom Draude, the assistant division commander, gave his speech on Marines in combat, it was just a damn good talk from a real warrior and a real gentleman.

The officers and staff NCOs of the battalion gathered under a camouflage net for what we figured was just another general coming to give us just another pep talk about the Corps and valor and history. What we heard couldn't have surprised us more, and it couldn't have moved me more. Draude spoke quietly, but with a passion unusual for Marine officers, about what he called the "four Fs"—fatigue, fear, failure, and feelings—and how each affect your performance and well-being in combat. I listened as passionately as he spoke, because for the first time, a Marine officer—a general no less—articulated what I had felt and all the things I had wondered about for so many years. Draude's words comforted me like a mother's lullaby as he talked about the love that men feel for each other in combat.

Marines don't die for glory or patriotic reasons, he said. Marines die for each other. They die for the ones they love, the men that have become their friends and their comrades. Some of the greatest acts of courage ever seen in combat, Draude said, came because of that bond, that feeling of "I can't let the others down."

Several times, I saw officers dab at the corners of their eyes. It seemed so incongruous to hear a man who served three tours in Vietnam talk about love, but at the same time, it made perfect sense.

And it makes even more sense today, as I remember those men that I served with nearly every day, especially the ones who didn't come back. The bond of combat is strong, and for better or worse, it is forever. The love that combat veterans feel for each other is every bit as deep, and every bit as different, as the love between a man and wife, which is probably why many wives don't understand it. It took me years to understand it, and there are times when I think I still don't, even after talking to other men who have experienced combat.

It is a bond of common suffering. In the case of the Desert Storm veteran, that closeness comes not so much from being under fire together, though many were, as a long period of misery during which every Marine had to depend on another for physical and emotional support. Marines may not like to talk about it, but the truth is we all needed somebody to lean on out there.

I'm not very good at names, but I can rattle off the names of the Marines who spent nearly nine months at my side. And I consider them among the most important people in my life. Only my family ranks higher than those Marines that were with me day by day.

Draude's words also vindicated some of my own feelings about how I perceived combat, and I gained great comfort knowing that I'd been at least partially right in the lessons I'd learned from reading S.L.A. Marshall's excellent books about men in combat, *The Soldier's Load and the Mobility of a Nation* and *Men Against Fire*. His words prompted me to write the following:

1 Dec 90

So I'm mentally, emotionally, and physically prepared for it. What remains is if I'm capable to endure it. It's a big, black, scary void out there, one impossible to fathom.

Besides speeches, reunions and moves, we also began to train, this time for real. In 1/12, we began to work on a concept we'd begun in Hawaii before Desert Shield, one that could pay huge dividends now, provided we did it right and didn't get anybody killed.

The idea was to use a "jump FDC," a miniaturized version of the battalion FDC, that jumped forward whenever the infantry moved. The concept was to put the jump right up against the infantry, move with the grunts, then set up a bare-bones FDC and take control of the firing batteries while the main battalion FDC got on the road and moved up to us.

Doing so would allow for continuous fire support for the grunts, because once the jump was set up and had control of the batteries, the main FDC was free to move. When it set up again, it would take control back from the jump FDC, which would leapfrog ahead to yet another position. The jump consisted of only two or three humvees, about half a dozen radios, a computer, and some maps.

It wasn't really a new concept. I'd learned about it a year earlier at Fort Sill. But 1/12 was still working out the bugs. Putting the jump right on the tail of the infantry was a little different, though. That was inherently more dangerous than simply sending the jump to a position to which the main FDC would move, but it would give us much more flexibility, as well as "eyes" on what the grunts were doing, which could affect how and where we emplaced our battalion.

There was one advantage, though, to being in the jump. It made one slightly less susceptible to being gassed than being in the main FDC— a primary target of the Iraqi artillery.

At least I hoped so, because Lt. Col. Rivers had named me as the FDO for the jump. GySgt. Robert Miller, some communicators, Chief Warrant Officer-2 Neal Noem — the battalion communications officer — and some FDC troops would make up the jump. All told, we had about ten Marines.

We got a chance to test the idea immediately, as the battalion moved a few clicks toward the Abu Hadriyah cloverleaf. And, as usual, the move turned into a nightmare of confusion and chaos over the radio nets. In the jump FDC, we all knew we had a lot of work to do.

0716, Fri., 7 Dec 90

Have had some classes on breaching ops lately — our most likely mission would be to clear the two minefields on the Kuwaiti border. It's a mission rife w/potential disaster. To even get through the defensive belts, we'll have to take out their artillery, a nearly impossible task because (1) there's so damn much of it, (2) they can outrange our artillery, and (3) resupply of ammo is a nightmare (9 hours to resupply a battalion!).

Then there are the obstacles themselves to deal with. A belt of trenches, initially, followed by a belt of wire, then mines, and finally fortified positions. After that belt, there are two more just like it. The trenches/wire aren't too much worry, but the mines are. They cannot be sympathetically detonated by artillery; they are Italian-made plastic mines. Which means they have to be cleared slowly by infantry and engineers.

One battalion per belt is estimated, w/an estimated 50% casualties. After the breach is made, a battalion of tanks will form the exploitation force on the far bank — w/the jump FDC right behind, for control while 1/12 moves fwd.

This has been practiced at Ft. Irwin [California], where an Iraqi obstacle belt was rebuilt from satellite photos. Typical counterfire

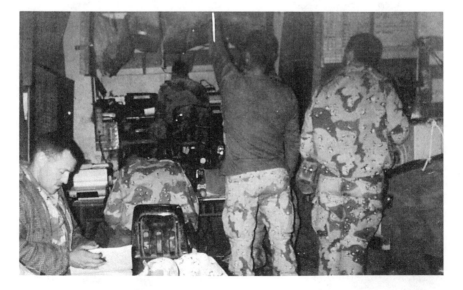

The main fire direction center. CWO-2 Neal Noem keeps an eye on communicators and fire direction men during an exercise.

Top: The "jump FDC" was a scaled-version of the battalion's main fire direction center. This set-up, in December 1990, would be further reduced in size in preparation for the ground assault. (Capt. Neal Noem, USMC) *Bottom:* Just another day at the office. Inside the "jump FDC"—the back of my humvee—I update our tactical map.

target received approx. 160 DPICM rounds. They say it takes approx.
1/2 hr for each belt, if the artillery can fire constantly, and not get
acquired and neutralized by counterbattery fire. The risk is stagger-
ing. And I'll be right in the middle of it, up front w/the maneuver
forces. Needless to say, it has been weighing heavily on my mind lately.

It is pure madness to attack in this fashion. This, of course, does
not take into account 2 factors: (1) the preliminary aerial bombard-
ment, and (2) the alleged report that the southernmost positions are
not even occupied anymore. Plus, the Commanding Gen. has ordered
max effort on destroying enemy artillery prior to the breach. Still, it
is an overwhelmingly grim mission. We could be bled white on this
one. Those flyboys better earn their damn pay. The casualties could
be like Tarawa or Iwo Jima.

The Iraqi minefields terrified most Marines, myself included. We were
hit daily with grim assessments of our chances, our equipment, our tactics, our defenses against chemical weapons, public support, you name it.

Every newspaper we got seemed to carry headlines that screamed
doom. No matter how we looked at it, we saw a division of Marines
jammed up against an obstacle belt under heavy fire, trying to clutch at a
foothold that would buy us time and safety. Our desert version of the
Tarawa beachhead. We paid attention in the classes, studied all the sand
tables, and looked for ways to clear mines more quickly than sending engineers in to blast out a corridor through which to shoehorn the division.
We also worked day after day to come up with a plan to keep our howitzers firing while holding the Iraqi guns at bay. We knew it would be an
uphill fight, since we were outgunned and outranged.

It wasn't encouraging, and we took it seriously enough to become
zealots in the art of minefield breaching. We talked about it constantly,
voiced all kinds of crazy ideas, and privately fretted about the possibility
of being blown to pieces by the most evil of all weapons, a cowardly,
unseen, and unfair beast that, if you were lucky, killed you, and if you
weren't, sent you home maimed. Truth be told, I don't think any of us
expected to make it through that ordeal whole. Everywhere we turned, we
kept hearing "Fifty percent casualties estimated."

We heard many reports of eroding public support back home, which
we attributed to the fact that the public really had no idea what we were facing. We were wrong on both counts. Many of Angie's letters indicated that
the public was, in fact, being informed of the grim possibilities of a frontal
assault against a defended minefield, but that didn't cause support to fade.
In fact, our support remained steadfast throughout the deployment.

The importance of that support cannot be overlooked, not only from
a political standpoint, but from a morale standpoint as well. The last thing

we wanted was to start a ground war with Americans turning a blind eye to us, or worse, becoming horrified by casualty counts and turning against us.

1200, Mon., 10 Dec 90

Not a lot of mail lately. Last thing I got was an anniversary card from Angie a few days ago. Bn is moving for a Regimental FireEx 11-17 Dec.

1913, Tues., 11 Dec 90

In position now for the regimental shoot. Got in at 0015; hit the rack at 0130, got up at 0530.

2039

Golf 3/11 just shot out, putting a damper on the evening. Shot a Charge 8, rather than a Charge 7 and put a round about 500 meters away from the Regimental FDC, which is south of the range, and along the gun-target line, for some reason. An inherently dangerous spot, as the battalions are to the north, firing south. Think Reg't just found out how dangerous it is there. Golf shot over the entire impact area. Big stink at 11th Marines, as to be expected. "G" Btry cold for the rest of the night. Reg't CO called a meeting at 0800 tomorrow for all battalion COs, plus "G" Btry CO Glad I'm not in his shoes. There are three types of artillerymen: (1) Those who have shot out; (2) those who are going to shoot out; (3) those who lie.

The impact area for this regimental firing exercise was square-shaped, with the batteries of three artillery battalions arrayed on three sides firing toward the fourth.

The regimental FDC, for reasons that I never learned, decided to emplace itself beyond this fourth side, straight down the gun-target line, or the imaginary line drawn from the howitzers' positions to a target.

In other words, every battery in the exercise was essentially aimed in the general direction of the regimental FDC. This is not exactly the preferred location when firing artillery, as evidenced by "G" Battery's erroneous shot.

The battery made a mistake in the amount of propellant — gunpowder — placed behind the projectile. In this case, the cannoneers loaded too much propellant, a Charge 8 instead of the less-powerful Charge 7. Thus, the round sailed over the impact area. Luckily, no one was injured.

"Firing incidents," as these types of mistakes are called, are the most serious incidents that can befall a battery during training. Because of the inherent danger of firing artillery and the inevitable case of human error, safety is paramount to artillerymen and is taken very seriously. Layer upon layer of safety measures are imposed upon firing exercises.

Yet, shit happens, as the saying goes. Usually, after a firing incident, the battery commander, a captain, is relieved of his command. In the Marine Corps, the commander is responsible for everything his unit does or fails to do, and the price for that responsibility is his command.

I should know. After the war, in April 1991, I took command of "A" Battery, 1/12, in Hawaii. The following August, my battery was involved in a similar firing incident at the Army's Schofield Barracks range on Oahu. There were no injuries and no property damage. In fact, no irrefutable evidence that my battery in fact "shot out" was ever found, although there was a great deal of circumstantial evidence that a 105mm shell sailed completely over the impact area, over a mountain, and onto a steep slope on the populated side of the mountain range.

No matter. The commanding general of 1st MEB, Brig. Gen. Coleman D. Kuhn, ordered my relief, even though the investigating officer, himself an artillery officer, recommended that I retain my command and be reprimanded in writing. Actually, Kuhn ordered my regimental commander, Col. Wayne Rollings, to relieve me. Kuhn, who had never met me, couldn't have picked me out of a police line-up, yet he relieved me by proxy.

I had lost the most precious possession an officer can ever be granted, a command. The relief, which came after an agonizing month of investigation, devastated me, and not just because my career was destroyed. I'd never really given much thought to my career. I wasn't after a twenty-year career with a military pension at the end. I joined the Marine Corps for one reason — to prove that I was capable of leading Marines. I'd done that, and I'd had a lot of fun doing it. That was all the job satisfaction I ever needed.

All that ended with one pull of a howitzer lanyard.

I felt I'd betrayed the Marines who were under my command, by failing them as a commander. And I felt betrayed by people I thought were my friends. Officers in the battalion who just days earlier would have stopped by my office to invite me to the club for a beer now changed directions when they saw me coming. Senior officers who swore their commitment to keeping me in my job suddenly couldn't remember such a commitment, and said their hands were tied.

Part of it, of course, was that no one really knows what to say to an officer who suffers such a blow. But another, more disturbing, part of my ostracism was that I'd become tainted. I had been stained, if not with incompetence, with the manifestation of their own fears— that it could happen to anyone, maybe even them. That was a possibility they didn't want to admit, because to do so smacks of self-doubt. Like a diseased steer, I'd been cut out of the herd, both figuratively and literally. Too often, officers are quick to judge a colleague who makes a mistake, believing themselves to be impervious to the same fate. Any officer who does this is terribly mistaken.

The burden of command is a heavy one in the Marine Corps. One mistake and your career is finished. That's always been the case, regardless of how much lip service is paid to the campaign against the "zero-defects mentality." And after the Persian Gulf War, that mentality thrived in the middle of a drawdown that had many officers running scared.

Ultimately, losing my command was a fatal blow to my career. In 1996, after twice failing to be selected for promotion to major, I was separated from the Marine Corps. By that time, I was as ready to get out of the Corps as it was to get rid of me.

I do not recall if the "G" Battery commander was relieved. I do know the battery was immediately shut down — put in a "cold" status, as I wrote in my journal. I hoped then, and still do, that the commander was not relieved. There were no injuries, and I'm willing to bet that the Marines involved certainly learned a valuable lesson from the experience.

After the shoot ended, we moved into position for another exercise, this time a division TEWT. The one-two pace of the training was proof that we were operating at a markedly different level than a few months earlier.

About this time, we got the word that 2nd Marine Division had begun arriving in-country from Camp Lejeune, North Carolina, which set off waves of grumbling throughout 1st MARDIV. We'd been evicted out of Haii 3 to make room for them, so there wasn't much of a welcome wagon waiting for our Lejeune brethren.

But what really irritated us was what the commandant, Gen. Al Gray, had said to the nation before dispatching 2nd MARDIV. Gray, who had previously commanded II MEF, of which the division is a part, said as the division left North Carolina, "I'm sending in the A-team now."

The comment rankled those of us in 1st MARDIV, partly because we'd been rotting in the desert for months, but also because of the intense rivalry that has existed between the two divisions for years. 2nd Marine Division prides itself on being the "Carolina MAGTF" at the pointy end of the spear, always deployed, always ready. They look upon 1st Marine Division with disdain that borders on contempt, derisively referring to the West Coast Marines as "Hollywood Marines."

In California, the sentiment is returned. After meeting a Marine from the East Coast, many a 1st MARDIV Marine has been heard to say, "Man, are those guys uptight!" Themselves always deployed, always ready, the Marines of 1st Marine Division call themselves part of the Corps' "heavy MEF" and consider their division to be the best.

When we heard about Gray's comment, a running joke rippled through the ranks that when 2nd MARDIV arrived, we just might have the largest intramural firefight in the history of warfare. I heard several Marines say they'd rather attack 2nd Marine Division than the Iraqis.

0935, Thurs., 20 Dec 90

TEWT ended yesterday; practiced minefield breaching. "Jump" moved out in the morning. We were close enough to the grunts to see the line charges detonate. Loud as hell. Moved to main position at dusk — around 1600 nowadays. Left this morning to move thru the breach w/TF Taro. We're sitting on the "home bank" now, watching the air show, waiting for Taro to get thru. Hurry up and wait. Just got the word to saddle up.

Very cold last week, and I got a case of the shits yesterday. Belly still griping today. Bet I've lost five pounds, just from head calls.

Line charges are bags of high explosives strung together, then fired from an AAV across a minefield to blast out a lane for vehicles. From a distance, it's like watching bags of sugar being fired from a cannon inside an amtrack. The ensuing powerful explosion creates quite an attention-getter.

In keeping with our "ride the infantry's ass" philosophy for the "jump FDC," we clung to the end of their convoy to the breaching site, and when the first infantry units began to filter through the narrow lane carved out by the line charges, we holed up near the simulated minefield to await the main FDC. Our position, nestled under the lip of a broad, slightly sloping dune, gave us a fantastic view of the exercise. About two miles away, the infantry, mounted in trucks and amphibious tractors, labored as they ground their way through the soft sand. Ahead of them, at the second simulated minefield, combat engineers blasted out another lane with line charges. Pillars of dark-brown smoke *karumphed* into the gray sky. Gunny Miller, Neal Noem, and I relaxed in the back of my humvee as we watched the spectacle, sipping coffee brewed on my propane stove, and wisecracking about the exercise.

When our turn came, we jammed ourselves into the Headquarters Battery convoy and clawed our way through the ten-foot-wide breach. Most of the division had passed through ahead of us, and the vehicles had turned the lane into a sandy chute about six feet deep.

There was absolutely no danger involved in the exercise, but we were tense as we passed through the breach to the "far bank." Most of that tension was caused by the casualty predictions we had heard for this operation when we did it for real. We expected most of our casualties to come from Iraqi artillery, which we assumed would rain upon us as we crowded into the breach lanes.

Once on the other side of the minefield, my stomach ailment, which seemed to flare up at the worst of times, provided a moment of levity. My stomach began cramping, which I knew was my early-warning system. I grabbed an entrenching tool and scuttled away from my vehicle, looking for a dip in the ground that would give me some semblance of privacy.

Unfortunately, we had set up our position on a bare hillside. I scrambled over the crest and down the reverse slope until I found The Spot.

The Spot is that one place you find when you're looking to dig a cat hole and give a little something back to the earth. It's hard to find The Spot, because you never know exactly what you're looking for, but you know it when you see it. Like art. And finding The Spot is an art. You're looking for a place a respectable distance away from your fellow Marines, but not so far away that you couldn't run back to safety if you start taking incoming. Concealment is preferred, even ideal, but not always available, so you make the best with what you have, a rock or a bush, even a dead camel, if need be.

I had no concealment whatsoever, but I did have privacy. There wasn't a human being for miles. I hastily dug a hole and squatted over The Spot, facing uphill.

No sooner had I dropped my trousers when I heard the all-too-familiar jet-engine whine of an amtrack. Actually, many amtracks. I craned my neck around. Downhill, a company of trackers rumbled past as I squatted, bare ass in the wind. I could see their goggled and grinning faces as they lumbered by me.

In the sedate, polite Real World, this would have been a mortifying experience. But I didn't even attempt to move. Months of living in the field had turned me into just another mammal relieving itself in the wild.

When we finished the "breachex," we dragged ourselves into yet another position. In contrast to the summer, we were moving so often now that I couldn't keep up with the locations. We were now somewhere north of Abu Hadriyah, but still south of Al-Mishab, a small intersection of roads a few miles south of Khafji.

1606, Fri., 21 Dec 90

3rd Mar is being considered for a mission that is causing great apprehension. Basically, 3rd Mar would be the "raid regiment." The idea is to helo the reg't over the border a short way, prior to the breach. Once in Kuwait, 1/12 would support them while they disrupt/destroy the artillery brigade that would be firing upon the breach site. There are several light infantry brigades in the area that could possibly threaten the mission. Dicey mission at best, particularly for 1/12.

Of all the rumors and dumbass orders I heard during Desert Shield and Desert Storm, this was without a doubt the stupidest idea I'd heard. And it would only get worse.

The object of this foray, which was apparently dreamed up by someone on the division staff, was to place 3rd Marines, including 1/12 in a position inside Kuwait from which the regiment could attack a "high-payoff" target, which in this case was supposed to be a corps headquarters.

Lifting an entire regiment by helicopter is a Herculean task for the Marine Corps, since the Marine Corps doesn't even own enough helos to pick up an entire regiment at once. Under combat conditions, it becomes nearly impossible, to the point of almost being ludicrous. Added to the difficulty factor would be the lifting of the M198 155mm towed howitzer, a cumbersome beast that weighs 16,000 pounds. In fact, the "Niner-Eight" is so heavy that only one helo in the Marine Corps inventory can lift it, the CH-53E.

In December 1990, we had about 20 operable howitzers in the battalion. Finding 20 53Es — much less dedicating them — to lift our guns would be another near impossibility. And that didn't count the helos needed to lift ammunition, the various FDC crews and communicators, and the security element that would be needed that deep in Iraqi territory.

And that was just the artillery. That didn't include all the helicopters needed to lift the grunts of 3rd Marines.

And, assuming we could get in, the method for getting out, presumably either under fire or direct attack, was none too appealing. If we were under "pressure," we were to spike the howitzers with thermite grenades and get the crews out, which would eliminate a battalion of artillery for the remainder of the war.

I sat open-mouthed in the FDC tent as Lt. Col. Rivers outlined this plan. I regained my composure enough to join the rapid-fire questions being hurled at him. He raised his hands in surrender. He then informed us that the regiment had already realized all the drawbacks of the plan and that, unfortunately, had drawn up the initial plans without much input whatsoever from an artilleryman. Thus, the grunts had come up with their own solution to our lack of helicopters.

The answer was to trade in our "Niner-Eights" for 105mm howitzers, much lighter — and much less powerful — pieces. If we did that, we would give up nearly five kilometers in range. We also lost an immense capability in munitions, as the M101A1 105mm howitzer had no DPICM, rocket-assisted projectiles, or laser-guided Copperhead rounds. The RAP rounds extended the M198's range from 14.7 kilometers to thirty.

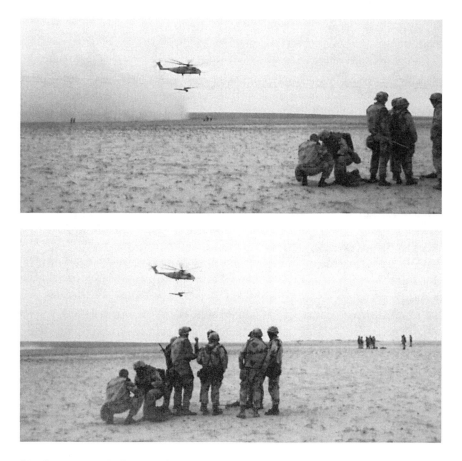

"Task Force Gecko" trains for its short-lived raid mission shortly after the battle of Khafji. In the distance, a CH-53E Super Stallion lifts an M198 155mm howitzer. Note Marines in front of cloud of sand caused by rotor wash.

So, to cover all the bases, we planned on a battalion-sized insertion for both types of howitzers. Rivers put me in charge of conducting all the classes for the operation. He also designated me as the "security team commander," one of the first ones in the battalion landing zone. The mission of the security team was to hit the deck first and secure the landing zone for the rest of the battalion. Of course, the noise of our helicopters would likely alert every Iraqi in Kuwait, so we fully expected to be met by the entire Iraqi Army when we hit the LZ.

I wasn't exactly thrilled with that prospect, but I said "Aye, aye sir," and carried on, even though I could not fathom the reason for sending a whole regiment behind enemy lines at a known target that could easily be hit w/B-52s, RAP, or Tomahawks. Or the 16-inch guns of a battleship, for that matter.

I understood the necessity of taking some of the pressure off the forces that would breach the Iraqi minefields, which we would do by going after the Iraqi artillery brigade that would be delivering indirect fire to the breach or a corps headquarters, or any number of other targets. But I thought it could be done without dropping a light regiment among six or so enemy divisions, some of which were mechanized or armored.

Whatever the reason, I put in many long hours over the next few days trying to figure out how to pull it off. On Christmas Eve I held an afternoon sand-table class on heliborne operations. It was a very broad look at what would be needed to get the battalion into a landing zone in enemy-held territory. There were several thoughtful comments from the staff NCOs and officers, none of whom were thrilled with the assignment. I answered them as best I could, trying to keep my own skepticism out of my voice.

Col. Howard was there, too, and he was very frank and gentlemanly in his comments, as usual. He said he talked to Col. Admire and hoped to convince him that there were other ways to provide fire support to 3rd Marines without sending 1/12 over the border in helos, a statement that drew the wholehearted agreement of the two dozen or so Marines around him. He was also averse to giving up the '98s for 105s, and when he expressed that sentiment, he drew a wave of helmeted nods from the Marines around him.

Later that day, I looked for a respite from the stress and apprehension of the last few days. I made my way to the camouflage net that was, for a day, a chapel in our position. Bundled up against a nippy desert wind in my "night ninja jacket," the night parka we all loved, I picked my way through a tangle of legs and sat on the cold sand to listen to a service by our new chaplain, Navy Lt. Grady Pennell.

As I listened to him speak in his soft Texas twang about the real meaning of Christmas, I was struck by the irony of the moment. I was sitting in the land of Islam, celebrating the birth of Christ. Grady was not even allowed to wear on his collar the symbol of his faith, a cross, yet we celebrated the birth of Christ.

I thought back to Thanksgiving Day, and realized that this service was proof that I'd rediscovered my faith in God, and again I took solace in God's will. I thought of Psalm 40: "I waited patiently for the Lord, He inclined to me and heard my cry."

Grady's honest, heartfelt sermon touched us all, and several of us had to fight back tears, an incongruous sight in a bunch of Marines. As I stepped out into a purple sky and made my way back to my fighting hole, I felt a peace I'd not felt in a long time.

My faith would be tested again and again in the next few weeks. I would lose a friend. Another would lose a limb. I would fall to my knees and curse at the death of a Marine, and I would hug the ground, afraid, as artillery rounds exploded nearby. I would cause death and destruction by uttering a few words into a radio handset. But on this one, cold night, I was at peace.

I awoke to the coldest morning of the entire deployment on Christmas morning. Ice had formed in patches on the sand. I shivered through breakfast — an MRE heated up over my propane camp stove — then met with Lt. Col. Rivers, who told me we could be moving on the 28th to Al-Mishab, about 40 kilometers north. That would put us within range of Iraqi rockets, called FROG — Free Rocket, Over Ground.

I had a lucky encounter the next day, when I drove south to the airport at Jubayl for a conference with a helicopter squadron, which I hoped would coordinate some training for our insane insertion mission.

While I was there, Gen. Gray showed up. He was met by a host of clean and pressed field-grade officers and pilots in clean, cute "zoom bags"—flight suits. I was grubby after about two weeks without a shower. Gray spoke off the cuff for about 20 minutes, whacked a few Marines on the arm in his trademark greeting, then hung out for photo ops. He almost bowled me over as he left in a rush.

In the field, we listened for word that we'd move all the way to Mishab, but the word kept changing. We'd become accustomed to that, and to moving with absolutely no notice at all. Personally, I didn't mind the moving. The desert winter had become surprisingly cold — the temperature the night of December 27 dipped to 39 degrees, 27 with the wind chill factor. None of us had expected Saudi weather to be that cold. I awoke at 0430 shivering in my sleeping bag, even though I was in thermal underwear and wrapped in a poncho liner, and couldn't get back to sleep.

Another thing we'd finally become used to was the food. The Marine cooks had broken the code apparently, because now we were getting chow that was not only tasty, it was actually hot when we got it. Neither had been the case in previous weeks. In fact, our twice-daily deliveries of hot chow were becoming the highlights of our day. When the chow trucks rolled into the position, Marines gravitated toward them, like moths to a flame. Officers usually clumped themselves near the edge of the activity, with staff NCOs a little closer, so they could supervise the NCOs, who supervised the troops, who — in keeping with the Marine Corps leadership philosophy — always ate first.

That philosophy required the commanding officer to eat last, because Marine officers never eat before their Marines, and only after everyone has been fed. It is a small part of leadership that pays huge dividends, and it sums up the Marine Corps ethos in one gesture: leaders take care of their troops first, then themselves.

It's also a great way for officers to keep each other in line. I can imagine the upbraiding an officer would have gotten from his peers if he had cut in a chow line.

My after-dinner hours were usually spent in the FDC tent, unless the weather was pleasant enough to remain outside. Neal Noem, Chief Warrant Officer-2 Lynn Nesbit, and I passed the time talking about the latest news from the United States and speculating about what Saddam would do next. The reports we read to each other showed that Saddam had given absolutely no indication of pulling out of Kuwait.

The papers were full of contradictory reports. Half said we wouldn't be ready to launch an attack on January 15; the other half said we would. Half said Bush would start the bombing on January 15; the other half said we wouldn't do anything until February. By the end of December, I'd quit paying attention. Nobody in the desert seemed to think we'd do anything on January 15. 11th Marines was even planning another regimental FIREX for January 12-16.

I'd gotten a letter from my sister, Renee, that included an article from the *Wall Street Journal*. The article discussed an air attack against Iraq and the stupidity of attacking the defenses of Kuwait.

And there we sat, planning to do just that by breaching a minefield.

The article suggested completely bypassing Kuwait and driving toward Baghdad, containing/isolating the forces in Kuwait. At the time, it was an intriguing plan, but seemed impossible.

1909, Sat., 29 Dec 90
Finally warmed up enough to run the showers (NBC decon apparatus). Cold again now. Days are getting longer, a welcome occurrence.

In the weeks since we moved permanently to the field from Haii 3, we'd become extremely nasty. Showers in the field were never easy — and by this time I was far, far away from Haddad's solar-powered camp shower. Plus, the cold weather made the very idea of getting undressed seem like torture.

There had been a few sunny days that had coaxed me out of my clothes long enough to heat water on my propane stove and squat on the cold sand to make an attempt at getting clean. On those days, Gunny Miller and I would also spread our smelly poncho liners and sleeping bags in the sun to air out.

The Iraqis' chemical warfare might have been enough to make us don gas masks, but after spending weeks in the same clothes—long underwear included—we were killing each other with our own body odors. At least at first. After a few days, the stench of unwashed bodies and sour clothes ceased to raise any olfactory alarms. We stunk, and we knew it, so we dealt with it.

But, the nuclear, biological, and chemical defense crew provided a chance at cleanliness for those who dared brave the cutting wind and near-freezing temperatures. The crew set up its decontamination shower for field tests, and some of us took advantage of it.

The decon shower was designed to clean the human body of NBC agents. The apparatus was nothing more than a spindly set of piping with a few crude shower heads at the top. A fine spray of water blasted out of tiny fittings in the overhead pipe. The contraption resembled a giant staple embedded into the ground. The water came from a nearby rubber or canvas bladder and was heated—but only barely—as it coursed its way up the piping and through the shower head.

The NBC crew offered showers to all comers. It sounded like a good idea to me until I saw where and how the crew had set up the apparatus. The giant staple was smack in the middle of our position. Underneath the shower heads were wooden ammo pallets to stand on, but there were no privacy screens or hooks on which to hang clothes and gear. Anyone taking a shower would be doing so in full view of all of Headquarters Battery.

I balked at first, when I realized that to avail myself of the rumored hot water, I'd have to undress under my camo net, then walk naked nearly a hundred yards to the shower, lather up, rinse, dry off, and walk back.

And that's when I saw somebody doing just that. I don't remember who—most likely Miller or Neal Noem—but that dissolved my inhibitions. I shucked my clothes, grabbed a towel and soap and headed for the showers, wearing nothing but my boots and a grin.

The water coming out of the shower head alternated between scalding and frigid, but I didn't care, nor did the growing number of naked and semi-naked Marines around me. Clean is clean, and I scrubbed myself pink before surrendering my spot to another grubby Marine.

Satisfied, I strolled back to my vehicle and dressed slowly, savoring the feeling of being clean for the first time in weeks. I wanted to enjoy it, because I had no idea when my next hot shower would be.

Later that day, I spoke with a corporal, one of the several wiremen in our communications section. He had gotten a real surprise in the morning mail—a handwritten note from Maj. Gen. Myatt.

A few days earlier, this NCO had sent Myatt some plastic soldiers he received from his 14-year-old niece, along with a note explaining that the general could use them for planning and sand-table models and that he hoped the general wouldn't forget that we weren't really toy soldiers. It was meant as a joke.

The 1st MARDIV sand table, incidentally, had become legendary for its enormous size. It had started out a little bigger than a card table, but had grown to a ten-foot square, maybe even larger.

Our wireman also wrote Myatt that he hoped the general had a sense of humor about the whole thing. I was intrigued by this story. It took a lot of guts to say something like that to your commanding general.

Myatt, in one of the classiest moves I've ever seen, responded in a handwritten note. He wrote that he was indeed keeping a sense of humor and that he kept a couple of the plastic figures in his shaving kit to remind him that his Marines were real people.

We were all surprised by the gentlemanly move by Myatt. I'd been impressed by Myatt's straightforward approach before, and this incident said a lot about him. In 1999, I spoke with Myatt, who is retired from the Marine Corps. When I mentioned the incident, he chuckled.

"I remember that one distinctly," he said.

CHAPTER SEVEN

In 1990, the fact that nearly half the Corps' strength was in the Gulf was shocking. Today, the fact that there were nearly 198,000 Marines then is in itself shocking.

The postwar drawdown was so quick and so savage in its quest to reduce the Corps to 174,000 that it's hard to imagine, even after only a decade, that the Corps once had the luxury of such numbers.

On January 1, I made a point of listening to U2's song, "New Year's Day," mostly to remind me of my goal: to make it home to Angie in one piece. Then I was back at work, coordinating a helicopter exercise for our still-unpopular raid mission.

I'd spent my New Year's Eve in the airport in Jubayl with Marine Air Group-16 and the CH-46 drivers of Marine Medium Helicopter Squadron-165, trying to explain to a very skeptical group of rotor jocks what we wanted to do and why. They weren't buying it, for the obvious reasons. I was further hamstrung by the fact that they just didn't understand the logistical aspect of artillery.

To most of these pilots—mostly captains—moving artillery simply meant sling-loading an M198 howitzer underneath a CH-53E at Point A and flying it to Point B. But they didn't think about ammo for the howitzers, the FDC, the security team itself, and the cannoneers who would man the guns. As I explained, their understanding grew, slowly, and with it, their skepticism. I really couldn't blame them.

After that meeting, which only reinforced a sense of futility, I drove back to the battalion's position and collected 126 Marines who'd be lucky

The nuclear, biological and chemical decontamination showers offered us a handy way to shower, if one didn't mind doing so in plain view of your fellow Marines. CWO-2 Neal Noem lathers up. (Capt. Neal Noem, USMC)

enough to be picked for what was becoming known as the "suicide mission." I gave the Marines a walk-through, giving them every bit of information I had in an attempt to allay their fears—and my own, I suppose. I don't think it worked. Marines aren't dumb.

I've always thought that one key element of leadership is to bring all your people in on the mission, so that every single Marine understands his role in the "big picture." I did that now, knowing I'd be a lightning rod for the angry and suspicious Marines who were convinced that the officers in this lash-up didn't know their asses from deep left field, and this mission was proof positive of that.

I explained how the helos would be inserted, how we'd land and exit the birds, how we'd set up. I discussed the possible fire missions we'd receive, and our plans to leave with our howitzers if possible, without them if necessary. I then opened the discussion up for questions.

I got several dubious looks, and even more dubious questions, but for the most part, the Marines asked professional questions about ammo resupply (there would be none) or how we would get the howitzers out (we most likely wouldn't, and we'd spike them where they sat with a thermite grenade in the breech).

It was a thoroughly unpleasant experience. I felt I'd failed to motivate the Marines properly, and felt I had most likely let them down, paradoxically, by being too honest in my assessment of the situation. It still seemed like suicide to me to toss away a battalion of artillery — and, more importantly, the Marines manning those guns — for such a low-priority target.

I dismissed the Marines and trudged back to the FDC tent, where Lt. Col. Rivers was preparing to drive north for a meeting. We discussed the mission again, and I offhandedly commented, "Sir, if I make it out of this thing alive, I'm putting myself in for a medal."

"Thompson," came his reply, "if you make it back from this one, I'll put you in for the Medal of Honor myself."

Not exactly the vote of confidence I was looking for.

While Rivers was gone, we got the word that we'd be moving out the next day to a position near Mishab. But throwing a kink in that plan was the fact that I had helos scheduled to train the security force until 1300, and division forbade us from moving at night. I knew it was going to be a nightmare and pleaded with Matthews, the S-3 officer, to either advise Rivers to postpone the move or the helicopter training, but he wasn't budging from what Rivers had told him, nor did I feel he was making any effort to improve the situation. Frustrated, I sat heavily on a chair in the FDC, too tired to argue any further.

Then, one Marine reminded me of why I put up with so much frustration and bullshit. LCpl. Ewing, one of the FDC radio operators, walked up to me and asked if he could speak to me. Sure, I said. I always tried to make time for a Marine who wanted to talk.

Ewing, who'd been at the security team briefing, surprised me by thanking me for "always being upbeat and straightforward and caring about the troops." He climbed into the comm vehicle to stand his watch, leaving me dumbfounded. It was unexpected, and it made me feel good. And it humbled me.

Later that day, CWO-2 Lynn Nesbit, the battalion intel officer, told me about an incident that had taken place the previous night. Around midnight, two NCOs had driven up from the logistics train in a humvee, with a corporal at the wheel. They drove through Headquarters Battery position without a ground guide, a cardinal sin in an artillery unit. Ground guides walk in front of vehicles at night with a red-lens flashlight, guiding them into position and preventing accidents. I commented to Nesbit that these two Marines probably figured they didn't need one because of the New Year's Eve full moon.

They drove to the "antenna farm" — the cluster of antennas for the battalion's radio networks — where they first backed into a camouflage net, then ran over — literally — a Marine sleeping on the ground. The tire went over the Marine's chest, not once but twice. Miraculously, he was not seriously injured, although he was medevacked to Fleet Hospital near Jubayl.

There were speculations that the driver was driving under the influence of alcohol. The corporal, Nesbit said, was even given a blood test. Nesbit, who had been on watch when the accident occurred, found a water bottle with a small amount of juice in it near the vehicle. A shakedown of the log train, however, revealed nothing.

For months, jokes and rumors about Marines making their own bootleg hooch with fruit and sugar had floated through the battalion. My own driver, LCpl. Rob Martin, had said something to me the week before about there being homemade brew in the log train, but I dismissed it as a rumor, saying that if it were true, they'd better (1) get rid of it, (2) not get caught. Martin tended to be a rumor hound at times.

When I heard about this incident, though, I knew I shouldn't have dismissed it so quickly.

South of Mishab, 1200, Thurs., 3 Jan 91
We are a few klicks south and west of Al-Mishab, about 60-70 miles from the Kuwaiti border, in direct support of TF Shepherd, the LAVs. Dug in deep last night. We're not quite in artillery range yet, but I'm not going to take any chances.

The day before, I drove to the helicopter landing zone, north of Jubayl, with "Task Force Gecko" loaded up on five-ton trucks behind me. Partly out of sarcasm and partly as a means of giving my suicide crew some morale and identity, I'd dubbed them the night before as Task Force Gecko, in deference to our Hawaiian home. It seemed that everybody and his brother in the 1st Marine Division had his own task force, so why not me?

Only four of the planned eight helos showed up, so I immediately had to alter my training plan. Plus, the weather turned nasty as the wind kicked up to add a maelstrom of blowing sand to the helos' rotor wash. I quickly briefed the pilots that we needed to do two identical runs shorter than originally planned, to give all my Marines a chance to embark the helo, then land, disembark and practice running to set up a security perimeter and tie in with other elements to their flanks.

We spent about three hours battling the sandstorm and lumbering through deep sand before everybody had had enough. The helo drivers gave us a last run, then thumped their way through the cold air back to Jubayl. I loaded up Task Force Gecko and headed back to the battalion position to prepare to move.

The battalion CP was in a state of confusion. Rivers was north of us, reconnoitering our new position, and nobody in the CP seemed to know what the plan for moving the battalion was. Exasperated, the battery commanders seized the initiative and put their Marines on the road, figuring any action was better than inaction. I agreed and told the jump FDC to saddle up.

By the time we got into position after a difficult, confused, disorganized move in the dark, rain had fallen for hours, and we still had holes to dig. Martin and I dug in as the rain poured. By the time we finished, we were soaked and covered in mud.

Next morning, on the 3rd, I tried to dry out and convince myself that Saddam would leave Kuwait and we could all go home. But I wasn't doing a very good job. The weather had brought with it bad moods for everyone.

That night, at 2100, Rivers told me that Col. Admire had directed a regimental helo ex for the 7th. We had a saying for such spur-of-the-moment pronouncements: "Once more through our asses."

I drove to the 3rd Marines CP the next morning to participate in the planning for exercise. We were informed that we'd have no CH-53Es, only D models. We were told to have the helos lift ammo instead, which was worthless training because the load riggers on the ground and the pilots knew how to pick up cargo. They needed to practice picking up a howitzer.

In any case, we had four 53Ds and four CH-46s planned for the 7th. The exercise would take place about thirty-five miles west of Mishab, our current locale. That distance was two-thirds the distance between Mishab and Kuwait City, roughly where our targets were located. Following that bit of news from the 3rd Marines staff, the meeting took a bizarre turn.

3rd Marines had been scheduled to strike the headquarters of the Iraqi III Corps. The plan, I was now told by the regimental S-3, was to be on the ground for 2½ hours at the most. That negated taking an artillery battalion—we'd barely have time to get the entire battalion set up, especially since the grunts wanted everyone to move in one massive wave. The S-3 then told me they weren't planning on taking artillery anyway. Shocked, I told him that was news to me, then asked why was 1/12 even involved in this exercise. He shrugged and replied Col. Admire had deemed it so.

Personally, I agreed with the regimental planners' thinking, and so did Col. Howard. We were one-fifth of the division's artillery. And we'd planned to leave the howitzers in the LZ when we left. It was unlikely that we'd willingly sacrifice that many cannons. I knew I wouldn't do it willingly.

Breaching a minefield began to look better every day. Plus, we really weren't designing the exercise to resemble the actual mission. Little by little, because of too little time and too few assets, we whittled away the exercise, to a training evolution that bore no resemblance to how we'd really do it. We had gone from an exercise in which our howitzers, crews, and ammo would be lifted and moved two-thirds of the actual distance to a few helos picking up pallets of ammo, just for practice. That troubled me greatly, because we were ten days from a war deadline and we were unable to even plan an exercise without playing bullshit stateside training games.

Several of us in 1/12 began to ask ourselves, "When does the training end and the preparation for war begin?" We didn't seem to be doing anything in the way of preparing to kick off a war, such as reconnaissance or pre-positioning ammo. Sure, I knew somebody was doing that, but it wasn't us. We were still training and going to the all-important meetings. I feared that when the war came, we'd be leaping through hoops again, and Marines would get killed because of it.

Marshall and I talked about this for hours and agreed that somebody had to say "OK, that's it. No more training. From here on, it's real."

1748, Sun., 6 Jan 91

Yet another meeting at 0730, this one at Jubayl Airport w/HMM-161, the helo squadron that is lifting us tomorrow. Had to get up at 0400 to make it. But, it was worth it; had an awesome double cheeseburger from the AAFES snack bar there (those pilots get all the bennies) and, best of all, I got to call Angie.

We talked for almost an hour and a half (damn the cost) and it was absolutely great. She's been blue lately and was so happy she cried. Otherwise a wonderful conversation. For the rest of the day I've been on cloud nine.

The cheeseburger and the conversation with Angie made the 0400 reveille worthwhile, and it gave me a diversion in what was becoming an incredibly stressful environment. But it only lasted a day. Next morning, as I watched our first-big-now-small helo exercise unfold, I was exhausted and frustrated.

I don't understand how a Marine on the ground can say to a pilot, "I want to go to grid so-and-so" and all the pilot hears is "anywhere on the ground." But that's what happens much of the time. I was furious with the pilots when they unloaded the ammo and Marines 1500 meters from the landing zone, after showing up hours late. I sat in the real landing zone with the rest of the Marines, who waited for their colleagues on the helo to trudge a mile back to the vehicles. Luckily, Neal got his communicators busy in a commex so that the entire morning wouldn't be wasted.

After a long ride back to the regimental headquarters, we had another long debrief of the exercise. The debrief was almost longer than the exercise itself. I then drove back and sat in a hole that was rapidly filling up with water from the sheets of rain that had begun after nightfall. I'd strung a poncho over my hole to stay dry, but the rain blew in horizontally, drenching me and my sleeping bag as I read two letters from Angie in the dark. I scribbled out a response, then collapsed.

The next day's training was canceled when the helos, for whatever reason, couldn't make it. Instead, helicopter support teams practiced rigging loads of equipment. 3rd Marines rescheduled the helos for a few days later. Again we drove out to the designated landing zone, but again the helicopters didn't show. Finally, we drove back to the battalion position, grubby, tired, and hungry. Three days had been wasted trying to train for an exceedingly dangerous mission. When we got back to the battalion position, our Army exchange officer, Maj. Carl Cook [*pseudonym*], was waiting.

Originally assigned to an artillery battalion in the 25th Infantry Division at Schofield Barracks on Oahu, Cook was part of a one-for-one officer exchange program in which an officer from 1/12 went to the 25th and one of theirs came to us. Cook worked as the assistant fire support coordinator, and he'd been assigned by 3rd Marines to go to Bahrain to make liaison with the battleship *Wisconsin*, in the event we pushed north into Kuwait up the coastal highway, which in early January seemed our most likely approach. So, we needed to talk to the people who'd be lobbing 16-inch shells over our heads.

I saw an opportunity. I had been aboard the *Missouri* for two years and knew *Iowa*-class battleships inside and out. I'd also been to naval gunfire school in 1987. Cook was an Army officer, and as such didn't know anything about ships or naval gunfire and admitted as much. Who better then, I suggested to Rivers, to go and translate for Cook than me?

I put the hard sell on Rivers and finally convinced him that I should go. Grinning, I piled into Cook's humvee, filthy from days of living in a muddy hole, still in my flak jacket and helmet. Cook was only slightly less dirty.

Normally, the humming of the tires on the asphalt would have put me to sleep as we made our way south past Jubayl toward Dhahran and Bahrain, but I was too intrigued by the countryside and too afraid I might miss something. That notion was soon put out of my head, however, as I realized that, in Saudi Arabia, if you've seen one city, you've seen them all. Dhahran was just another scruffy, dusty city. We drove on.

We finally crossed the causeway — a modern highway — into Bahrain in the late afternoon, just in time to catch a view of a gleaming white modern city bathed in golden twilight and teeming with activity. Our driver threaded his way through loud traffic and shouting drivers, past the *souk*— the market — to the pier.

The pier was about as modern as any I'd ever seen, and it was packed with staff cars and American servicemen in civvies, freshly scrubbed and headed into town on liberty. Cook and I suddenly felt conspicuous in our grubby utilities and war gear, but at the same time we took a perverse pride in being the dirtiest SOBs in the country.

We saw the low-slung *Wisconsin* to our right, anchored in the harbor, her guns a flat gray against the royal blue ocean. While we searched for a liberty boat to ferry us out to the battleship, I heard someone call my name.

Incredulous, I whirled around to see Navy Lt. Chris Walker coming toward me, in freshly pressed civvies and reeking of soap. I was dumbfounded. Walker and I had served together on the *Missouri* for about a year. He had been the public affairs officer, the same gig he had now on some admiral's staff. We played catch-up for a few minutes before he disappeared into the civilized world beyond the pier.

When I returned to Cook, he was staring awestruck at a huge, white cruise liner moored on our left. We'd found the infamous "Love Boat."

The Love Boat looked just like the one on the old TV show, and had been moored in Bahrain to provide American servicemen a getaway weekend. The ship had come over from the States as somebody's great idea to buck up morale. We'd first heard of it back in the early fall. The deal was that troops of all services would rotate to the ship for a weekend of rest and relaxation, maybe a couple of beers and, for the very lucky, a chance to talk to a female service member or two. The troops would go first, then more senior people until eventually even the officers would be able to get a weekend aboard. Nobody I knew ever made it aboard.

Cook and I wandered over to the gangway for a closer look. We saw a rowdy bunch of service men and women carousing on the weather decks about 40 feet above us. At the bottom of the gangway stood an Army specialist.

I don't speak much Army, so Cook asked him which unit was aboard. The specialist rattled off a nomenclature with which I wasn't familiar, and Cook asked him what one had to do to get aboard. I don't think Cook actually wanted to go aboard; he was simply curious.

The specialist, who was decked out in starched utilities, his helmet cocked back at just enough of an angle to be declared rakish, snorted and said, "Hell, you gotta be a real war fighter! These guys here just came from the front lines!"

Cook looked at me with a dirt-encrusted grin and shrugged in his flak jacket and war gear. I shrugged back, wondering who those "real war fighters" must be. We resumed our search for a ride out to the battleship.

The sun was slipping away as we requested permission to come aboard *Wisconsin*. I was in the lead, as Cook didn't speak much Navy. We were welcomed by an officer in working khakis who hustled us into the wardroom. I felt as if I were back aboard the *Missouri*, as the layout of the ship was identical.

Once in the wardroom, it was obvious the Navy was extremely uncomfortable at the sight of the weapons strapped to us—even though there was an entire detachment of armed Marines aboard.

The command duty officer, a lieutenant commander, wanted us to turn over our weapons to him. We essentially told him to piss off, and for a brief moment we glared at each other. We finally reached a compromise. Cook and I agreed to check our weapons, along with our driver's, but only to the Marines in the Marine Detachment armory. That accomplished, we tromped back up to the wardroom.

The Navy officers gathered around, staring at us as if we had just been chipped out of a glacier. One very officious lieutenant who appeared to be in charge began rapid-firing us a brief on the ship and the next day's itinerary. He then offered us food, which we heartily accepted.

We sat with about a half-dozen officers at the linen-covered wardroom table as well-turned-out stewards—a part of the Navy I never got used to and never agreed with—brought us piles of food on china plates. Reflexively, I reached for the long brown plastic MRE spoon I always carried on a loop on my flak jacket. Without thinking, I wiped the spoon on my sleeve and dug in to my chow. Cook did the same. Then we noticed the horrified looks on the faces of the Navy officers.

I grinned through a mouthful of food and shrugged. So much for wardroom etiquette. We also listened to the officers bitch through mouthfuls of soft-serve ice cream about their hardships on their deployment while they continued to stare at us dirty-ass field troops.

After chow, the officious lieutenant spoke again, and in a manner I figured could only mean he was trying to impress us. He told us where our sleeping quarters would be and that someone would show us the way soon. He was having a great time speaking Navy jargon in front of an Army officer and a jarhead, and I'm sure he thought he was confusing the hell out of us.

If we needed him, he said, he'd be in his stateroom, then rattled off a compartment number, a confusing series of letters and numbers used by the Navy to designate all the spaces on a ship. For, example, "3-111-4-L" means that the compartment is on the third deck below the main deck, 111 frames from the bow. The third number (4) indicates whether the compartment is on the port or starboard side and its relation to the ship's centerline. Odd numbers on the starboard side, even numbers to port. In this example, the compartment is on the port side. The letter indicates the type of compartment, in this case "L" for "living space." The numbers are pronounced with the hyphen indicated as "tack," i.e., 3 TACK 111 TACK 4 TACK LIMA (the phonetic designation for the letter "L").

Once you know how to read them, figuring out where a space is located is easy, but until you do, it sounds like a foreign language.

The lieutenant looked at us smugly, waiting for us to ask the obvious question — "Where the hell is that?"

"Oh," I said. "Second deck, across from the forward ship's store on the port side."

His mouth fell open. "How the —"

I smiled. "I was the MARDET XO on the *Missouri* up until a year and a half ago. We're going to head up to our racks now."

We didn't get any more trouble out of him.

Cook and I climbed the ladder just aft of the wardroom on the port side and threw our gear into a two-man room on the second level. We then took as long a "Hollywood shower" as we dared — with as much hot water as we could stand. It was the first real shower I'd had since leaving Haii 3 in early December, not counting the NBC shower, and I was going to make it last as long as possible.

We also availed ourselves of the officers' laundry and washed our utilities. I threw in my poncho liner for good measure, to wash out weeks of sweat and rainwater. We finally collapsed in a real rack, with crisp white sheets, luxuriating in the feel of a full belly and clean linen.

We spent most of the next day in the combat information center, discussing naval gunfire, target lists, payloads, and the like, for eastern Kuwait and Kuwait City. The briefings were very informative, and I had to give the Navy credit for doing its homework and preparation. We talked to the ship's intelligence officer about the air campaign. According to him, there would be three phases, as noted in my journal:

> I. A six-day strike against national strategic targets in Iraq. This would involve up to 1300 daily sorties hitting political infrastructure, dams, highways, power plants, and communications centers. Three hundred Tomahawks would go downrange on day one. Supposedly, even Saddam's mistress's house had been targeted.

II. An eight-day strike against the Republican Guards, twice-a-day Rockeye cluster-bomb runs. Carpet-bombing runs by B-52s would be included.

III. A four- to 14-day strike on the regular army in southern Kuwait, designed to pound the army into submission. Stealth fighters would continue to take out Scud sites located in Phase I.

When we left the ship that afternoon, I almost felt sorry for any Iraqi unit that came into the *Wisconsin*'s cross hairs.

By the time we crossed the causeway back to Saudi Arabia on the 10th, the sun had set. I was in the back of the humvee. Cook rode shotgun.

Two guards stopped us on the Bahrain side of the causeway. We presumed they were part of the Bahrainian military, whatever that was. One, a burly guy with a beard, leaned into the vehicle and began speaking in broken English, asking where we were going and if we had any Michael Jackson tapes, of all things.

His partner, I noticed, had begun walking around the back of the vehicle toward Cook. I nudged Cook. He looked as nervous as I felt. Then the burly guard abruptly walked back into the guard shack. We could see him talking to another Arab through the shack's plate glass window.

Cook said he wondered what the hell they were talking about and why we couldn't go. I decided to provide a soundtrack for the conversation, and in my best stereotypical Arab accent, I said, "He's in there telling his boss, 'Four son of bitch in truck. Need *beeger* sword!'"

The thick Arab accent wasn't really that funny, but we were all tense and tired, and Cook couldn't stop laughing. Burly Guard's partner inched closer, and the burly one came out of the guard shack in a hurry. He stuck his head back into our humvee so quickly that I unholstered my pistol. Our driver, a Marine whose name today escapes me, reached for his M16A2. There was no way in hell, we all decided at once, that we were going to be jumped on a highway in Bahfuckingrain.

I kept my pistol out of sight, but I kept my eyes on the smaller of the two guards. I could hear Cook's ragged breathing in front of me, and I could feel the driver tense up. The burly one grinned at us and simply said, "You may go."

Relieved, we hauled ass across the causeway without looking back.

0846, Sun., 13 Jan 91
Hot news this morning is that Congress authorized the use of force against Iraq if Saddam does not pull out of Kuwait by Tues. The new

word has me fired up. Getting in the mental state necessary for it, and I'm tired of fucking around and I'm ready to get going. The time for hope, fear, and contemplation is over.

I've done everything possible to get to this point; all that remains is the doing. People are starting to get motivated and are anxious for the bombing to start. I'm ready to start dumping some DPICM on these assholes.

We'd gotten reports that the Iraqis were shifting their forces and — astonishingly — had pulled back considerably from the border. If the intel was accurate, it meant the Iraqis had left their first defensive belt virtually unguarded. Supposedly, only two brigades of light infantry remained in the vicinity of the minefield, and those brigades were reported to be about fifteen kilometers behind the minefield.

We also knew that they had pulled their artillery back, but to where no one knew. The Iraqi troops on the border seemed to have vanished, and our satellite coverage was being hampered by cloudy weather, with three more days of foul weather predicted. That posed a problem for our counterfire plan.

Counterfire differs from counterbattery fire in that the former is more deliberate, and hopefully preemptive, while the latter is more reactive and immediate.

Counterfire involves locating enemy fire systems and weapons — tanks, artillery, missiles, rockets, and the like — and eliminating them with friendly indirect-fire assets, including artillery fire, bombs, and mortar fire. Even naval gunfire and attack aircraft can be considered as counterfire.

Counterbattery fire is simply fire, usually artillery, delivered for the purpose of destroying or neutralizing indirect-fire weapon systems such as artillery, missiles, and rockets. Counterbattery is usually reactive. For example, if an enemy artillery unit fires and is located, friendly artillery units will immediately fire upon the enemy unit.

Before Desert Storm began, we focused on counterfire, but we had to locate the Iraqi weapon systems before we could attack them. As Desert Storm's Scud hunt showed, finding those assets was no easy task.

By the afternoon of the 13th, when I made that day's journal entry, the weather had turned miserable. Rain had begun falling at 0430 and continued without let-up all day. Everything I owned was wet. This time, I didn't even try to keep the water out of my hole. I simply crawled in my bag, pulled a poncho over my head and fell asleep in the mud.

• CHAPTER EIGHT •

Tues., 15 Jan 91

Today is the day. Heard last night that the Iraqi government gave Saddam its "blessing" to "stand up to American tyranny."

Now that the deadline is upon us, the Marines are showing their traditional esprit de corps. They're eager and expectant, ready to do battle. There is definitely a warrior spirit prevailing. That plus a heavy feeling of agitation, from doing nothing for five months, and especially after the last three days of the most miserable weather anyone has seen in years. There is the belief that someone has to pay for this shit.

I share the same feeling. The time for worry and fear is past. Now it is time to gear up to do our job — grim as it may be. Nobody knows when the bombing will start, but most feel that it will be soon.

There is talk of our moving into an assembly area near the 20th. That would put us just outside Iraqi artillery range. From there, we'd go into an attack position a few klicks from the border, and up to the breach site, whenever the breach happens. But that may not be for a while, because the plan is to bomb for at least 3 weeks before starting the ground attack.

According to the intelligence reports we were getting from the *Wisconsin*, the chances were 90% that the war would begin between January 16-20, the new moon phases for the month of January. I hoped it was true. As far as I was concerned, the sooner the better.

But on the morning of January 15, it was hard to tell that we had passed a deadline that would unleash the American military machine in a fury not seen since World War II. The FDC radios were quiet, and Marines moved throughout the position in their normal routines. We all had our thoughts, but we kept them to ourselves.

When I spoke at all, it was to Neal Noem, who had become a very good friend in a very short amount of time. Neal worked with me in the jump FDC, which gave us an opportunity to spend hours together, especially in the lull after a move while we waited for the rest of the battalion to close on us. Neal had become the one person I could talk to about anything. His wife, Stacey, sought out Angie on Oahu, and because their husbands were getting to know each other, they found themselves becoming friends as well. That friendship continues today.

Neal and I probably talked that day about the deadline and the implications of what it meant. We had spent hour upon hour in the previous weeks speculating about our future, so I'm sure we did that day too.

Those kinds of conversations had occasionally taken weird, even macabre, turns, too. At one point, I fell into a discussion with Marshall and Miller about being wounded. We were telling each other how awful it would be to be wounded. We soon began discussing where we'd want to be hit, if we had to be hit at all. This soon led us to say what body part we'd be willing to give up to live.

What had started as an honest, almost embarrassing, discussion of one of our biggest fears had taken on a life of its own. Now we seemed to be making an indirect plea to God to spare us, to just name a price that we'd be willing to pay for the chance to return home alive. It was some sort of weird incantation, a desert mojo that would somehow keep us alive if we admitted it.

It didn't seem bizarre at the time, this disturbing talk, and I'm still not sure that it was, even after years have passed, and even though, except for a very few instances, I never faced the real possibility of being wounded. At the time, it seemed perfectly natural — evolutionary, perhaps — that we'd come to this discussion, not in some John Wayne, macho-man way, but intellectually, matter-of-factly, looking at our options and possibilities and trying to put on the best face possible, though deep down inside we knew we were powerless to control the one piece of sizzling metal that might take our lives. So I decided I could do without my left foot, as I am right-handed, terribly so.

I had a much more difficult time reacting intellectually to my separation from Angie. Where she is concerned, I have always reacted emotionally. I'd spent so much time away from her, first in the Mojave Desert with 5/11, then at sea aboard the *Missouri*, and now in Saudi Arabia. That time was catching up to me now.

The strength of her letters amazed me. She had learned about the reality of deployments over the years and had learned to be tough — a realization that made me feel even more selfish.

After the war, we would marvel at how well our relationship had fared, how it had actually intensified. This was a contrast to the first time I deployed to the Persian Gulf, in 1987. That deployment, and the ensuing two-year tour aboard the *Missouri*, had almost cost us our marriage.

But this time we became stronger during the separation. The difference? This time we knew it was worth it. We'd already passed through this crucible, and we knew that our respective places were with each other. We never doubted it.

And in those fearful uncertain days, Angie did more than just touch my life. She helped transform it.

0645, Thurs., 17 Jan 91
The bombing has begun. And the initial hysteria. Martin woke me up at 0550 w/news that it started at 0300. I'd heard impacts about 0400, but had gone back to sleep. Thought it was one of the ranges. Typical. But I didn't sleep that well.

FDC is abuzz now. Go on watch at 0900. The news is hopelessly fucked up. Pres. Bush announced it to the nation; Cheney said Desert Shield is over and Desert Storm has begun; we are bombing Baghdad at this minute; I can hear and feel the bombs falling inside Kuwait — we're close enough for that.

When Martin woke me, I angrily dismissed him and tried to go back to sleep. That proved impossible, as my ears recorded every distant thump of falling bombs. When I awoke fully, the sound was electrifying.

Charged with adrenaline, I scrambled into my clothes and joined Neal, Rivers, and the rest of the crew in the FDC, the nerve center of an artillery unit. It was now a squawking, static-filled madhouse of utterly unnecessary radio traffic. Unnecessary because we — Task Force Taro/Poi — were playing absolutely no part in the massive bombardment happening miles to our front.

And it was a massive bombardment. As one Marine put it, we were "bombing the shit out of 'em." We heard an incessant stream of muted thumps as Tomahawk cruise missiles and laser-guided missiles rained on the hapless Iraqis. Occasionally an exceptionally powerful or close explosion — we couldn't tell the difference — would rattle the plastic tent shell of the FDC, causing everyone to suck in their breath and look at each other, frightened but trying to hide it.

From the radio traffic that first morning, I heard a very early report that all Scud missiles pointed at Israel had been taken out, and there was a report of five Scuds being fired at us, which was later disproved.

From the news being broadcast through transistor and portable radios, we heard that U.S. planes had encountered only antiaircraft fire on their runs into Baghdad, and no losses were reported. The "Mighty Mo" and the *Wisconsin* fired their Tomahawks, along with hundreds of others fired at Iraq. The only information we weren't getting was the damage being inflicted on the Iraqi army. There was general agreement that people in the States knew more than we did because they had CNN.

It was hard to stay calm in those first few sweaty-palm hours. Things were happening so fast, and the information was so mixed up that I didn't know what to make of half of what I was hearing. As my ears strained against the radio static, I recalled that, the night before, I'd seen bumper-to-bumper traffic on the highway going north, toward Khafji. Presumably the vehicles were American combat vehicles and logistics trains. I wandered outside to a dune to get a daytime look at the highway.

There was a beeline of Saudi traffic — many expensive automobiles— streaking south. The residents of Khafji were fleeing for their lives. It made me wonder if they were running away from the Iraqis or us.

At 0659, CNN reported that the entire Iraqi Air Force had been destroyed, and, a few minutes later, that the Republican Guard had been destroyed. I was incredulous. There were about 120,000 troops in the Republican Guard. I also heard a report that the Pentagon claimed the success so far had been far better than expected.

By mid-afternoon, we were still listening to the news and the bombs, but we'd relaxed quite a bit. At least two bombing runs had been made, and Saddam continued to issue vitriolic statements. He also claimed the Iraqi forces had shot down 14 planes; our spokesmen countered with a loss estimate of one.

By then, we had learned that the attack had started with Tomahawk strikes in Baghdad, followed by planes. There was "scant resistance" to the pilots on the second run.

A Marine reconnaissance team checked in via radio from Khafji that afternoon. The team was believed to be the only Americans in the area. The Iraqis fired artillery into the city the morning of the 17th, hitting an oil refinery and setting it on fire. That barrage prompted the exodus I saw on the highway. The refinery still burned as the sun set.

At 1836, the news reported that the artillery unit firing on Khafji had been silenced that afternoon, apparently by an American bombing run. I recalled that I had heard what sounded like a whole rackload of bombs hit the deck mid-afternoon. It had made everybody in the FDC look up, and Neal and I exchanged glances, shaking our heads in amazement.

At 2234, 3rd Marines got hit with indirect fire, either artillery or rockets. I happened to be relieving myself, facing north, when I saw several very bright flashes of light, followed closely — less than four seconds — by the familiar *karumph* of artillery. The explosions were very loud, and felt very close.

Gunny Miller was in the jump FDC, and when he heard it, he scrambled out the back of the humvee. I called out that it looked like incoming. I ran to the FDC, where all hell was breaking loose.

"A" Battery, to our northeast, had taken rounds east of them; "F" Battery, to our northwest and near 3rd Marines, also had rounds landing nearby. Both units donned gas masks. 3rd Marines called and needlessly told us to go to "full alert."

Matthews was already in the FDC, trying to gain control of the situation, his voice quaking and his eyes wide and shiny. One of our intelligence NCOs, a corporal, bless his soul, was scared right out of his mind. I wasn't far behind, but luckily I could concentrate on the fire-direction radio nets and block it out. Several more huge concussions rocked the FDC.

Shortly after I arrived, Rivers, who had been asleep when the shooting started, burst into the FDC, blinking from the painful intrusion of light into his eyes and dressed in his long johns, flak jacket, and helmet. I had to suppress a smile. Rivers seemed unfazed. He glanced at me, and I nodded. He nodded at me and stood back, doing his job by letting his Marines do theirs.

Marshall, who had the watch, and I were puzzled by the attack. We knew the Iraqis didn't have any weapon systems that could range us from where their artillery was supposedly located. We broke out manuals and cheat sheets, checking and rechecking ranges of Soviet and Chinese artillery. We even double-checked our own, admitting that, for all we knew, the Iraqis could have a couple of American-made howitzers up there.

Our only conclusion that night was that it had to have been a mobile rocket launcher of some sort, but we had no idea what could have created such enormous explosions. We found out later that the Iraqis had acquired a 200mm rocket system of Brazilian origin, called the "Astral." I learned to hate that weapon.

The only other scare we had that night was one panicked 3rd Marines report of 25 Soviet BTR-60 combat vehicles moving south on the coastal highway. They turned out to be more Saudis getting the hell out of Dodge.

Al-Jubayl Airport, 1102, Fri., 18 Jan 91

"A" took incoming at 0530; M8 alarms went off; we went to MOPP *2, but no gas, thank God; overnight Iraq fired Scuds into Israel, chemical*

variant rumored to have been fired. Rumor of 1-5 fired at us, all taken out by our Patriot missiles.

Also, 1/12 is to move west tomorrow, firing two battalion missions on the way at targets as of yet undetermined. The whole mission/move is tentative right now. Schedule is accelerated. Now there is talk of a ground attack by the 25th or 27th. East of Al-Wafrah oilfield.

At a helo planning conference now. 3rd Marines is supposed to be lifted to the same area we are going to tomorrow.

Talked to Jim Thorp, classmate from Ole Miss, earlier. That was a surprise. He's a Cobra pilot now, and said they are taking out targets of opportunity — arty OP. Batteries shooting at Khafji yesterday were silenced, but not enough to prevent "A"s incoming this morning. Thorp said the Cobras are shooting "lots of people." Last night's enemy shooter — a multiple-rocket battery — was located by ANGLICO. A-10s rolled in but couldn't find it. They did get a POL [Petroleum, Oil, and Lubricants] site, though.

CO briefed last night that 72 B-52s are inbound this a.m. to work over southern Kuwait and the breach site.

Much has been made of the chemical detection alarms since the end of the war, especially with the growing numbers of veterans claiming to be affected by the mysterious ailments known as Gulf War Syndrome. "A" Battery was the first in the battalion to experience the alarms, and the accompanying terror.

It wouldn't be the last time during Desert Storm that the alarms would sound. But in each case, further tests and sampling of the air indicated absolutely no traces of chemical agents. We wrote it off to over-sensitive alarms that were susceptible to concussion — especially the large Astral rockets that were being launched from the border.

In 1997 and 1998, I was interviewed about these alarm incidents numerous times by the federal task force charged with investigating all chemical reports during the war. I came away unimpressed with the efforts of the investigators, all active-duty officers and senior enlisted people.

Navigating through faulty memories, sea stories, and factual errors was difficult enough, but it was made more so by the investigators. They seemed more intent on proving that the Marine Corps and the 1st Marine Division were not to blame for erroneous chemical reports than on proving whether or not we were exposed to chemical weapons.

A typical line of questioning: "When the M8 alarms went off, did you file an NBC (nuclear, biological, chemical) report in accordance with 1st Marine Division standard operating procedures?"

The implication was that if we did not, then we were in error because we failed to follow proper procedures. Another typical question: "Did you log in the activation of the alarm in your communications logbooks?"

Typical answer: "Not always. Sometimes we were too busy."

"Too busy? Doing what?"

"Fighting."

Again and again, the investigators asked loaded questions: Did you receive in-country NBC training? (No.); Why are your records incomplete? (Because we weren't concerned with the paperwork in a combat zone.); Why does your recollection differ so dramatically from other witnesses? (Because we each had our own point of view.)

During two hour-long interviews, I was asked only once if I thought we had been exposed to chemical weapons.

I don't think we were, but the point is, nobody even bothered to ask the question. When I responded, "No, I don't think we were exposed to chemical weapons, but I do think we were exposed to something that is making people sick," I got puzzled looks from under furrowed brows.

Repeatedly, I heard, "We're trying to get to the bottom of this," but I was never sure exactly what "this" was.

And in the end, the report said that nobody got exposed to chemicals and that, essentially, everything had been resolved. Actually, the report resolved little. Veterans are still sick, and doctors still don't have answers. I still believe that we were exposed to something that is, in fact, affecting some veterans.

In the first few months after I returned stateside, I watched with apprehension as reports of sick vets hit the media. In 1991 and 1992, most veterans claiming to be ill all generally had one thing in common: they were located in the rear areas during the war. I don't recall any large number of front-line troops claiming to be sick, at least not initially.

I began to wonder, and I still do, if location didn't have a lot to do with the illnesses. Jubayl, for example, was a refinery town — we called it the Saudi version of Houston — where toxins spewed into the air round the clock. The Saudis don't have an Environmental Protection Agency, so the air is not as regulated as American air. Saudi Arabia, especially the wilds of the desert, is a wilderness of dirt, dust, flies, animal carcasses, and oil toxins — none of which is familiar to the American immune system.

That, and the nerve-agent antidote pills we were issued — rumored to be "experimental" — and the unhealthy fumes from the hundreds of oil fires during Desert Storm must be taken into account in any investigation of Gulf War illnesses.

Jim Thorp was the last person I expected to see in Saudi Arabia. The first thing I noticed about him was that he'd lost a lot of weight. I was of course oblivious to the weight I'd lost. Jim's flight suit hung off him and his face looked gaunt.

But it was great to see him. Jim was a mustang — a former enlisted Marine — and one of the finest Marines I'd ever met. He had come to Ole Miss under the Marine Enlisted Commissioning Education Program, or MECEP, in my sophomore year. Then a sergeant, he made an immediate impression, not only with the NROTC students who viewed him as something of a god — a real no-shit Marine from the Fleet Marine Force — but from the faculty as well. Quiet, mature, and easygoing, Jim was easy to like. And although we hadn't been exceptionally close, I considered him to be not only a friend, but someone to admire as well.

Jim was excited that day in Jubayl, the first time I had seen him in about six and a half years. He'd been doing "a lot of flyin' and a lot of shootin'."

In great spirits, his eyes twinkling under his close-cropped blond hair, he told stories of flying low and fast to his targets, which were mostly Iraqi artillery observation posts, then hovering to light them up with 2.75-inch Zuni rockets or the nasty 20-millimeter Gatling gun slung underneath the nose of the helicopter.

I was enthralled by the news, since my participation in the war so far had been listening to bombs hit the deck.

We parted, promising each other to "get together sometime." I told him I'd look him up the next time I came to Jubayl.

I never got the chance.

A few days after I returned to Hawaii, in late April, Jeff Speights called with the news that Jim had been killed in a helicopter crash February 3, a few days after we'd spoken at the Jubayl airport.

I was standing in the kitchen of our house as Jeff told me, and his words felt like a kick to the head. I sank to the floor in the dark, absorbing the awful news.

Because I'd seen him just days before he died — the last Ole Miss classmate to see him — I felt connected to his death. It's a connection I've never shaken, and Jim's smiling face in the airport haunts me to this day. Part of it, I've come to realize, is what doctors call "survivor's guilt."

Jim's death, like so many, was so pointless and was such a waste that it is hard to justify. He had been an outstanding officer with a great future, and he had been the salt of the earth. He didn't deserve to die.

Mishab, 0650, Sat., 19 Jan 91

Only sporadic shelling last night. 3rd Marines had a volley land somewhere northwest of their pos.

The bombing continues. B-52s that the CO said were coming tomorrow are actually coming today. Hope we hear some of that.

"F" Btry was going to do a raid today — a battery 12-round mission on an artillery OP, but 11th Marines canceled it. We may move "C" up to Khafji today, if 3/3 goes up to establish a blocking position. I thought they were moving west on the 21st, but now I guess Col. Admire is considering putting 3/3 at Khafji.

2246

Waiting for a possible rocket attack anytime now. Got the word from 3rd Mar at 2218 of an attack being possible within the next 20 minutes.

"F" took incoming at 2007. Closer than last time, but still not close enough to cause casualties. 3rd Mar got it pretty close — "F" isn't too far from them. This shelling sounded a hell of a lot closer! It shook the tent here in the FDC— I've been on watch since 1800. At first I thought "C" Btry was getting nailed — they're about 1500m E of us, and we're about 14 Km S of "F" and "A." But the rounds sounded much closer. We were almost diving to the deck.

MEF cleared a mission about 1 hr. later. Apparently, hell obviously, the air strikes didn't completely silence the MRL battery (or batteries) that are doing this shooting, so the MEF gave TF Taro a mission to do an "artillery ambush."

The shelling tonight came from almost the exact spot "F" would have hit today, had they done their raid, the one that got canceled by MEF. The CO was going to move "F" today, too, because he suspected that something like tonight might happen. He did order "A" to move, which they did this afternoon, but he held off on "F." Almost had the chance to regret that decision. Those rounds landed about 300m from the battery. Amazing that there were no casualties anywhere. I did, however, hear a rumor that 3rd Mar took 3 WIAs on the night of the 17th. Nothing serious, 2 USMC and one corpsman got hit w/fragments.

Get off watch at midnight, and I'll be glad to be in my fucking hole. I do not like this sitting-here-taking-incoming shit.

2311

I'm starting to understand what the vets are talking about when they say that being shot at by artillery sucks. Being an artilleryman, I find it professionally humiliating to have to sit here and take incoming artillery fire, and not be able to return the favor. Not to mention that it's nerve-wracking as hell. When I say we, though, I mean the battalion. HQ Battery is out of range, I believe. Think the Iraqis are just lobbing rounds as far as they can and hoping for the best. Nothing has come this far south yet. Luckily. That doesn't, of course, make us impervious.

To say that all hell broke loose when Desert Storm began would be an understatement of British proportions.

In just two days we received so much information — and what CWO-2 Lynn Nesbit and I began calling "counterinformation"— that we truly had no idea what the hell was going on, as these journal entries indicate.

Fox Battery's raid would have exercised what was being touted as a "new" concept in artillery, basically an artillery ambush.

The Corps had had some success in loading up a 105mm howitzer and crew and ammo aboard a helo and flying them to an advantageous position, from where the crew would fire, then beat feet out of the area aboard a helo.

In Saudi Arabia, we sought to accomplish the same thing with a ground raid — hauling the M198s into position by five-ton truck. A ground raid had a distinct advantage: We could move an entire battery, the jump FDC, and a security force into position and deliver a crippling punch.

The disadvantage, however, was just as distinct: We were slow and couldn't get to faraway targets quickly. Another disadvantage was the noise created by more than a dozen trucks and humvees rumbling through the darkness across an open desert.

But we didn't have to worry about faraway targets. We had plenty just north of us, opposite the Saudi border town of Khafji. That town had become the focal point of 3rd Marines and the division. Khafji offered the Iraqis a lucrative target — a Saudi city that could be easily taken by their mechanized forces, which could roll south out of Kuwait along the coastal highway.

Those Iraqi units faced less than half the distance to travel than we. If the Iraqis were to seize and hold Khafji, they would have an excellent avenue of approach to strike deep into Saudi Arabia. In doing so, they would run smack into 3rd Marines. Sensing this, Admire wanted to establish a presence that would discourage any such Iraqi foray, hence his consideration to move 3/3 north. It must have been on the minds of the I MEF staff, too, given their order to us to plan for a raid, an order that was canceled after only a few hours.

Meanwhile, Thorp and his Cobra buddies were hitting the observation posts responsible for directing Iraqi artillery, the delivery of which I took as an insult more than anything else. For an artilleryman, there are few things worse than being forced to suffer the indignity of enemy artillery. That indignity manifested itself in the way we cringed at sounds of incoming rounds that, in the cold still air, felt dangerously close.

I'm sure we were a comical sight, crouch-squatting in the dim glow of chem-lights and Coleman lanterns, eyes darting about as we tried to look less frightened than those around us and failing miserably.

Except for Neal Noem. He was the original cool customer. I have no memory of his facial expression ever changing from its usual patient, almost doleful, look. There were times when I tried to crawl completely inside my helmet, but Neal never even looked up from whatever book he happened to be reading. It was both a comfort and an annoyance.

But within 24 hours, I would tap into Neal's cool and try to make it my own.

BOOK II

OPERATION DESERT STORM

Part One

Air War

· C H A P T E R   N I N E ·

0640, Sun., 20 January 91

MEF raid mission approved. Got briefed about 0215. We leave for 3rd Mar at 0730 to brief, pick up RPVs (our eyes) and "C" Battery. Fox will go up to an assembly area today, then move into position right at nightfall, FIRECAP NLT 1900. The position is about 5 Km from the border. We'll be a few klicks back of them w/the jump and RPVs;

"C" will be behind the jump ready to support "F" withdrawal with RAP, if need be. "A" not playing.

Target is an Astral battalion that apparently has been firing at us. The plan is to get RPVs up, let him shoot—he usually does around 2000—locate him, then hit him w/DPICM and WP from "F," a battery 10 or 12. Then haul ass.

There's a lot to hope for: cloud cover, that the enemy is actually there; that he indeed shoots tonight, etc. Have some secondary targets in case he's a no-show.

1010

This mission is getting all fucked up. MEF got involved, so now the MEF CG is giving orders directly to 1/12 CO. RIDICULOUS. They told us where to fire from, which is bullshit.

And MEF wants us to establish a CBR site 4 Km south of the jump, which is actually a good idea. Counterbattery radar can get a good acquisition when they fire, then we can call in A-10s on these fuckers. Haven't left 3rd Marines yet. We'll be in position by dark.

I Marine Expeditionary Force ordered 1/12 to conduct an artillery raid on an Iraqi Astral rocket unit, presumably the unit responsible for the incoming TF Taro had received the previous few nights.

By the time Desert Storm started, nearly everyone had dug a hole for protection in the event of incoming fire. Note grenade sump between my feet.

I MEF intelligence indicated this unit had a pattern of firing a volley each night around 2000, then departing before being located by American counterbattery radar or other detection units. So far, this tactic had worked. We received fire on a somewhat regular basis from the first night of the air war, and we had been unable to return fire.

We welcomed the mission. The nightly rocket and artillery attacks unnerved everyone in TF Taro, especially since the 200-millimeter rockets were fairly accurate. Fox Battery, having taken some rounds near its position on previous nights, was more than happy to have the chance to give some back to the Iraqis.

An artillery raid is simple in concept, but it can be extremely difficult to execute. Once an artillery battery fires on today's modern battlefield, which is scoured by all sorts of radar and other detection systems, the whole world knows where that battery is. To remain in position is to sign your own death warrant.

1105, Mon., 21 Jan 91

Last night was a fucking fiasco. We shot all right, but we have no idea if we hit the target. No surveillance (BDA), no observers. But, as of now, I believe I'm the first USMC FDO to actually issue a fire order. Too bad I feel like shit about it.

2100 came and went, and division told us to stay put until 2230 to engage "alternate targets." MRLS never showed, so we waited and waited. Div wanted us to engage a convoy—that was 2 mapsheets out of range.

I was worried about being discovered. God knows we were putting out enough radio transmissions for any half-assed DF unit to find us.

At 2135 we were discovered. Took about 6 rounds of arty, not very well-placed. No casualties, but I know the Iraqis DFed us. We were on the radios way too much.

Played the waiting game until 0300—the whole time I was either falling asleep or waiting for a second, more accurate, volley to hit us. Then, the CO decided enough was enough. We sent a TOT for 0345 to Fox; 12 rounds of DPICM at an infantry CP. No sooner had we sent it than 3rd Marines sent an immediate fire mission to us—an Iraqi artillery battery firing into Khafji.

Then Fox had enormous problems, still don't know details. Wouldn't acknowledge me on BCT or radio, took over 6 minutes to fire. Fired 10 rounds DPICM — 70 total. Have no idea if they hit anything. They took so long that the battery had probably already displaced.

Haven't slept since about 0300 yesterday, except for catnaps in the vehicle. Pounding headache now. Gen. Draude coming for debrief at noon.

1959

Brig. Gen. Draude has come and gone; apparently he & the division CG are "immensely pleased" w/our raid last night, even if I am not. No BDA, but apparently the sequence of events was as follows:

> *(1) Khafji receives fire from Iraqi artillery; ANGLICO locates target, radios 3rd Marines.*
> *(2) We receive fire mission & shoot Fox at the artillery battery.*
> *(3) ANGLICO reports no more activity from pos we fired at.*
> *(4) Khafji receives rocket fire; ANGLICO locates target north of arty position; calls in A-6s.*
> *(5) A-6s strike, report numerous secondary explosions.*

Brig. Gen. Draude said division thought it might have been a ruse by the Iraqis—present a target by firing the artillery, knowing we would fire counterbattery, then leave the area. Once we were out of the area, the rockets could fire w/o a counterbattery threat. However, there was a counterfire threat they didn't know about — the A-6 flight — and got nailed because of it. Also, Draude said that it could also be we missed, but even if we did, we set them up for the A-6s, thus actually accomplishing the objective of destroying the battery. RPVs went up to take a look this afternoon to see what we hit.

In any case, he congratulated us on the raid and being the first ground unit in the Marine Corps (and of course, in the 1st Marine Division) to fire in anger. So, I actually was the first FDO to fire in combat (in USMC) in Saudi Arabia.

More notes: We were definitely acquired & the incoming was intended for us. The question is whether it was by DF or RPV. Draude is checking to see if it was a DF acquisition or not. God knows we had enough radio traffic to give them a chance. I cringed at every transmission, esp. after the incoming. That shit was close enough, thank you. Draude also said that 1/12 now definitely qualifies for a Combat Action Ribbon. We were shot at, and we shot back. That's the requirement.

I was scared to death. Every mile closer to the border, I got more & more scared. Just plain old scared. Never experienced that kind of terror. Tried to compare it to something, but nothing fit. There is a certain exhilaration, no doubt, but not like that you get, say, anticipating a big football game. A unique excitement that I guess comes from realizing that you are going out to find the enemy and kill him. But just as strong, if not stronger, is an unbelievable fear that grips you. It can consume you if you let your guard down. And last night was fairly easy! We weren't advancing under fire. But I really had to control the fear the whole way up. Can't describe it accurately enough. Proved an old theory that combat — or the inherent fear — makes one extremely thirsty. Drank water all night. So did Gunny.

We talked about how scared we were today. While we were doing so, I noticed my hands shaking. Better now, had a good rest this afternoon, blew off a little steam. But there is only one emotion in combat — controlled fear.

Several things are essential in an artillery raid. First, of course, is stealth. The battery must get into position undetected and remain so by minimizing radio transmissions — both voice and digital. Anybody with a sixth-grade education can set up a direction-finding, or DF, apparatus.

I am convinced that the Iraqis found us that night with DF gear, even though we never received any official word from Brig. Gen. Draude. We poured a steady stream of transmissions into the night air. It seemed that every officer in the MEF near a radio wanted to talk.

Another essential item in a raid is an accurately located target. There is only one opportunity to fire in a raid; there is no adjusting a second volley. Thus, the target must be located as accurately as possible, preferably before the mission even commences.

All we had was a general area for the Iraqi artillery battery, but we thought the use of the MEF's remotely piloted vehicles would overcome this deficiency.

Lt. Col. Rivers, Miller, Marshall, and I felt we had a good plan. We would move "F" and "C" batteries to positions near the border, with Fox being the primary shooter. Charlie would support Fox if needed, and would serve as a standby should Fox become unable to fire. "A" Battery remained behind, but on call.

The jump FDC would provide fire direction and command and control on the move. I would issue the fire order once the target presented itself and RPVs located it.

Because we had very little time for planning, we picked our positions and the route to them by what I called the "scratch and sniff" method: a combination of first-hand knowledge from the battery commanders, reports, from the Saudis and 3rd Marines, intelligence reports and map studies. None of us had been that far north; we had no idea what the roads would be like, especially since we had received quite a bit of rain in the previous days.

The headquarters element pulled out of 1/12's main position in mid-afternoon under cloudy skies. My humvee — the jump FDC — was accompanied by several other vehicles, mostly communications vehicles.

We stopped at 3rd Marines' position to pick up a heavy weapons detachment. It gave me great comfort to see a TOW missile and a .50-caliber machine gun, both mounted on humvees. We also took aboard Capt. Tim Massey, who would communicate with and monitor the RPV team that would provide us with aerial images throughout the night.

The drive north was nerve-wracking, to say the least. My driver, LCpl. Rob Martin, and I usually maintained a conversational banter when we were on the road, but not this night. We spoke only when necessary, both absorbed in our own thoughts and fears. In the back of the vehicle, Gunny Miller and PFC Kyle Schneider, an FDC Marine, did the same.

As the daylight faded, I felt the creeping sensation of fear ease closer and closer. Eight years after I wrote that night's journal entry, those words are still the most accurate record of the fear we experienced that night. It seemed as if every rotation of the tires brought more anxiety.

At about 1800, we stopped to allow the batteries an opportunity to ease into position and to wait for complete darkness to fall. As we dismounted from our vehicles, I saw Marines immediately grab shovels and start digging. I smiled at this because, during peacetime training, artillery Marines rarely dig fighting positions. It's just something we never did, and it usually took all sorts of vile threats to get Marines to do it. That night, however, my Marines dug furiously, not needing to be told, and not caring about how long they would be in that position. I was impressed and thankful that they understood the gravity of our situation.

We pulled out after about half an hour and approached our position in the inky blackness, only about eight to ten klicks from enemy observation posts. In that desert, headlights—even blackout lights—can be seen for miles, so we drove solely on the illumination of night-vision goggles.

Our position was the reverse slope—that is, the side away from the enemy—of a small rise, at the bottom of which was an abandoned Bedouin camp. It looked like a mini-ranch, with stables and a small, barn-like building. We swept this camp before occupying the ground immediately adjacent to it. It seems ridiculous now, a bunch of us dashing like SWAT team members into this camp, weapons at the ready, peeking around corners, hearts pounding, not really knowing what the hell we would do if we actually found any Iraqis or Bedouins in there. As I sprinted from my vehicle to the building, I had the absurd thought that I might step on a mine. We found nothing.

As the night wore on, our nerves frayed almost to the breaking point. By definition, raids are supposed to be quick affairs. Sitting in one position for hours is, in artillery parlance, a deliberate occupation. Rivers, Noem, and Massey crouched over a video monitor in Massey's humvee, watching RPV images of a multitude of targets. None were approved by I MEF, much to Rivers' irritation. Miller and I chided and swore at "F" Battery, which struggled to maintain comm with us. If they could communicate digitally, they couldn't communicate by voice, and vice versa. Though this is fairly typical—perfect comm just doesn't exist—the added stress of being so close to the Iraqis only exacerbated the matter.

I heard the incoming, as did Miller, just before the rounds landed. We locked eyes, terrified. We knew we were screwed, sitting in the back of the humvee, about four feet off the ground with only a sheet of vinyl to protect us from shrapnel. There was no way we could make it to a hole in time. We clamped a hand on our helmets and braced ourselves.

The concussion slammed into the humvee and jarred us. I opened my eyes, realized I was still alive, and dove out the back of the vehicle. I had no idea where the rounds had landed or how closely. Lynn Nesbit who had seen the rounds land, walked up, said, "Close." Noem appeared out of the darkness and indicated that the rounds had landed off to our left front, in the general direction of Fox Battery. He'd actually seen the impact of the rounds, and thought they had landed between us and Fox. Later, Capt. Bruce Kowalski, the CO of Fox Battery, said the same thing.

I checked my Marines, all of whom were in holes, some trying to dig with their teeth, one praying out loud. Relieved that no one was wounded, I climbed back into the humvee and resumed waiting for this mission — which was becoming more and more screwed up — to get moving. Miller and I talked for a few minutes and agreed that we had been discovered from our radio transmissions.

I informed division; we were told to stay in place. Miller and I shook our heads in disbelief and discussed whether or not the Iraqis would adjust their first volley and fire again. We agreed that they'd have to be crazy not to. Luckily, they did not.

I don't know why the Iraqis chose not to adjust, but the answer may lie in their tactics. Lacking the sophisticated counterbattery radars the U.S. military possesses, the Iraqis used a more primitive method.

An artillery battalion commander would place his batteries and draw a graphic which depicted his howitzers' maximum range on a map, essentially a collection of fans— one from each howitzer — that looked like pie wedges. He would then study the map and determine, in his judgment, where the likely spots for enemy artillery were. He would inform his battery FDCS, which would compute firing data.

If the battalion received incoming artillery fire, the commander would most likely order the FDCS to fire at all the targets at once. If the battalion commander knew his stuff, it could be a very effective method.

That night, however, the Iraqis fired first. Perhaps they acquired us from our radio transmissions and lit up the nearest target. Maybe somebody just decided to crank a couple of rounds downrange. Maybe they were just lousy shots. Years later, I learned that an Egyptian tank unit had been operating to our left flank that night, creating a huge amount of noise and even driving with headlights on. Some of the Marines with us that night surmised that the Egyptians had drawn the fire, not the jump FDC or Fox Battery.

In any case, it scared the hell out of me. For the first time, I knew that there were people out there trying to kill me specifically.

Miller and I became more irritated as the night wore on. We were exhausted and scared, and angry at the officers at division and MEF who would inform us of ridiculous targets, then countermand their own orders almost immediately. It was both frustrating and infuriating.

I felt like bait being dangled in front of the Iraqis, as if our only purpose was to draw them out to shoot at us so MEF could hit them with an air strike. This feeling intensified when division told us to wait for alternate targets, even though Rivers and Massey had found numerous suitable targets from the RPV monitor, which Massey had brought along just for that purpose. When that call came, we had been in position for four hours and had already been fired at once.

When we finally did fire, chaos erupted. The Marine Corps calls it the "fog of war," which is another way of saying, "If it can get screwed up, it will."

Miller sent the fire mission via computer to "F" Battery. Inexplicably, the battery's terminal froze up at that moment. It took several seconds to realize this, and another several minutes to try — vainly — to retransmit the firing data.

Finally, I grabbed the radio and called Fox Battery. The FDO, a lieutenant, was near panic. I was near rage. I keyed the handset and passed the entire fire mission over the radio, even though I knew the lengthy transmission would give even Zippy the Chimp enough time to DF us. At this point, however, that was a secondary concern.

The battery FDC outdid itself computing the data and transmitting it to the gun line. We expected to hear the report of the howitzers a minute later. Instead, we agonized through the longest six minutes of my life. Later, I heard several stories about the reasons for this delay, but I could never verify them. Whatever the cause, the delay nearly drove me, and Rivers, to wits' end.

As soon as Fox reported "Rounds complete," I gave them the order to CSMO — close station, march order, or in artilleryspeak, "Collect shit, move out." Instantly, LCpls. Gates and Reed, my trusty radio operators, started ripping comm wire out of my humvee so we could haul ass ourselves. We got on the road in record time.

But "on the road" is a relative term. We tried to find the sandy track with night-vision glasses before every Iraqi in the world learned where we were. It turned our return trip into an adventure. Our inability to do a route recon before the raid now resulted in several vehicles becoming mired in deep mud, the result of the recent rains. Compounding this was the lack of moonlight and dense fog. By the time we made it back to the battalion pos, I was too strung out to sleep. I relaxed with a cup of coffee in the FDC instead, trying to calm down as the sun chased the purple morning sky.

When we returned to the battalion position, Gunny Miller and I went over the entire mission again, critiquing the bad parts and taking note of the good. I actually felt better than I indicated in my journal. I was being too hard on myself, a habit of mine, and I was exhausted.

Next morning, Gunny Miller and I straightened up the back of the jump FDC humvee. During our housekeeping, we talked for a long time about the raid and our emotions during it, specifically the fear. We were both amazed that we had drunk so much water. I had heard about the phenomenon of being thirsty in battle; now I had experienced it. I drank at least five liters of water in as many hours.

I was surprised to find my hands shaking when I raised my coffee cup to my lips as we talked. Miller laughed until he realized his were shaking, too.

Meanwhile, Rivers was able to reconstruct the fire mission from the RPV crew, and learned that our rounds had missed the multiple-launch rocket battery we fired at, but, in one of those oddities of war, we did hit the resupply column that was pulling into the position at the time of the fire mission. As our rounds blew up the resupply convoy, the secondary explosions caused more explosions among the rocket battery, destroying it.

1420, Tues., 22 Jan 91

1st MARDIV is making a very big deal about our raid. A couple of hours ago, I got interviewed by NBC TV and a reporter for Vignette News Services. I was kind of overwhelmed; it was an on-the-spot kind of thing.

I was trying to get them steered down to Fox, the guys who did all the real work, & someone told them I was "directly involved" in the raid, so they descended on me. Should be on TV in the next couple of days. No way to tell Angie; hope she sees it. Or reads it. The Vignette guy says the Honolulu paper is on his beat.

The television interview gained me my "fifteen minutes of fame." By the time I got a chance to call Angie, she'd already seen it, along with, apparently, every other household in America. She had received about fifty phone calls from friends around the country. The interview, which quoted Rivers and me, as well some Marines from "F" Battery, was shown on all three networks and CNN. I even got letters of encouragement from as far away as South Africa.

And for the first time in about four days, we received no incoming.

1253, Wed., 23 Jan 91

I just found out that we just got assigned another raid — for tonight. No planning, just leap through your ass and do it.

We didn't even get to debrief the division on the one 2 days ago!

1409

Not only do we not have a target, we are going to the same area as two nights ago! If this isn't stupid enough, the Iraqis have placed a radar on the border. It has a range of 30K. There is no fucking way we'll get there undetected! The CO is aware of this, but still plans on going back to the same spot. Somebody is going to get hurt tonight.

First to fight. CWO-2 Neal Noem stands behind the first Marine howitzer to fire at Iraqi forces during the Persian Gulf War. The howitzer belongs to Fox Battery, 2nd Battalion, 12th Marines.

Luckily no one got hurt on the second raid, but we got a very up-close-and-personal look at the war. And the Iraqi radar proved to be yet another rumor.

With such little time for planning, we made the raid up as we went along. The original plan was for Alpha and Fox to fire on targets, with Charlie Battery backing them up. However, on the way to a firing position, Morgan's Charlie Battery got hopelessly bogged down in a *sabhka*—a dry lake bed that wasn't so dry anymore—and spent the night digging its vehicles out of hip-deep mud—mud we probably would have avoided had we had enough time to check out the roads ahead of us.

In some ways, the raid went better than the first, in other ways it was worse. We managed to convince the powers that be that going back into the same area as before, miles west of Khafji, wasn't prudent, and selected a position farther to the east, closer to Khafji and our battalion position.

We used a more direct approach, going up the coastal highway, then going off-road for a few miles for the final leg. Our intended position was right in the middle of the war, and we didn't even know it until the Saudis unexpectedly fired a salvo of rockets from a Multiple-Launch Rocket System battery not long after we had settled in.

The American-made MLRS is a devastating piece of artillery. Each rocket in the "six-pack," mounted on a tracked vehicle, carries the same firepower as a battery of cannon artillery firing one round from each of its eight tubes. And when it fires, it will wake the dead, as the rocket motors sound like jet engines and leave a huge trail of white smoke behind.

I had no idea that the Saudis were anywhere near us, so when they launched a rocket from only a few hundred meters away, I nearly jumped out of my skin. All around me, Marines shouted their favorite obscenity and dove for the ground, thinking we were taking incoming again.

Minutes later, the Iraqis returned the favor with a FROG rocket of their own. The impact of that rocket sent us scuttling for cover as someone yelled "Incoming!"—a word we were getting used to in a very short amount of time. The concussion rocked my humvee before I could leap out the back.

The incoming prompted Rivers to move the jump from our position among a craggy outcropping of rocks to a position slightly farther away from the Saudis. By 2015 we were in position, a small north-south dune from which we had a dazzling view of the air war being conducted in Kuwait, just a few miles to our front.

Green and red tracers stitched the black sky like insane spider webs, and antiaircraft fire blossomed in deadly orange clouds. On the ground, American and British bombs backlit the show with a strobe effect accompanied by the throaty rumble of explosions.

On this raid, we were calmer, and we were smarter as a battalion. We stayed off the radios and allowed what Marshall called the "trust factor" to have a play. We knew what the batteries were doing, so there was no need to talk about it on the radio. But our compressed time schedule meant that only Fox had a preplanned target, and they got that on the road via radio. Fox found its position, set up its guns, fired on an Iraqi BM-21 artillery battalion, then headed south to the 3rd Marines perimeter. The RPVs confirmed that the rounds hit the target.

"A" Battery, on the other hand, had no target until the battery pulled into position. I had the RPV controllers with me in the jump, and we wasted hours looking for a target, not a good idea on a raid. Once we located a target—another mobile rocket unit—with the RPV, it took another hour to verify, by which time the unit had disappeared.

Finally, the RPV crew gave us a target, but the description—a mobile artillery unit—didn't match the location, which looked like a police station on my map. After a short conference with Rivers and a check of our watches, I sent "A" Battery a fire order, and the cannoneers fired several volleys. From the surveillance that the RPV crew gave us after Alpha fired, it appeared that the battery was way off target.

I was skeptical of that report, because I didn't trust the grid the RPVs had in the first place, and I knew that "A" Battery was by far our most accurate battery. I noted in my journal that I thought Alpha hit the grid they were given, but that I wasn't sure the enemy had been there. We received word from division, via ANGLICO, a few days later that Alpha had indeed hit the target at which it had aimed, but there wasn't much evidence of any Iraqi presence in the area.

Meanwhile, American A-6 Intruders dropped rackloads of bombs on unseen targets, causing Miller and I to shake our heads, almost feeling sorry for the Iraqis underneath all that steel. Occasionally, the ground beneath our humvee would shake from the impact, and the vinyl covering on our humvee would rattle loudly.

At midnight, we got the word to pull out for what became a 4½ hour drive back to the battalion over unfamiliar terrain. As we left, I heard a series of explosions behind us. We were already on the road, about two hundred meters from our just-vacated position. I heard the noise and, being the last vehicle in our convoy, glanced in my passenger-side rear-view mirror. I saw several brilliant flashes of orange light just behind the small rise that only minutes before had been our position. Loud rumblings made their way to my vehicle, and I slumped back in my seat, not knowing if the noise was outgoing or incoming. Either way, I was glad to be leaving the area. When we got back to the battalion position, I headed straight to my hole for some much-needed sleep.

After a few hours of fitful sleep, I awoke to discover that three new officers had arrived in the battalion while we had been on the road. One, a captain, was sent immediately to the rear to serve as our adjutant.

The other two officers were majors. One was sent to our logistics train to become the battalion S-4. The other, Mike Jeffcoat, was to be our S-3, which would put Matthews out of a job. He was reassigned as the liaison officer to 3rd Battalion, 11th Marines.

But I also viewed Jeffcoat with suspicion, for he came dragging a cartload of rumors behind him. He was assigned as the Marine Option Instructor at Old Dominion University, a cushy job by anyone's standards, and he was basically TAD to the war — on temporary additional duty.

The word from the rumor mill was that Jeffcoat was a "fast-tracker," a political animal looking to get his ticket punched and some "trigger time." According to his legend, which grew by the hour, he had been selected for lieutenant colonel a year early and had commanded five artillery batteries, a near impossibility.

My first impression of the short, combative major with a shaved pate was to not ever piss him off— which I would invariably do in the days to come. Jeffcoat, from the moment I met him, was a straightforward, no-bullshit officer.

Just before 2100 that night, we started scrambling again. This time, the attention was focused on Khafji, the little town that had become a huge thorn in the side of the 1st Marine Division.

Division had already reported that we might be in for an attack for that night. Ostensibly, the Iraqis wanted to take Khafji and emplace artillery there, but, to my knowledge, 11th Marines had no intelligence or indicators of an attack. Col. Admire decided to get his own intelligence, and ordered 3rd Battalion, 3rd Marines, to conduct a reconnaissance in force to secure, and defend if necessary, Khafji. That task fell to India Company, 3/3. Screening to the north of India Company would be LAV units, presumably from Task Force Shepherd.

Rivers ordered "C" Battery to the west of Khafji and "A" to the south. "F" stood ready to rush their ammo trucks forward, if need be. I sent Marshall and the jump FDC forward to coordinate the moves at 2000. I was exhausted and suffering the after-effects of a cold. More importantly, if we were to shoot, I wanted Marshall to get the experience, as he had yet to issue a combat fire order, though certainly not from lack of desire. Rivers and I planned to relieve the jump crew at first light.

But we never had to. As happened so often, once the plan got set in motion, it was immediately canceled. When the division got better intelligence, the staff decided that the Iraqis weren't after Khafji at all and told everybody to stand down.

Marshall came back visibly disappointed, but convinced that we should have stayed in Khafji.

· CHAPTER TEN ·

2040, 28 Jan 91

Maj. V. (Maj. Mike Vontungeln, battalion XO) left 1/12 today; his retirement orders finally came in. Sad to see him go; he's one of the finest men I've ever met.

Very quiet last night. No incoming at all, & no Scud launches. Nor did anyone get shot at on the 25th, the night everybody thought the Iraqis were going to attack Khafji. But, as I write this, we are receiving word of a Scud launch. The game continues.

Surely, Saddam must see that he can't win. Over 13,000 sorties have been flown — over 1,000 a day. His "elite" RGFC are getting hammered hourly w/Rockeye [cluster bombs]. Even if they are dug in, they can only take so much pounding. Troops facing us are faring no better; B-52s carpet-bombing them. Some are defecting. They are in sorry shape, covered w/lice & half-starved.

The border troops have pulled back considerably. The first defensive belt is now manned by a few scattered light infantry companies. Lots of artillery covering the obstacles, though. If it is still there. That's the #1 priority of the tactical bombing campaign. Guess we'll see. It's just hard to believe that Saddam is going to let his people get the hell bombed out of them.

We have a raid scheduled for the 30th, a joint operation w/the Saudi artillery. We're going to use Copperhead to take out 2 artillery observation towers along the border.

Marshall was the one who found them and started the planning. It's only right that he go as the battalion FDO on this one. I'll man the rail here in the main FDC.

2146, 29 Jan 91
Received a report from 11th Mar a few minutes ago that a mech bat-
talion was moving south along the coastal road. No further info.
Nothing has materialized yet.

Raid is put on hold—apparently the Saudis are causing a prob-
lem. Don't know a lot about that.

The pilots are finding that they can't knock out Iraqi artillery units,
no matter how hard they try. Wonderful. And there is a lot of move-
ment in south Kuwait; what is here now, isn't an hour later. And all
Iraqi officers have been ordered north.

2152
Just got a report that TF Shepherd is engaging tanks in W corner of
Kuwait.

The battle of Khafji had begun. Jack Marshall had been right that the
Iraqis were interested in the town.

The Iraqis attacked in three columns: the 1st Mechanized Division
attacked the western "dogleg" area of Kuwait, where Task Force Shepherd
operated; the 3rd Armored Division moved south from the Al-Wafrah
oilfield; and the 5th Mechanized Division moved down the coastal road
into Khafji, north of 3rd Marines.

We began hearing explosions to our north, but no one at 3rd Marines
would or could confirm the cause. Just before midnight, somebody at 3rd
Marines screamed "Gas!" over the radio and scared the living hell out of
everybody in the FDC. It turned out to be a false alarm.

In the early morning hours before sunup on the 30th, the situation
was incredibly screwed up. Utter chaos reigned on the radios, and the FDC
was alive with radio traffic and Marines, all talking excitedly, most passing on rumors. We did, however, receive reports of Allied aircraft circling
overhead, preparing to drop ordnance on the advancing Iraqis. Within
hours, the pilots were getting a workout making runs over the armored
columns.

By mid-morning, the Iraqis had held Khafji for almost five hours with
a mechanized brigade, and we had not fired a shot at them. We were getting plenty of reports of Iraqis moving south, mostly false. I listened, and
then discounted reports of self-propelled artillery, then T-55 tanks moving toward us.

By 0430 on January 30, I'd spent nearly twelve hours straight in the
FDC, most of that time on watch. I'd caught only about an hour and a half
of sleep in a corner of the FDC.

3rd Marines had launched its tank-killing "CAAT teams"—counterar-
mor, antitank—some time in the middle of the night. Their mission was

to speed up to the approaches to Khafji and cover the route south in an attempt to blunt any further incursions south by the Iraqis.

CAAT teams were essentially Marines with shoulder-launched antitank missiles loaded up in humvees and TOW-missile humvees. At daybreak, Admire came on the radio to remind them that he had not heard a peep out of them in "six fucking hours."

Likewise, Qatari tanks, which had been posted to our rear with Saudis as a sort of Pan-Arab mishmash of units, moved up in the night, but did not engage any targets.

Out west, Shepherd took artillery fire and engaged tanks w/LAVs, TOWs, and air all night, according to their reports that filtered back to our radio nets. Their engagements included one LAV that was struck by a missile, believed to be an American Maverick, killing seven Marines.

Meanwhile on the coast, Saudi refugees fled south, complicating our ability to tell friend from foe in the dark. The town had been evacuated, we knew, days before the attack, but judging from the stream of traffic headed south, there were still plenty of civilians in the area. My biggest fear was that the Iraqi Army would be clever enough to turn on its headlights and mingle in with the civilian automobiles.

We also had reports, which seemed to make no sense to our current dilemma, that a large number of vehicles were moving east of the Al-Wafrah oil field in Kuwait. Nobody seemed to know why. Later we learned this force, the middle-attacking column, had been chopped to pieces by American planes.

I found it hard to believe that the division had been taken by surprise, especially after our "dress rehearsal" a few days earlier. But that's exactly what it seemed like: like we'd been caught with our pants down.

1/12 used the dress rehearsal to its advantage. We sent "A" and "C" batteries up north with the jump FDC. Marshall and Jeffcoat went with the new XO, Maj. Barry Hardy [*pseudonym*], and the usual crew. I stayed in the main FDC with GySgt. Quint Avenetti. The main reason for the personnel switch was that I'd had my opportunity to fire in combat; now it was Marshall's turn, and he was chomping at the bit to see some action.

Once those pieces were set in motion, there wasn't much for me to do, so I took advantage of the lull and slept from about 0600 to 1100. By the time I returned to the FDC, the Saudis were closing on Khafji from three sides. 1st Tanks had set up a blocking position south of the city. "C" Battery had fired more than 100 rounds of DPICM at Iraqi convoys and a mechanized battalion.

In the early afternoon, the Iraqis made an odd, and fatal, error. About eighty vehicles, which we estimated to be about two battalions of mechanized infantry, appeared to want to surrender, according to the American ANGLICO team that had accompanied the Saudis. Marshall told me via radio that he was receiving reports of the vehicles moving across an open area west of town, with their main guns pointed at the ground or rotated over the back of the turrets.

But as they moved south, it became clear to the Saudis that the Iraqis had no intention of surrendering. Realizing the ruse, 3rd Marines requested permission from division to fire on the Iraqis. The ensuing coordination took nearly an hour as division staffers argued with the regimental fire support coordination center over whether the troops being targeted were in fact the enemy.

The regiment didn't get clearance, but "C" Battery was still sending rounds downrange, as it continued to take calls for fire from a recon team that had become trapped in the city as the Iraqis poured in. It seemed that every time I looked up, Charlie Battery was firing. And in those first few hours during the battle, there wasn't much more than that one artillery battery, commanded by my friend Steve Morgan, between the Iraqi Army and 1st MARDIV.

This team would become our focal point during the remainder of the battle, and a priority of the division. Besides kicking the Iraqis back across the border, division wanted that recon team back within friendly lines. The team had to play a terrifying game of "hide and seek" with the Iraqis infesting the town. At one point, the Marines were on the second floor of a building, whispering their fire missions to us because the Iraqis were on the floor below them.

I had no idea who the recon team was, but I was glad they were in the city. They were our "eyes" and called in target after target for us. Division's priority may have been their return, and it was a priority for us, too, but my concern was eliminating as many targets as possible inside Khafji.

We eventually had to order more ammo to Morgan's battery, and sent 340 more rounds of DPICM up the highway. We also moved "A" Battery – the most accurate battery in the battalion — north, to put another battery within range of the town.

Aircraft clogged the skies above as attack pilots, fighter jocks, and helo drivers all jockeyed for position to drop ordnance on the Iraqis, who were, by the afternoon of the 30th, lodged in Khafji. F/A-18s and Cobras, in particular, worked over everything on the ground. What we didn't know at the time was that the air wingers had already slaughtered hundreds of Iraqis north of the border as their mechanized forces moved south along the highway.

By 1700, we were getting better intelligence, mainly because Saudis, Qataris, Americans, and the pilots were now viewing the battlefield. We received word that the Iraqis would attack again that night, with two mechanized battalions in our sector and with the 3rd Armored Division near the Al-Wafrah oil field.

In the main FDC, Rivers and I listened to the radio traffic and agreed that Saddam was making it easy for us. We knew that if he put an armored division on the road, our A-10 Warthogs and Marine Harriers would eat his tanks up.

I was surprised that Saddam attacked at all. As long as he sat under the American bombs, he could claim to be a victim, but by attacking us, he became the bad guy. Not that I minded. My reasoning was that if we stopped this upcoming attack, and destroyed an armored division or more, it might cause him to rethink his alternatives. My only fear was that if we started to hammer him hard, he might gas us.

Grid Coordinates TM 605 253 [Just south of Khafji] 1226, 31 Jan 91

Exhausted. Relieved Marshall in the jump 2000 last night. Gunny Avenetti & I are the fire direction team. Went to MOPP 2, started taking nerve antidote pills. Fucking experimental drug. Looked very likely that we would get gassed (but didn't).

Usual confusing reports throughout the night. Allies destroyed better part of an Iraqi battalion yesterday. A force of company/battalion-size still in Khafji at nightfall. Recon Marines still trapped in the city — we're the only ones they can call for fire support. Marshall's crew made his day. He had an APC & 20 troops nearby. 1/12 shot 1 round HE, scored a direct hit. Pure luck, but it blew the shit out of the Iraqis! Recon guy said we were great — "I love you arty guys!"

3/3 and Saudi tanks attempted to rescue him last night, but were turned back, for some unknown reason. CAAT teams everywhere. Air on station most of the night. Around 2330, we fired a prep for 3/3 with "A" Btry, a Platoon 1 of DPICM a min. for 15 min.

This morning about 0700, we got a call from our recon friend — 17 tanks staging. Nailed them w/a battalion 4 from "C" and "A."

His BDA: "Holy shit! All 17 tanks destroyed and abandoned. Hatches open, troops running!"

We hit them again w/a battery 1 from "A," DPICM, converged sheaf, knocking down more troops. "A" then fired a WP marking round for an AV-8B making a strike on the troops. Those guys were fucked. We killed an entire tank company.

The attack reported to come last night actually began today, by way of infiltration. Currently there is another tank company (T-55s) and a mech company closing on Khafji from the north. B-52s have already hit one big convoy on the border. Our pos is right next to the MSR, south of Khafji, and I just watched an Allied tank company (M60s) and a mech company go north. Maybe this is the decisive effort.

½ dozen Cobras (USMC) accompanied them. Thought that last night, too, only to see Saudis drive their British tanks up and down the road.

My first night near Khafji was one of the most frightening of my life.

Sometime after nightfall, we got word over the division radio net that the Iraqis were planning a big push into Khafji, ostensibly to reinforce the now-depleted forces already around the town. We were expecting at least a mechanized brigade, maybe a division.

Then I got one of the most chilling radio messages I'd ever heard, though none of the Marines that heard it can remember exactly who passed it — but it was either the MEF CG, Lt. Gen. Walt Boomer or, more likely, our division commander, Maj. Gen. Mike Myatt. But the general came on the air and ordered us into MOPP level 2 — wearing protective suits and carrying gas masks. He also told us that our intelligence showed every indication that the Iraqis intended to launch chemical rounds into Khafji that night, as they were believed to have rushed all such weapons in the sector to the Khafji front.

As we listened, Avenetti and I just looked at each other, speechless. We had been given the nerve agent antidote pills, but nobody had been thrilled about taking them. Somebody told us to start taking them, but I don't remember who. I took one, just to be on the safe side, even as Neal Noem refused to even consider it.

At that point I didn't know what to think. I had a battalion to shoot and wanted to concentrate on that. The knowledge that we would likely be attacked and gassed was not helping matters. Avenetti and I spent most of the night listening to radio traffic and straining our ears for sounds of vehicles moving or incoming rounds. I fell asleep at some point, but not for long. I awoke with a start and realized that the Iraqis weren't going to attack after all. By sunup, I was communicating with the recon team in the town. I could hardly hear one Marine's transmissions because he had to whisper. The Iraqis were on the first floor of the building the team occupied.

The fire mission in which we shot up the tank company was a contentious one. The 3rd Marines Fire Support Coordination Center cleared the mission, and I began formulating fire orders while Avenetti started analyzing the target. We alerted "A" and "C" batteries of the fire mission and the grid location of the target. Avenetti noticed that the location was a road and the target description was "tanks staging."

Avenetti, as good an FDC Marine as I ever saw, immediately asked for the target "attitude," while I stared at him in amazement. I knew what he was trying to do, but I couldn't believe he was actually trying to do it in the middle of combat. He quickly figured the "attitude," essentially the direction of the long axis of such a long, narrow target as a single file of tanks on a road. With that info, he computed data for a "linear sheaf" with lightning speed. Instead of aiming the howitzers so that the rounds made a circular pattern over the target, which was the norm, he was trying to inflict maximum damage on the column by having the rounds fall in a single-file down the road over the target.

It worked.

"A" and "C" began firing, and within seconds hundreds of DPICM bomblets rained down on the Iraqi column.

Then the regimental FSCC called "checkfiring," immediately halting the mission. They said we would be shooting friendlies, presumably Qataris. The FSCC then denied clearing the mission. I started arguing with the FSCC, demanding clearance to resume firing—Charlie Battery was screaming that they still had rounds in the tubes. I told them over and over that I'd received the call for fire from the recon team in Khafji. The FSSC was unconvinced.

3rd Marines' hesitance came from its confusion over whether ANGLICO, working as a liaison for Arab allies, knew about the mission and if the recon team was sure the tanks were those of the enemy. The FSCC finally called ANGLICO, only to learn that they were the ones who told the recon team about the tanks—which turned out to be Chinese-made, wheeled combat vehicles—in the first place. Jeffcoat was with me when I handled the fire mission. He watched and listened, and being new, his head was spinning from the activity. Rivers was with him. While haggling with 3rd Marines, I explained the situation to them. Jeffcoat asked me one question: "Are you sure?" I nodded and looked at Rivers, who nodded back.

I gave the batteries the order to resume firing. The "battalion 4" to which I referred in my journal meant that each howitzer in "A" and "C" batteries fired four rounds of DPICM. In other words, we hit the Iraqi column with about 64 rounds, but we were only about halfway through. It turned out that Charlie Battery didn't have rounds in any of its howitzers after all, so Alpha Battery finished firing its portion of the barrage.

The first volley had shattered the column. So much smoke and flame erupted that the recon Marine had to wait a few minutes to tell us the effects of our fire, even though I was practically screaming at him to give us some indication of our effectiveness. When he told us there were troops running away, Avenetti and I decided to go after the survivors. We both trembled from the excitement, and the world outside our humvee seemed to cease to exist. I didn't have to tell Avenetti to switch to a converged sheaf—he was ordering it before I could even get the words out of my mouth. Damn, I thought, this guy is good.

A converged sheaf compresses the area covered by a volley of artillery and puts more shrapnel in a smaller area, much like a "full choke" shotgun. Converged sheaves are very effective on small targets.

We fired according to the adjustments coming over the radio. Our second volley was just as effective, as hundreds of DPICM bomblets showered the fleeing Iraqis, killing more enemy soldiers. Our recon Marine continued to update us, and told us that a Harrier was rolling in over the spot where the Iraqis were fleeing. We fired a white-phosphorous round to mark the target for the Harrier. By the time the Harrier dove in, there wasn't much left to attack.

Avenetti and I leaned back and grinned at each other, the adrenaline jag dropping off sharply. We'd gotten so wrapped up in the excitement of actually pinpointing and destroying the enemy we were unaware that we'd been practically yelling at each other, though we were nearly nose-to-nose in the humvee.

The mission and the argument with 3rd Marines demonstrated Marshall's "trust factor," but for a few moments after 3rd Marines started screaming I felt sick, thinking the worst had happened and that we'd killed friendlies, but I was convinced I was right. Had I not been, I wouldn't have looked to Rivers for approval. When it was over, an obviously relieved Jeffcoat draped an arm over my shoulder and said, "That was one of the ballsiest things I've ever seen."

But 3rd Marines won something of a victory in the argument. The FSCC forbade us from firing into Khafji anymore unless the mission originated from ANGLICO. Conversely, any call we received from ANGLICO was automatically cleared to fire. That edict shut down much of our shooting, but by that time, most of the fighting in Khafji was over. The air wing had had a field day making bombing runs along the highway in Kuwait, and we had put enough artillery fire into the city to make the Iraqis start easing back across the border. We heard that the air wingers had destroyed most of a division on the road—the division that we'd been warned about was heading our way, presumably to gas us.

3/3, the Saudis and the Qataris helped them along with tank and machine-gun fire. Our late-night abortive prep fires didn't do much good, mainly because the Saudis, with 3/3 along for "moral support," skedaddled when they received machine-gun, evoking snorts of derision from us and plaintive, frustrated reports from 3/3 officers.

But the Saudi army had never been in battle before Khafji, a fight that would have huge ramifications, not just for Desert Storm, but for Saudi

Arabia's stability. Khafji became a watershed moment for the Saudis. It proved that the Iraqis were not invincible and that the Saudi army could and would fight.

Leading them was a colorful officer we knew only as Col. Turqii. Admire worked closely with him to "convince" him that the Saudis could wrest control of the town from the enemy. His nudgings worked, because the Saudis did eventually move into town on the morning of the 30th, a move that bolstered their confidence immensely. In fact their success at Khafji was a key factor in the Saudi decision to advance up the coastal road into Kuwait City when the ground war started, while the 1st Marine Division moved to the west for an attack.

We did have one more hair-raising incident that morning. There wasn't much happening in the town, so most of us were lounging around the vehicles. A couple of Marines disassembled our lone machine gun and began cleaning it in its position just off the highway.

Then shots rang out to our front, and the unmistakable deep cough told us the weapon firing was a .50-cal. We dashed behind the low dunes that hid the vehicles and toward the machine gun, where the two Marines scrambled to reassemble the piece. We heard more shots, nearer us than the previous burst.

As the enlisted Marines chambered rounds in their rifles, I wished I had more to fight with than a 9mm pistol.

Then we heard the rumblings of tracked vehicles and the whine of engines. To our north, a group of ten armored personnel carriers came barreling toward us. Oh shit, I thought, we're going to get hit. Another burst of fire sent us diving again, then a Marine noticed that the shooters were aiming at the sky. About that time a radio operator yelled out, "They're Qataris!"

The jubilant Qataris were celebrating their victory by firing their machine guns skyward. They very nearly got shot up by a group of very pissed-off artillery Marines. Several Marines grumbled as the convoy of APCs rolled past. I went back to the main FDC for a few hours the afternoon of the 30th. While there, I heard a report that the Corps had taken twelve casualties, while the Iraqis had lost hundreds. I then collapsed for nearly eleven hours of uninterrupted sleep, which in itself was a miracle.

By February 1, the Saudis controlled the southern portion of Khafji. We heard a steady stream of reports, through the airwaves and through our official channels, that the Iraqis had lost hundreds of troops and vehicles. Two hundred and eighty vehicles were confirmed as destroyed between Khafji and the Al-Wafrah oilfield. Those vehicles, we presumed, had made up a large portion of the armored division that was supposed to attack Marine positions west of us.

We also heard a report that a convoy of a hundred or so vehicles got caught on the road in "the elbow," the southwestern corner of Kuwait. At least 40 were reported to have been killed outright; the remainder — less than 50 — was seen fleeing north.

These losses were in addition to the convoy, rumored to have been 13½ miles long, hit by B-52s on the border above Khafji. This was most likely the second tank and/or mechanized division we expected to attack and gas us, but which never materialized at Khafji.

Best of all, the recon team that had been trapped in the city, and that had provided us with so much good target intelligence, made it back to 3rd Marines safely. I was at the 3rd Marines CP the morning of February 1 and bumped into Capt. Pete McCarthy, the reconnaissance company commander and an acquaintance of mine. Pete thanked me — and 1/12 — personally and profusely. His first sergeant, a giant, bald Marine, nearly tore my arm off pumping it in appreciation. It was one of the very few moments during Desert Storm that I actually felt proud and felt like I had accomplished something. My battalion had saved Marines' lives, and that felt good.

A few months after the war, *People* magazine interviewed one of the recon team members, who praised "that artillery battalion from Hawaii."

Later that day, I drove into the city to take a look at the damage. Many of the vehicles that had been knocked out, including some of the ones 1/12 had destroyed, had been hauled away or pushed off the side of the road. Those that remained had been killed several times, as the attacking Saudis and Qataris put another projectile into them, just to make sure.

The town was a shambles. Bullet holes scored nearly every building, and fire had gutted several. The streets were pockmarked with holes from machine-gun fire and artillery rounds. The Cobras' handiwork was evident at several towers near the edge of the city, their walls shredded by 20mm rounds. The buildings that had been left intact had been looted and trashed.

Interrogator-translator teams roamed the city in a humvee, making sure no Iraqis had been left behind, either intentionally or unintentionally. None were ever found in the rubble.

The twisted, scorched metal of the destroyed vehicles was a gruesome testimony to the effectiveness of Allied fire. Debris and blood littered their scorched hulls. I left the scene with a shudder, simply thankful that at that moment an Iraqi soldier wasn't surveying the burnt remains of my vehicle.

At 3rd Marines, I learned that the Saudis had taken about 300 prisoners of war, about two companies' worth of troops. That made a total of

Qatari armored vehicles speed up the coastal highway into Khafji. Supported by allied airpower and Marine artillery and infantry, the Qataris and Saudis retook the town.

one battalion destroyed, one tank company destroyed, nearly another battalion captured, the better part of a division wiped out in Kuwait, and an undetermined number believed destroyed as a result of the Iraqi incursion into Khafji.

The intelligence people posted general estimates of at least a brigade lost by the Iraqis at Khafji and a division out west.

· CHAPTER ELEVEN ·

The days following the fight at Khafji were dull compared to the days before the Iraqis made their foray across the border.

I was still on the hook for training Task Force Gecko, but I had to admit I was even less motivated to carry out the mission, which seemed sillier — and less important — by the day.

Rivers debriefed us on the damage inflicted on the Iraqis, and it was sobering. As usual, I was skeptical of the body counts and estimations, but even if I ruled out the fudge factor, I knew we'd killed quite a few Iraqis. Division credited 1/12 with 280 KIA, mostly from missions Marshall orchestrated early on in the battle. That didn't include the estimated 80 or so killed when I ordered the fire mission on the convoy of vehicles on the highway.

Listening to the numbers roll effortlessly from Rivers's mouth, I began to realize the gravity of the moment, and the reality of what we were doing out there. We were killing people, plain and simple. And enjoying it. The thought disturbed me, and I struggled to sort out my feelings. Avenetti and I had celebrated the destruction of the convoy of vehicles we'd shot at. Now I began to feel ashamed of that, and more than a little ghoulish.

The thought occurred to me that I — so desperate to return to my wife's side — had killed, or at the least caused the death of, somebody's husband, or son, or brother, or father. That thought rattled me, and I promised myself that I would not look an Iraqi in the eyes, that I would not go souvenir hunting on any Iraqi corpses that I happened to run across.

The reason was simple, although I could not have articulated it at the time. I didn't want the enemy to have a face. I wanted to objectify the enemy, to dehumanize him, to regard him as a thing, not unlike a bug, to be exterminated. As long as I fired at *things*, not people, I would not feel guilty. Already feeling the sting of my conscience, I did not want to come face to face with the reality that the men we were killing had families and lives, too. And someone waiting for them to return.

This was a horrible realization for me, and one that I rationalized with the thought, "It was them or me, kill or be killed." The rationalization worked at the time, and necessarily so. It still does. I was already learning that thinking too deeply while under so much stress could be dangerous—both to me and to those around me. My mind had already begun the process of compartmentalizing emotions, registering them, but not quite processing them. I sealed them off to be dealt with later, thinking it would be easier when I had time to sort them out. I didn't realize it would just be more difficult.

That's not to say I feel guilty about participating in the destruction of the enemy. I'm quite comfortable admitting that I'm glad it didn't turn out the other way around. I did my job and I'm proud of that, but that pride is tinged with sadness that it had to be done in the first place. But it's not tinged with guilt.

I got more bad news on February 2. The night before, while conducting a raid, Sierra Battery, 5/11—SSgt. Mike Almanza's battery, the old November 5/12—had been bombed by one of our own aircraft, killing two marines and wounding three. The news shook me, because I knew so many marines in that battery and feared that the dead and wounded were people I knew.

I was right, but I didn't know it at the time. We didn't get the names of the casualties, but we did hear that one marine was wounded when he climbed atop one of the self-propelled howitzers and fired a .50-caliber machine-gun at the attacking plane. *Sounds like something Almanza would do*, I thought.

Almanza was, in fact, wounded that night, I learned weeks later, while wasting away in Manifa Bay awaiting a flight out of Saudi Arabia after the war. A lieutenant from the battery stopped by the 1/12 officers' tent one day, and I asked him about that night. When he told me that Almanza had been medevacked, a chill passed through me. I felt sick as he told me that Almanza had lost an arm and possibly an eye from the bombs, which the battery believed came from a Navy A-6 Intruder.

There was one more friendly-fire incident that I heard about that day. The LAV that had been struck in the battle out west had indeed been hit by a Maverick missile, just as we'd suspected. Apparently, the missile came from an A-10, but that was not widely reported by the American media.

I hit the rack that night thoroughly depressed.

The sudden slow pace after the adrenaline surge of Khafji, followed by the news of marines being killed by our own fire left me thinking of the worst possible scenarios for our future. Neal and I talked often, and we were both skeptical of much of the "news" we heard. And we trusted even less of the intelligence we were getting, much to Nesbit's irritation. We were guilty of killing the messenger when he told us the Iraqis had only a brigade left on the border, then less than twenty-four hours later reported we'd be facing a division.

It was a time of conflicting, boiling emotions for all of us. Most of us were impatient because we weren't doing much in the way of bringing the war to a close, save the brief action at Khafji. In my eyes, every day that passed was just another day away from home. That caused restlessness, and the inaction led to frustration. But even a desire to go into full-scale warfare against the Iraqis seemed to contradict itself, because as restless and impatient as I was to finish the war, I hoped a ground attack wouldn't be necessary. I was perfectly willing to sit in the desert, inactive and frustrated, and let the planes bomb until the end of time or until Saddam quit.

It was an emotional Jekyll and Hyde that many of us played. Plus, I was becoming angry and bitter for having to live for five months in a country that looked down its nose at the very people it begged for protection. The Saudis seemed less interested in defending their country than in hiring someone to protect their wealth. That old mercenary feeling was coming back.

I had not lost my faith in the justness of the mission. The best proof of that was in the face of an officer who had joined the battalion just days before. He was a lieutenant from the ousted Kuwaiti army, and he would serve as our interpreter as we invaded his country. The instant I met him, I knew what the war was about, and it wasn't oil. One look at his face told me this was a war to give a country back to its rightful owners. To right a wrong. And, deep down inside, I was glad to be a part of such a monumental undertaking. Still, the months in-country were taking a toll on my patience, temper, and motivation.

I also disagreed with those who thought we'd roll over the Iraqis. I had no idea how wrong I would be, or I wouldn't have argued with Marshall for hours over what I thought the nature of the war would be. I envisaged a dirty war of attrition, one in which we'd have to root out Iraqi troops and vehicles, à la World War II in the South Pacific.

A quiet moment after the action at Khafji. I resumed training Task Force Gecko in the days after the town was retaken.

Marshall thought that, once we made the breach, thousands would surrender. He was convinced that the Iraqis would crumble almost immediately once the ground war began. After the war, I couldn't believe how right he had been.

I still feared Saddam's chemicals, and I was not alone. Though we knew we were pounding the hell out of the Republican Guards—the smallest amount of ordnance we'd dropped in a single day had been 320 *tons*—we still fretted over Saddam's chemical capability.

We spent several days being told to prepare to move about a hundred miles to the west, to Al-Qaraah, only to have the order rescinded several times. With Task Force Taro hugging the coast, there had begun a high-level debate over where or if we should move.

We spent the first two weeks of February being ordered to move west, then being ordered to stay put, then being ordered to prepare to support the Arab forces as they moved north. It gave us the feeling of lurching, as a battalion, across the desert. 1/12 had gotten caught in the middle of a tug-of-war, of sorts. Task Force Taro—and the nascent Task Force

Gecko—had at long last been ordered off its helicopter assault mission. Instead, the division assigned Taro the mission of infiltrating into Kuwait—on foot—through the first minefield.

I was shocked when Maj. Cook told me of this, and not at all surprised when he added that Col. Admire was furious with being assigned the ignominious job of mine-finder. Cook said Admire commented that he was ready to stay with the Saudis, who had been asking for 3rd Marines' company since Khafji, especially 1/12.

Col. Turqii, Rivers said, had asked for 1/12 to support him during the ground offensive. Admire was reported to have said he planned to propose a Marine-Saudi drive up the coast. This little debate lasted for about two days, then passed like a cloud. Soon enough, we were back to planning for a big move to the central part of Saudi Arabia to positions near the "elbow" of western Kuwait. These positions, we were told, would be our preinvasion positions.

We did have a bit of excitement the night of February 9. I was dozing in my hole at about 2200 when I heard a machine gun open up to our left front, to the northwest. I flew out of my rack and into my flak jacket and helmet as a chorus of automatic rifles and smaller-caliber machine guns joined the heavy machine gun that had started the fracas. The crackling staccato of the small-arms fire was punctuated every other second by a short cough from a .50-cal.

When I gathered my senses, I poked my head up into the night, expecting to see tracers crisscrossing the sky. I saw none, and I finally realized that the gunfire was coming from the direction of a Saudi unit, at least half a click away. Irritated at both the Saudis and myself, I stripped off my gear and went back to sleep.

Next morning, Marshall told me 3rd Marines had received an erroneous report of vehicles closing in on our old stomping ground, Khafji. That report apparently spooked the already jumpy Saudis, causing a few nervous trigger fingers.

We continued to fret and speculate over the steady stream of news reports "confirming" the number of destroyed tanks, howitzers, and units in Kuwait and Iraq. We were also keenly interested in the fair number of reports of the flurry of diplomatic missions being conducted in an attempt to stave off the coming ground offensive.

These reports gave us fits and sent our emotions skyrocketing one minute and plummeting the next. Jeffcoat and I talked incessantly about how ridiculous the political jockeying was and what it meant for our chances of getting home anytime soon. We spent hours hunched over coffee cups under his camouflage net trying to figure out what the politicians were up to.

In mid-February, when the Soviets opened negotiations with Saddam, our hopes for a peaceful resolution soared. Surely, we thought, Saddam's biggest sponsor could talk some sense into him. In just a few short days, though, those hopes crashed to earth as the Soviets reported that Saddam wouldn't budge.

Between the worrying and the contradictory orders, we were still trying to train. 11th Marines organized another command-post exercise. The problem was that 11th Marines, with the rest of 1st Marine Division, had already moved about a hundred kilometers to our west. Task Force Taro hung off the division's flank like an appendix.

On the afternoon of February 15, during the CPX, we heard electrifying news. The Iraqi Security Council, the radio announcer intoned, had voted unanimously to comply with all United Nations resolutions, which, of course, included the immediate withdrawal of all forces from Kuwait.

I listened to the broadcast with several marines, hunched over the radio during a lull in the CPX. The news, we all thought, was too good to be true.

For the briefest of moments, my eyes swept the brown desert, flat as a tabletop. I let the bright sun warm my face as I tried to convince myself that we'd be going home. I couldn't, and it was a good thing that I couldn't. It turned out to be what President Bush later called a "cruel hoax." As we had so many times in the past months, we shook off the bad news and went back to planning the destruction of the Iraqi army.

Our objective for the first day — which we were informed would be February 24 — was an airfield in southwest Kuwait named Al-Jaber. Seizing this objective would require the division to make a huge left turn, away from the Al-Burqan oilfield, as it breached the second defensive belt. For the moment, 3rd Marines was assigned to the division's right flank, what Marshall and I called the "backwater of the war."

Once through the second breach site, 1/12 would then follow the division north to Kuwait City, presumably leaving 3rd Marines to its own devices.

Meanwhile, 2nd Division, to our left, would attack a few hours after 1st Division kicked off. The Army would dash straight at Baghdad to lure the RGFC out of its holes, then turn into the enemy and smash them on the open desert. This maneuver would later be referred to as Schwarzkopf's "Sunday punch."

CHAPTER TWELVE

On February 20, 1/12 moved to within six miles of the Kuwaiti border to join 3rd Marines. We had been told to move up as stealthily as possible and remain undetected until G-day, the first day of the ground offensive. By nightfall, we were in place.

Almost immediately, however, 3rd Marines—who had told us to be quiet—called in a fire mission, prompting irritated looks all around the FDC. To me, "remaining undetected" implied not shooting.

But recon teams had supposedly found an enemy armored personnel carrier and were practically demanding we fire at it. A TOW unit reported that it could identify the target with its thermal sights. Marshall, his temper rising, suggested to Maj. Hardy that if the TOW team could see the target, it should simply fire one of its missiles at the vehicle.

Or send a patrol out to knock it out with an AT-4, I added. In our eyes, the mission was a ridiculous waste of artillery, one that needlessly exposed our position.

But when one receives orders, one follows them, if one intends to remain employed. We fired a "Platoon One"—one round each from the four guns of an artillery platoon—of DPICM. I cringed as the howitzers thumped in the night, waiting for counterbattery fire, which, thankfully, never came.

The whole mission set my teeth on edge, and I wrote in my journal that " ... *it is so frustrating to have to take this shit from a bunch of overzealous senior officers who just can't wait to take credit for getting some trigger time.*"

The vigilant TOW team radioed back that we had hit the APC, to which I simply shrugged, happy to be done with it. But our success only encouraged the grunts. 3rd Marines immediately requested a "time on target" mission — a scheduled fire mission — for 0300 the next morning at an unobserved target.

This was even worse than the first mission. Unobserved targets are practically worthless. With no way to observe the target, it is impossible to tell if it is accurately located or if the rounds even hit anything.

Frustrated, I ordered "C" Battery to fire a "Platoon One" and set the time, which was still about four hours away. And, early the next morning, the battery did indeed fire. Five minutes too soon, a cardinal sin in the artillery.

I exploded into a rage at about the same time as the watch officer at 3rd Marines. While I was screaming into a handset at the lieutenant who had screwed up the fire mission, the watch officer's voice screeched through a loudspeaker: "Hey, you gotta let us know when you're going to do that! We got people buckin' and jivin' thinking they're taking incoming!" He was referring to the recon teams in the area, who, like the rest of us, expected the rounds to hit the deck at 0300, *not* 0255.

"I had no fucking idea they were going to shoot five minutes early!" I yelled back at the officer, a fellow captain who was actually a friend of mine. "And I don't need anybody up there telling me how to conduct a fire mission."

I slammed the phone down, swearing I'd give him a bigger piece of my mind as soon as I finished chewing the ass off the lieutenant in Charlie Battery. We did talk about it much later and even chuckled about it. But the incident served as a great example of how a hundred "atta boys" can get wiped away by one "oh shit." All the fine shooting we had done up to that point was immediately forgotten.

The battery's error could have been tragic. A TOT mission is intentionally precise, and firing five minutes early could have killed or wounded any marines in the target area who thought they still had five minutes before having to clear out. Luckily, no one was hurt.

I spent most of the next day, February 21, trying to sleep, having been up most of the night with "C" Battery's fire mission. But, my slumber was interrupted when I got the word to turn in my chemical protective suit.

Months earlier, we'd been issued British MOPP suits as our second MOPP suit. We were now required to turn them in for American suits, these compressed into a plastic bag about the size of an MRE. Also, these weren't the standard green, but a desert camouflage pattern.

I returned from the suit exchange to find Jeff Speights waiting for me. He had managed to locate 1/12 as his Hawk battalion moved north.

Seeing Jeff cheered me up immediately. By now, he'd heard about 1/12 and our raids and work at Khafji, and he was visibly impressed that we'd actually gotten some "trigger time" and had done so well. We talked for a couple of hours, mostly catching up on our families back in The World and what each of us had been doing since we last met in the summer. A hush then settled over us, as each of us contemplated our future.

We both gazed northward, toward Kuwait. I told Jeff that we'd be crossing the border the next day, and that 1st Marine Division had changed our mission yet again. We were now ordered to reinforce 1st Battalion, 11th Marines, which supported Task Force Papa Bear—1st Marines and company. We were both nervous, even scared, of what lay ahead, but neither admitted it, and both of us tried to avoid the subject. It made the conversation awkward. Instead we told old jokes and recalled college memories. When the conversation wore itself out, Jeff and I shook hands and promised to call each other once we made it home.

After the war, Jeff recalled this conversation and said that he had left our position shaken, convinced that he'd never see me again, especially since I would be crossing the border a day before the ground war was set to begin — most people are unaware that 1st Marine Division moved several units into Kuwait, close to the first minefield, hours before the ground war even started.

The thought that I was spending my last night in Saudi Arabia had crossed my mind, too. It had weighed on me for days, but especially now that I'd been told that the jump FDC would move into Kuwait on the 22nd, behind elements of the 1st Marine Division. We had trained for this moment for weeks on end, but it still caused a bit of apprehension.

The jump FDC personnel had become incredibly close. Neal Noem and I had become very good friends, and we shared coffee and conversations that were almost like confession on a daily basis. I'd grown to admire him as I watched him work with his radio operators, training them with a level of competence and leadership that I'd never seen before and that I haven't seen since. Neal had, and still has, a special gift for leadership, and I respected his ability to get the most out of his people.

Maj. Mike Jeffcoat and I had also become close. Honest, tough, and occasionally irascible, Jeffcoat was like a big brother. He often joined Neal and I after evening chow for coffee and storytelling, and he had plenty of tales. He also loved old songs and sang them often. He even made me write down all the words to Bobbie Gentry's "Ode to Billie Joe" once he heard that I used to sing that song with my grandmother.

Our enlisted crew was one of the finest groups of marines I ever served with. Cpl. Sam Crowe, our radio chief, was always cheerful, hardworking and professional. Like his boss—Neal—Crowe knew how to lead people.

Radio operators LCpls. Reed and Gates—I called them the "salt and pepper gang" because one was black and one was white—had become indispensable to me. Not only were they crackerjack radio operators who never flinched under pressure, but they'd learned the nuances of the personalities of Miller and myself. So they anticipated our every move and usually had what we needed even before we asked for it. They knew exactly how to set the radios up in the jump FDC, according to our idiosyncracies. They probably even knew at what volume to set them. They heard everything passed over the nets and expertly kept track of huge amounts of information, all the while troubleshooting and maintaining radios.

Gunny Miller and I had bonded as a result of the raids we'd done. Our senses of humor played off each other and helped us keep our perspectives. I would have put his skills as a fire direction chief up against anyone in 11th Marines, and I was thankful to have him by my side. We spent hours poring over maps, looking for ways to improve our accuracy, movements, and artillery support. We read and reread the logs we kept on the raids, looking for ways to improve the battalion's shooting. We would relieve each other on watch without gripe and because we truly cared about each other.

My driver, LCpl. Rob Martin, and PFC Kyle Schneider were the jump FDC's fire direction controlmen. Both were just kids, barely out of their teens. Martin, who could bitch with the best of them, never failed to get me where I needed to go. Trying to navigate across the trackless desert at night, alone, with no real idea where the hell we were, forced us to work together. The long days and nights on the road also allowed us to get to know each other and talk about home and the future. Our ranks prevented us from ever becoming close, but our circumstances allowed us to get to know each other far better than most officer-enlisted marine acquaintances.

The same held for Schneider, who joined us in-country, fresh out of Fort Sill. Irreverent and quick-witted, Schneider fell right into our crowd of irreverent jokers. In no time, he was talking trash with the rest of the crew and working like a madman in the FDC.

We'd become jaunty and proud of our "lone wolf" crew and our seemingly dangerous mission of going ahead of the battalion into Indian country, either with the grunts or alone. More than one person remarked that you had to be a little crazy to take three humvees into enemy territory and set up a bunch of radio antennas, with only small arms and antitank rockets for protection.

We kept our vehicles away from the main FDC, ostensibly so we could make a quick exit to our next position, but really because we were becoming our own little clique, a world unto ourselves, one that did not tolerate outsiders.

And, on the evening of the 21st, the thought that we could all be dead within a few hours was one I didn't want to consider, even though I had a hard time blocking that thought out of my mind.

Luckily, I was distracted that evening by a call from division to attend to an "emergency" fire-support meeting. Martin and I loaded up for another difficult drive across the bleak, featureless, and now moonlit, desert.

We made it to the division command post—dozens of miles to our south—in time to see Maj. Gen. Myatt chew out the staff of 1st Battalion, 3rd Marines, which had been recently organized into yet another task force, "X-ray."

X-ray's mission was to serve as a heliborne maneuver element under the control of the division. The task force's fire-support plan had originally called for a battery of artillery for support, and 1/12 had been given that mission as an "on order," or on call, mission. Myatt disapproved that plan, and ordered X-ray to be supported by a battalion—1/12. I spent the next few hours shifting gears, going from our original mission of reinforcing 1/11—our *second* "original" mission, that is—to the new one. The division FSCC and 11th Marines decided to simply switch 1/12's priorities— we'd be in direct support of Task Force X-ray, with a secondary mission of reinforcing 1/11, a terribly confusing set of priorities, as we would learn once the ground war started.

I was exhausted by the time Martin and I made it back to the battalion after about two hours of groping along the pitch-black desert floor. All I wanted to do was sleep, but I had one bit of business left to take care of.

I crawled into the back of a humvee in the FDC and took a seat by Maj. Hardy, who was drawing in the dim light of the truck. On a yellow legal pad, I began writing a letter to Angie.

It was the most serious letter I'd ever written to her, and I spoke honestly and bluntly of what might lie ahead for us. I wrote that, on my last night in Saudi Arabia, my thoughts were with her. I also told her that I had lived my entire adult life for this night, and that I was ready to do my job.

I also pledged to her that we would discuss children when I got home, whenever that might be. And finally, I told her that, should I not return home, that she should keep my officer's sword: " ... *in case that someday you should have a son. I would like for you to give him my sword, and explain to him that it once belonged to a man who loved you very, very much."*

It was difficult to write those words, because doing so admitted my deepest fear, my own mortality. I was admitting to myself that I might not ever see my wife again. Several times I paused, pen hovering over the paper as I struggled to find the right words.

I finally finished, exhausted from the effort, and sealed the letter in an envelope, addressed it, and scrawled "FREE" where the stamp should go. I pushed myself to my feet and stepped out into the cold, early morning. Oddly, I felt relieved, cleansed, and clear-headed. Now, I thought, I'm ready for the war.

Part Two

Ground War

· C H A P T E R   T H I R T E E N ·

1644, 22 Feb 91

*Jump still hasn't moved and everybody's pissed off. Long day. This
a.m. we got a call for fire from 3/3 on 2 T-62s and 3 BMPS. It was totally
fucked up. We adjusted over 5K in range because of a terrible target
location by the FO. Plus, he kept correcting to a point inside Saudi
Arabia! In fact, when we recorded his final target, it was in Saudi Arabia. Marshall had a bad feeling about it — so close, across a boundary, insignificant target, etc. Was worried about hitting friendlies.*

*Sure enough, we damn near did. Engineers had a bulldozer behind
the border berm. The FO saw smoke coming up from behind the berm,
and assumed it was tanks — without ever actually seeing a tank. We
expended a total of 52 rounds (4 HE, 48 DPICM) on a fucking bulldozer! The FO even repeated on it! Don't know what he was smoking.*

*Later, he tried to shoot the same grid, but we wouldn't do it, and
got into a huge clusterfuck with 3rd Marines FSCC. They didn't seem
to have a clue. So back and forth we went. Ultimately, we ended the
msn.*

*We're still waiting to take the jump out. Four times Maj. J has said
he's ready to go, and we haven't left yet. We were supposed to leave
at 1100.*

*Heard the news last night at 0200 that Iraq is now saying that they
will accept the Soviet peace plan and drop the Palestinian issue. But
they want a 24-hour cease-fire to pull out, and once ¾ of the troops
are out of Kuwait, they want all UN sanctions lifted. Not sure, but
I think Bush said no again. I'm past the point of caring.*

*CO told us some units in 5th MEB (TF Troy) went in today on a
deception operation and encountered Iraqis hiding among herds of*

goats, wearing goat skins. Armed w/AK-47s and AT-4s and are ambushing convoys. We are going to recon by fire on any goat herds we see over the border.

The fire mission infuriated both Marshall and me, although I had little to do with it — I was sitting in my humvee at the time.

Marshall took the mission from 3rd Marines and immediately questioned it. I heard our howitzers fire in the distance and left my vehicle for the FDC. By the time I got there, Marshall was berating the FSCC, and Maj. Hardy was trying to make sense of the situation. I got a quick brief from Marshall and agreed with his assessment: The forward observer didn't know what the hell he was doing. His adjustments on our rounds were bringing the fire back toward us, into Saudi Arabia.

In between shouting matches with the FSCC, Marshall and I recommended to Hardy that we shut the mission down. He considered it, but reminded us that the mission was, after all, coming from the regiment. We showed him the map Marshall had been using to track the impact of the rounds, and he, too, became skeptical of the mission, after which Marshall shut the FO down — just as we heard about the bulldozer.

Once again, the incident showed just how quickly something can get out of hand. It is a miracle we didn't kill a Marine that day.

Strangely enough, we got to meet the bulldozer driver a few hours later. On our first night in Kuwait, February 23, the combat engineers sent dozers out to build hasty protective berms around our vehicles, basically a bunch of sand pushed up to protect us from shrapnel. The dozer driver met Marshall and asked him, "Sir, why the hell were you trying to kill me the other day?" Marshall explained and, luckily, the dozer driver bore no grudges.

It's hilarious now, but when we heard the wild rumor about Iraqis in goat skins, we took it as seriously as the gospel, especially Jeffcoat. He and I discussed it for quite a while and came up with a scheme even more harebrained than a bunch of Iraqis playing goat. We decided that once we made it through the minefield, we'd put Schneider on top of my humvee, which had been outfitted — courtesy of Miller's ingenuity — with a wooden box across the top of the cab, and arm him with the jump's one machine gun. He would sit in the box with the gun mounted on the edge. His job would be to light up every herd of goats between us and Kuwait City. Schneider listened as we told him, and he nodded seriously, as if we'd just told him he would single-handedly attack a battalion of tanks.

After four abortive attempts to cross the border, Neal and I relaxed near my vehicle as I wrote in my journal as the day wore on. But, as so often happened, as soon as I began to write, Jeffcoat approached and yelled, "Let's go! On the road!"

We all scrambled into our vehicles for our move into Kuwait. A new solemnity — and fear — swept over us. Martin and I exchanged a look as he fired up the humvee. He was unusually quiet, and I noticed he wasn't griping.

We moved out under heavy, slate-gray clouds that gathered in the afternoon daylight. My vehicle led the pack as we got our first glimpse of the Kuwait border, easily distinguishable by the double row of sand berms built, we had been told, by the Saudis years earlier. If its purpose was to serve as a Middle East variant of the Maginot Line, it had about as much success. The border itself was unguarded, making it an easy task for combat engineers to puncture the berms with bulldozers and clear a path for vehicles. We drove through silently. I took several photographs to record the moment, which filled me with an odd sense of history. I was part of an invasion of another country.

We found our position, about four kilometers south of the first obstacle belt, easily enough — other elements of 1st Marine Division had already moved ahead of us hours before, creating a clear trail for us to navigate.

Once inside Kuwait, our whole demeanor changed. The "smoking and joking" common among Marines in the field was replaced with a cool detachment. We even spoke to each other softly, as if a loud voice might alert the Iraqis, now only a few miles ahead of us.

We set up the jump FDC quietly and quickly, did our comm checks with the main FDC, and then posed for a group photo. Miller and I had adorned the wooden box over the cab of our humvee with seventeen black silhouettes, representing the vehicles we'd killed at Khafji, and we gathered under the decoration for our only group photo of the war.

While we were doing so, we heard the familiar thump of rotor blades in the distance, to the west. We scrambled around, grabbing rifles and looking for defilade. We heard another sound, too, but this one didn't sound like a helicopter. Nobody could make it out. Then, breaking out of the clouds, a Marine UH-1 Huey appeared, slowly flying across our field of vision.

Then we could make sense of the noise. We heard the unmistakable voice of Robert Plant belting out the lyrics to Led Zeppelin's "Black Dog."

It was a surreal moment, like something out of *Apocalypse Now*, hearing rock and roll blaring out of a flying war machine. The helo was, most likely, on a psychological-operations mission designed to rattle the Iraqis — as if the tons of bombs falling on their heads hourly weren't doing the job.

The "Jump FDC" crew crossed the border into Kuwait at about 1700 on 23 Feb 1990. Dunes at center are man-made berms built by Saudis years before Desert Shield.

The Marines loved it. Grinning like madmen, they threw their fists into the air, pumping them in time to the music. A couple used their rifles as air guitars. The helo crew chief saw us and waved lazily as the Huey flew past us and out of sight. We laughed about the visit for a while then settled in to await the arrival of the rest of the battalion.

The main FDC lumbered into our position about 1800, set up in orderly fashion, then went quiet as Marines broke out shovels and started to dig in. To our north, the bedlam of the air campaign continued, shaking the ground beneath us. Also to our north, 3rd Marines prepared for its infiltration of the first minefield.

0600, 24 Feb 91, Inside Kuwait

Took our first casualties last night. About 1920, I was standing at the jump w/Schneider and Martin when we all heard incoming, followed by a tremendous explosion. Dove into the hole and heard a helo overhead. Was more confused than scared. Then we heard that the radar HMMWV had been taken out. Crawled out of my hole and looked to see the radar totally consumed. Lots of people running around. Checked the holes; Marines were all scared shitless.

Immediate confusion as to the direction of the rocket. Cpl. Crowe and WO Noem saw it come in, I heard it and we all said it came from the northwest, the same direction I heard the helo come from. I knew it was friendly fire, possibly a HARM.

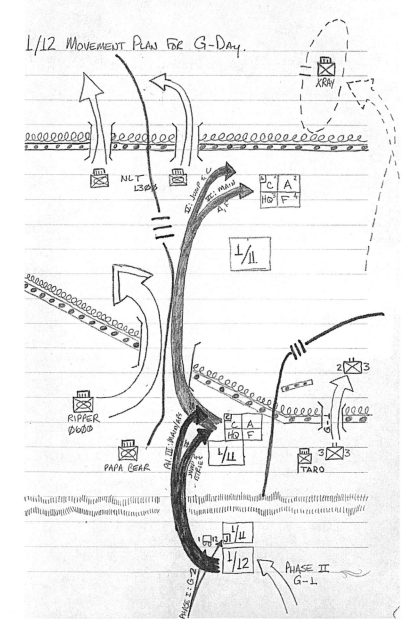

Most of 1st Marine Division moved into Kuwait one day before the ground war began, or G-1. As soon as was practicable, 1/12 expected to move to the second minefield on G-Day.

Papa Bear is in the breach now. Last night's bombing was just indescribable. It shook our hole and vehicle all night. We are very close to it. And it was incessant. Still going on; I'm jumpy as hell. We all flinch when we hear an impact, especially after last night. We go thru the breach in a few hours. We're in MOPP 1, *and doubly miserable because of the fucking rain.*

I was feeling pretty cocky the night Cpl. Aaron Pack died.

After the main body of the battalion moved into position, I spoke with Lt. Col. Rivers about our trip through the breach, scheduled for the next day. I'd enjoyed evening chow, which was actually pretty good, considering the cooks at regiment had been able to find us in Kuwait. All in all, things were going pretty well.

I had a cup of coffee in the main FDC with Jeffcoat, then walked to my vehicle to check on Martin and Schneider, who were understandably nervous on their first night in Kuwait.

I stepped under the canvas tarp stretched over the back of the humvee — we used it to keep light inside the vehicle. I briefed them on the next morning's activities. That's when I heard a shriek overhead, like the sound of a huge bedsheet being ripped, followed by the "tremendous explosion." At the same time, an enormous concussion slammed into the canvas, slapping my legs and nearly knocking me off balance. Without thinking, I dove outside toward my shallow hole, dragging Schneider with me. We landed heavily in the bottom, confused and frightened.

The "Jump FDC" group photo. Front row, left to right: CWO-2 Neal Noem is second from left in front row; Maj. Mike Jeffcoat second from left, back row. Author is at extreme right in back row. (Capt. Neal Noem, USMC)

When I looked up, I saw a huge ball of fire about 50 yards behind my vehicle. Our Q-38 counterbattery radar was completely engulfed in flames, along with the humvee next to it.

I swiveled my head around, thinking for some reason that we must be under attack from tanks. The thought didn't make sense, but it's all my mind would register. It sounded just like tank fire. I heard Marines screaming near the burning radar and saw silhouettes dashing around the flames.

I checked on Schneider and Martin. Both were in the hole and uninjured. I told them to stay put and scrambled away. I ran toward the burning vehicle, thinking there may be wounded Marines in the area. Neal Noem popped up in front of me, having climbed out of his hole a few yards away. We stopped and talked for a few seconds. He had two very scared radio operators in his hole, and we quickly took stock of our situation. Somebody said there had been a Marine in the humvee when the radar exploded.

By the time I got to the humvee, Jeffcoat was already there, pistol drawn, and staring grimly at the humvee. I had no idea who the dead Marine was, nor did anyone nearby.

Cpl. Pack had come to us from 11th Marines to man our counterbattery radar. Technically, he didn't belong to us, which explained why nobody in 1/12 immediately identified him. I stared for a long time at the fire, then walked slowly with Neal back to my vehicle.

I choked back anger and shock when I settled down in my hole, which Schneider had already begun to deepen. As he flung shovels of dirt into the night, I realized that we'd been hit by friendly fire. That realization angered me beyond description. To shrug it off, I helped Schneider dig.

Hours later, I finally decided to try to sleep, but that proved impossible. I curled up under a poncho liner in the bottom of our 6' hole, only to be jarred around like a pinball. The bombing, only about 4 miles distant, was like an evil chorus of hammers pounding at the earth, intent on destroying the Iraqis or driving them insane. It was driving me nuts, too. I lay in the damp earth in amazement of the maelstrom to my front and understood for the first time how combat troops get "shell shock." Dirt dribbled onto me every time a rackload of bombs hit the ground. The rolling barrage thundered unbroken, punctuated with crescendos and lulls.

Furious, I flung off my poncho liner and climbed into the back of my humvee, where it was just as noisy, but at least warmer. Mercifully, I dozed for a couple of hours before being rousted by Martin at dawn. He told me Rivers wanted me to do a crater analysis on the missile strike, a technique used to determine the direction of an incoming artillery round, rocket, or missile.

I met with Rivers and Jeffcoat in the main FDC for a few minutes. The night's bombing, and the missile strike, had taken a toll on all of us. We were all strung-out and jittery. At one point, we heard the high-pitched shriek of a jet aircraft flying very, very low. Jeffcoat and I locked eyes, then dove to the ground. Rivers followed suit. The plane passed overhead and we regained our seats, feeling sheepish.

I walked to the impact site. The destruction was sickening. About 15 yards from the humvee, I had to pick my way through equipment that had been shredded by hundreds of 5.56mm rounds that had cooked off following the explosion. An upturned Kevlar helmet demonstrated the effectiveness of its armor. Scores of bullet strikes covered the outside of the helmet, but none had penetrated. I studied the helmet, looking for a name, but found none. I began my work, studiously avoiding the gruesome sight of the humvee.

Crater analysis is a simple technique that requires examining the angle of the strike, any pieces of the round that remain, and the pattern of dirt and shrapnel spray.

In this case, the missile struck the ground less than 4' from the radar, ripping it to shreds. It had come from the northwest.

While I worked in drizzling rain, Miller and CWO-2 Tony Campagna, the battalion survey officer, showed up to help. I took a picture of Miller next to the crater, to give the shot some perspective. The photo turned out fuzzy and unusable, but that photo has a haunting quality to it that makes it hard for me to look at today.

From the bottom of the 3' deep crater, I pulled the remainder of a tail fin from a HARM missile, an American antiradar missile. Holding the piece of American hardware was like holding a hot coal as the confirmation hit me — Cpl. Pack had been killed by an American.

After I reported my findings to Rivers, I mentioned that Cpl. Pack's body was still in the vehicle. He ordered the corpsmen to retrieve him. I accompanied them, along with Maj. Hardy. The corpsmen, surprisingly, blanched at the sight, so Hardy and I, the only Marines there, took care of one of our own by retrieving him. I identified him from his dogtags and assisted the corpsmen in gathering the pertinent information to notify his next of kin.

I walked back to my vehicle overcome with despair. Perhaps I was still in shock, but I hadn't felt horrified or sickened by being face to face with my first combat death. My anguish came from knowing that Pack had been killed by an American missile. For years, the sight of his vehicle stayed in my mind.

Then, surprisingly, in early 1999, I was researching the Gulf War for an upcoming article in *Marine Corps Times*, where I worked as the managing editor. In the process, I came across a special supplement that *Army Times* had put together at the end of the war. One chapter dealt with the casualties, and the first page of the section opened with a two-column photo of Cpl. Pack taken the summer before he had been killed, during Desert Shield.

The photograph stunned me. My only memory of him was in death. At last, I had an image to remember him when he had been alive, young and happy.

· CHAPTER FOURTEEN ·

1320, 25 Feb 91

Crossed through the breach yesterday. It was somewhat disappointing. The "formidable" Iraqi defenses just weren't there. One thin minefield and single-strand concertina.

Unbelievable spectacle — vehicles from horizon to horizon going north. Ripper got through the second breach before Papa Bear was ever committed. They made it to Al-Jaber before midnight!

The trip through the first minefield was indeed anticlimactic, after months of preparing to slug our way through a wall of fire and shrapnel.

We got on the road in a cold drizzle just moments after receiving reports that 2nd Division had been gassed. The report rippled through the main FDC like electricity. Gunny Miller and I looked at each other and shook our heads as we heard the word passed on the radio. That report, we learned hours later, was false.

We got on the road shortly after and fell into a huge vehicle convoy. It seemed the entire 1st Marine Division was in single file, destination Kuwait City. Vehicles of all types stretched to the horizons, moving slowly but steadily.

As we approached the breach site — wearing MOPP suits and with sandbags in the floorboards to protect us against mines — I wondered what had become of the enemy. I saw numerous crumbling trench lines. Here and there a deteriorated bunker poked up from the undulating sand. We'd already heard reports of Iraqis appearing in these bunkers, hands up and hungry. What looked to be abandoned weapons emplacements dotted the landscape. Otherwise, southern Kuwait looked as desolate as the moon.

At the breach site, a Marine stood to the side of the now-sunken path through the minefield. He held up a very explicit photograph of a nude woman, obviously torn from a magazine. When he was sure he had our undivided attention, he turned the photograph around. On the back he had written in large red letters, "SLOW DOWN." I chuckled at his ingenuity.

Days before, Miller had rigged a couple of radio loudspeakers—"bitch boxes"—so that we could play cassette tapes through them. Miller opted to drive the vehicle through the minefield, so he and I listened to Pink Floyd's "The Wall" as we made our way through the breach. It seemed appropriate, given the unreal feel of the moment.

We sped up after we cleared the minefield and headed north. After what seemed like a couple of hours, we stopped on a rise within viewing distance of the second minefield. We had not heard a shot fired the entire time, and the radios had been surprisingly quiet.

Ahead of us, in what was supposed to be our next position, sat a cluster of AAVS and humvees. Marines were piled atop the AAVS smoking and joking. Curious, and a little irritated, I climbed out of my humvee and walked to the top of the rise, where a group of Marines peered into the valley below. When I asked what was going on, a Marine pointed.

On the valley floor sat a picket line of TOW humvees, idling. A few clicks in front of them, artillery rounds thudded into the sand, creating geysers of brown dirt.

Into the breach, literally. The "Jump FDC" passed through the first minefield early on G-Day, behind task forces Ripper and Papa Bear.

Startled, I asked no one in particular, "Who's doing the shooting?" I assumed the artillery was friendly, perhaps one of the 11th Marines battalions laying down a prep fire.

"Hell, sir, that's the Iraqis," called a grunt.

I thought, "What the hell?" and swiveled my head. To my left, several clicks away, I saw what looked like an Iraqi rocket or missile battery nestled behind a dune that hid it from the view of the TOW teams in the valley. Farther to my left, a pair of Cobras flitted like angry mosquitoes, spitting 20mm shells at the battery. I could see the tiny puffs of smoke erupt from the nose of the Cobras, followed by the strange ripping sound of the 20mm Gatling gun. Occasionally, I saw a bright orange blip near the Iraqi battery as one of the 20mm rounds found the mark.

It was the most surreal moment of the whole war. Dozens of Marines watched, as if at a football game, mildly curious as to the outcome of this duel between Marine air and Iraqi artillery. I popped a fresh pinch of Copenhagen in my lip, leaned against my humvee and became a spectator as well.

Then, the skies to my right began rumbling, and an AV-8B Harrier appeared, streaking across the valley floor. We all sat up, rapt, as the attack jet came at the Iraqis head-on. At the last second, the Harrier pulled up and released two bombs. We saw the silent orange blossom of a direct hit before we heard it, followed by a second hit, equally as devastating. Almost immediately, another Harrier repeated the attack, with exactly the same result. Scratch one Iraqi artillery unit. When the smoke settled, the dark forms that were the Iraqi unit were smoking and misshapen.

The attack evoked wild applause and cheering from the grunts and amtrackers, who scrambled back into their vehicles, fired up their engines and headed toward the second breach. The Cobras darted to and fro for a moment, then shot out of sight.

When they cleared out, we set up the jump and started coordinating fire missions, which were now coming quickly as Task Force Ripper closed on the MEF's intermediate objective, the airfield at Al-Jaber. Meanwhile, Task Force Papa Bear made its huge left turn out of the breach, in front of the massive Al-Burqan oilfield. Papa Bear got hit almost immediately by an Iraqi brigade that had been lurking in the nearby oilfield, which had been the reason for the sweeping turn in the first place.

By this time, the main FDC was up and running, and Miller and I scrambled to stay on top of the frantic radio calls coming across the nets. We got numerous reports from 1/11, also supporting Papa Bear, and at one time we believed that 1/11 had been attacked and had taken casualties. Initially, reports claimed that "A" Battery, 1/11, had been forced to engage

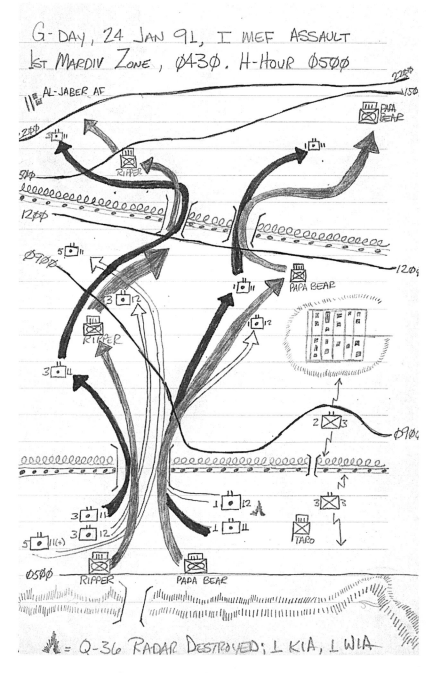

Movements of 1st Marine Division units on G-Day. Not to scale.

tanks with direct fire from its howitzers. This later proved to be false, the result of confusion by radio operators and forward observers. But at the time, we had no reason to doubt it. Papa Bear was duking it out with the Iraqis between the minefield and the oilfield at fairly close range. 3/11 and 5/11 were firing at a brisk rate, covering both Ripper and Papa Bear.

Soon, 1/12 was in the mix, processing and firing mission after mission. Throughout the day, 1/12 fired in support of three separate task forces, the only artillery battalion in the war to do so. At one point, we were actually processing three separate fire missions — simultaneously — for three separate task forces: Ripper, Papa Bear, and Taro, which kept all of us in the FDC on our toes. I lost count of the number of fire missions we coordinated. But at least three turned out to be right on the money. Soon after we arrived in position, I massed the battalion — in other words, ordered all the guns in the battalion to fire at once on the same target — on a mechanized brigade attempting to attack into Papa Bear's flank. The salvo stopped them cold as hundreds of DPICM bomblets rained down on them. Later, Marshall directed "A" Battery to fire rocket-assisted projectiles at an Iraqi bunker. The rounds destroyed it and prompted the survivors to surrender. Another accurate fire mission that day set the division CP abuzz. Under Marshall's direction, we caught another mechanized unit in the open, and we got the word that Maj. Gen. Myatt was talking about us.

While we fired, I saw Papa Bear fighting in the distance, the muzzle flashes from its M60 tanks lighting up the leaden sky. Hundreds of orange oil fires dotted the heavy, gray curtain of smoke on the horizon. Several times, I saw new orange flares blink into existence, which I presumed to be new oil fires started when the oil lines were punctured by tank rounds.

Once things settled down and Papa Bear began to overwhelm the Iraqis, I left the FDC to get some sleep. I was completely exhausted. Too tired to try and set up a hooch, I stopped at the first vehicle I came to, a pickup truck that belonged to our survey crew. I crawled under the tailgate, as "C" Battery, just meters to our front, opened fire. I fell asleep listening to rounds go downrange.

When I returned to the FDC three hours later, Marshall was on the radio with "C" Battery, who reported about 70 Iraqis to their front, arms up and ready to surrender. We quickly gathered them in and set up a "containment" area for them.

They were a ragged bunch. They looked like hell, and several had boots that were falling off their feet. Some had difficulty walking, a condition caused by the weeks of incessant bombing which had affected their equilibrium. A few had nosebleeds or bled from their ears. They hadn't eaten in days — every time a chow truck got on the road, it had been blown up. Marines, in a remarkable display of compassion, handed over MRES, field jackets, even poncho liners to the bedraggled soldiers, who hardly looked like the enemy. They just looked pitiful. We eventually got them fed and bedded down for the night. At daybreak, reserve Marines who were acting as POW control arrived to herd them south.

1130, 26 Feb 91

Events are happening too fast to keep up with. 270 tanks of the RGFC destroyed, and the general giving the brief to the media said that was a conservative estimate. Ripper went north of Al-Jaber at 0600, hoping to be about 5 Km south of Kuwait Internat'l by nightfall. They were there by 0830. No resistance, hardly, and we are surging forward. 3rd Marines took 20 POWs last night, dozens this a.m. The Iraqi 6th Mech Division was reportedly coming to counterattack at Al-Jaber last night — at 45% strength. That never materialized.

1/12 and Taro are in a "backwater." Everybody is ahead of us!

RGFC is FINALLY out of its holes moving south, and, in Col. Howard's words, being slaughtered. Air is wreaking havoc. Iraqis are killing civilians as they pull out of Kuwait City, probably so as not to leave witnesses of the atrocities. Lots of executions, decapitations, rapes. Fighting going on in Kuwait City. 22,000+ POWs. Last night the Iraqis reported that they "intend to pull out of Kuwait." We ignored them. Too late now. We'll push them out. Hell, they're retreating forward, into us, to surrender.

I could barely conceal my excitement as I scribbled furiously in my journal, trying to keep track of events, which seemed to be occurring at light speed.

Nesbit had given up trying to keep up with the situation map in the FDC. His felt-tip pen outlines of Iraqi units changed so often they looked like one big red smear. At one point, he said, "Ah fuck it," and swiped a rag across the acetate, obliterating half the Iraqi army. We all laughed loudly, realizing that Lynn had just provided the perfect metaphor for the destruction of Saddam's army.

It provided a break in the tension, which had built up for days, starting with Cpl. Pack's death. We were all exhausted and short-tempered. When Matthews, recently returned from liaison duty, came into the FDC flinging his web gear —complete with dangling grenades, John Wayne style — to the ground, I turned and screamed at him to "get the hell out of my FDC with those fucking grenades" before he killed somebody. He and I had never gotten along, and I wasn't about to start now, in the middle of fire missions.

Around noon we got the word to move out through the second breach, which we did quickly. The drive through the breach lanes was about as disappointing the second time, but the destruction before us was much more impressive. As we closed on the ominous oil fires belching acrid black smoke into the sky from the Al-Burqan oilfields, we passed two dead M60 tanks — Marine tanks, a subtle reminder that this war was very real, despite all the unreal moments we'd experienced.

We skirted around the southwestern edge of the oilfield, where Papa Bear had fought a brief but sharp fight, and through the remains of hundreds of Iraqi positions. The evidence of the battle was everywhere: blown-apart bunkers, gutted vehicles, discarded weapons and gear.

While we were making our way to our position, the radios came alive up and down the battalion column. Task Force Ripper had blown through the entire Iraqi army, impelling the division forward all the way to Kuwait City. We were told to follow and to close on the Kuwait International Airport to support an attack by the division. And we were to do so as fast as possible. Already, Marine and Iraqi tanks were exchanging fire in the vicinity of the airport. We still had nearly seventy kilometers to cover — through devastated terrain.

The Al-Burqan oilfield was an inferno. Hundreds of fires raged from ruptured pipelines, and waves of heat rippled over us, forcing us to turn

By G-2, the 1st Marine division was moving so fast we could hardly keep up with where the enemy was, or was supposed to be. Here, I jokingly point to our destination, Kuwait City. Note journal in my right hand.

our faces away. As we neared the steel-piping refinery structure, smoke enveloped us. The oil became so thick in the air that vehicles were covered in a black, sticky rain of crude oil. The day turned to an eerie twilight, even though it was only about 1500, as we picked our way through the devastation. At times it was hard to see beyond the hood of the humvee.

There were defenses around the oilfield, but they were pitiful—what there was left of them. We expected to see World War II-style concrete bunkers. The Iraqis had had six months to build what should have been impregnable defenses, but all we saw were fighting holes with parapets of sand. There was very little overheard cover left on any of the weapons emplacements. Some had been blown off by countless bombs; on others, it was obvious that no overhead protection had ever been erected. There wasn't even any evidence of construction materials, such as sandbags or timbers. The Iraqis, it appeared, had scrounged for cinder blocks, sheet metal, even footlockers filled with sand to stack around the edges of the holes as a parapet. One hole, for example, had *one sheet* of corrugated tin over it for overhead cover—the equivalent of a sheet of toilet paper against a B-52 raid.

The devastation of the battlefield was shocking. Rockeye cluster bomb canisters littered the ground. Tanks, APCs, trucks, and gear were strewn across the entire desert, mauled and burned, seemingly tossed about by a giant, invisible hand. I counted fifteen T-62 tanks and five other vehicles destroyed. The tanks were completely gutted. Smashed artillery pieces and antiaircraft guns lay with their muzzles pointed skyward. Everywhere I looked, I saw an ungodly tableau of destruction and death.

There were also bodies, in green uniforms, scattered across the desert, most probably long dead. One group near the dirt track leading us north had apparently been caught in the open near an APC, and had paid for it. Their bodies lay piled near the ramp of the vehicle. One soldier lay only feet from the road, alone, with his trousers unbuckled. Martin and I stared at his already blackening body riddled with wounds and surmised that he probably had walked off to relieve himself and gotten killed in the process. Interestingly, I saw lots of Iraqi gas masks lying around. They must have been in one hell of a hurry, I thought, to leave their masks behind.

We lumbered into a position near the airport well after dark, a darkness made impenetrable by the dense cloud of oil smoke. At one point, I thought it was raining and told Martin to turn on the windshield wipers. When the wipers smeared the glass, I stuck my hand outside the window, and pulled it back. It was covered in oil. I shook my head and prayed that the stuff wasn't poisonous.

The Al-Burqan oilfield was an inferno. Numerous fires caused thick clouds of smoke that drifted over the battlefield.

Around midnight, the wind shifted and blew in from the Gulf. It swept the clouds away and lit up the sky with the hellish glow of a thousand screaming oil wells. The midnight sky glowed bright orange. It was a spooky feeling, and Dante's Inferno kept coming to mind. The eerie glow would continue for a day or so as the wind turned daylight into night and nighttime into a glowing, orange day. We were able to at least see our surroundings, though. We were about seven kilometers south of the airport, in some kind of quarry, which made walking around the numerous pits a tricky feat in the darkness.

We fired one mission from that position. "C" Battery fired illumination rounds for an assault by Ripper that didn't amount to much. Exhausted beyond description but unable to sleep, Jeffcoat, Neal, and I talked until dawn, discussing the ongoing slaughter of the Republican Guards and the 21 Iraqi divisions in Kuwait. They were trapped, with only one way out — the road from Kuwait City that became known as the "Highway of Death." We also took pictures of each other, slathered in oil and soot, and hoisting captured AK-47s and machine guns. After the war, when those pictures were developed, I was shocked at my appearance. I was thinner than I had imagined, and appeared even more exhausted than I thought I was at the time.

When daylight finally came, we saw that we had occupied an Iraqi T-72 tank battalion position. We set about looting the bunkers for whatever souvenirs we could find, even after the grunts had undoubtedly picked

Top: A gutted T-62 Iraqi tank destroyed by Marine forces. Note burning oil well in background. *Bottom:* This destroyed Iraqi armored vehicle demonstrates the lethality of American firepower, as wielded by the 1st Marine division. (Capt. Neal Noem, USMC)

through them. All I was able to collect was an Iraqi uniform, cartridge belt, the epaulets of an Iraqi lieutenant, and a canteen — hardly war booty.

I was not impressed with the bunkers or the tanks. The tanks that were still in one piece probably couldn't have made it to the city — which we could see from our position — on their own power. The tracks were coated in rust, the insides were filthy, and none looked like they had seen a drop of grease in months. The crews never stood a chance.

While we meandered through the wreckage, somebody near the FDC began shouting. We trotted back just in time to hear a Marine yell "The war's over!" A dozen lusty cheers went up. I stopped in my tracks and said a silent prayer.

It was over in just two days. I was alive and I would be going home soon. I smiled. As I began walking back to the FDC, I began stripping off my sooty, foul-smelling MOPP suit.

Later that day, I loaded up half a dozen Marines in my humvee and took them into Kuwait City, the city we had liberated. We felt like conquering heroes, but we didn't know how to play the part. We were exhausted and filthy and in culture shock as we rolled down paved streets between modern buildings. I felt as if I had passed from one world to another, and in some ways I had.

We drove through the looted, destroyed city blocks, viewing the Iraqis' handiwork. All the pity I had felt for the prisoners we'd taken days before now turned to utter rage. Everything had been sacked. Expensive cars lay crippled on the roadside, their wheels torn off, doors missing, glass shattered. Stores had been completely emptied. I walked, in shock, past a shoe store that held nothing but a seven-foot pile of empty shoeboxes. Oddly enough — and in a revealing statement on the attackers — the bookstore

The "Jump" in action in Kuwait. Note the reduced size of the unit from December. By the time the ground war started, we were able to set up this miniaturized fire direction center in a matter of minutes. (Capt. Neal Noem, USMC)

The battalion's final position was an abandoned Iraqi tank unit's perimeter just outside Kuwait International Airport. These vehicles had been hit with what appeared to be tank rounds. (Capt. Neal Noem, USMC)

next door was left largely untouched, its rows of textbooks still neatly aligned on the shelves.

The heart of the city was alive, though. I saw a perfect symbol for the Kuwaitis' survival. Martin and I had pulled to the curb to get our bearings in the huge modern city. As he tried to make heads or tails of a tourist map, I noticed a scruffy, half-starved cat limp out of a building. The gray cat looked like he'd spent the last hour or so in a laundry dryer, but he managed to stroll down the street with aplomb, unfazed by the destruction around him.

After a few turns in the downtown portion of the city, we unexpectedly found ourselves driving through a huge, impromptu parade of screaming, singing, crying Filipinos and Arabs, all of whom wanted to hug us, kiss us, and press a small paper Kuwaiti flag in our hands. I was nearly pulled from the humvee as Martin tried to avoid the swarm of humanity. Young Filipino women mobbed us at every turn, and for a brief second, I thought I was in Manila, not Kuwait City. And I must have shaken the hands of a hundred old men that morning.

The spectacle before us was the reason we had come to this country. Huge Kuwaiti flags draped out nearly every apartment building and welcomed us in the gentle breeze. All the anger and frustration of the previous six months began melting away in the hundreds of smiles I now saw.

"Thank you for saving our country!"

Nearly every building in Kuwait City was sacked by Iraqi troops. Note sandbags at right. (Capt. Neal Noem, USMC)

"We love U.S. Marines!"

"We love USA!"

We heard it over and over. I could only smile and nod. I was afraid to speak. Somewhere along the line, someone gave me a ragged, soot-covered Kuwaiti flag, which I still have.

The trip to Kuwait City taught me a lot. It taught me that the human spirit knows no bounds, and cannot be defeated. People who had lost everything offered me something to drink. I realized these people had climbed from the pit of inhumanity, the depths of sorrow, to stand on their feet, not because they wanted to be seen, but because they only wanted to stand with dignity. In Kuwait City, ragged, thin children smiled and flashed the "V" sign, the same sign that a few months earlier had made me suspicious. Now, I couldn't have cared less. It was a "V" for victory, a peace sign, a symbol of the Palestinian struggle. It was a simple gesture that meant many things to many people. I smiled and returned the sign. Even today, I find myself flashing it to people, especially children.

As we left the city I reached into my trouser cargo pocket and took out the small green notebook that I had used for a journal, my little green friend.

I climbed into my vehicle and began to write as Martin began the drive back to the battalion position.

"Can't describe the relief I feel," I wrote, staring at the late-afternoon skyline of Kuwait City, alabaster against the oily black clouds. *"Relief at being alive, knowing that I'm going home whole and safe, not having the threat of injury or death hanging over my head. It's like being given a second chance at life, and it's something that I plan to take advantage of."*

· CHAPTER FIFTEEN ·

My war ended far more abruptly than it had begun.

We pulled out of Kuwait City on March 2, and picked our way past the destroyed Iraqi army along the coastal highway. Near Khafji and the Saudi border, I surveyed the remnants of the mechanized division that had tried to attack us, the division I'd helped destroy. The sight was gruesome and awe-inspiring. Blackened, twisted war machines, huge and grotesque, lay like elephant carcasses in the sand and across the asphalt. Death lay everywhere in piles of bloody rags, footprints, bloodstains, and broken weapons. Many men had died here, and their deaths had been violent and painful. The images stayed in my mind until we reached Manifa Bay. In our months in the Middle East, we had literally come full circle.

We thought we'd be home soon, but it would be another agonizing six weeks before we actually boarded a chartered plane out of a place I'd come to regard as a stinking hell-hole, Manifa Bay. Hundreds of Marines were crammed into tents in this dustbowl near the coast. At times, the frustration and inaction — and the bullshit of a military bureaucracy — pushed all of us to the edge of insanity.

Luckily, I had the wise counsel of Neal Noem and Lynn Nesbit, two warrant officers I had come to regard as close friends. Neal and I spent hour upon hour reading, listening to music and talking in musty, cramped, dirty tents as we watched dozens of units head home ahead of us, a frustrating experience that seemed to have no end. The policy of "First in, first out," didn't seem to apply to 1/12. Days turned into weeks, and soon the entire battalion was in a state of near-mutiny as we watched units that had come to Saudi Arabia long after we did board planes bound for the United States. Neal's mature perspective and patient ear kept me grounded and allowed me to keep my perspective, even when I didn't want to.

Finally, after nearly six weeks of waiting, we got the word to break camp and move to Jubayl airport.

1807, 13 Apr 1991

Currently over Alexandria, Egypt, and the Nile on a beautiful, crystal-clear evening. Heading across the Med to Brussels, then on to Bangor, Maine, for a "heroes welcome," whatever that is. Supposed to be a big deal, to hear the stews tell it. They have sandwiches and beer waiting for us. That will be awesome. From there, we go to San Francisco, then to Hickam AFB.

Can't believe we're actually going home! Sitting in first class on a 747, kicked way back in a seat, w/a full belly, watching a movie with Morgan. Big-time culture shock just being around flushing toilets again. The crew is giving us the royal treatment. I'll not soon forget the sound of 400 Marines cheering their brains out as we left the ground.

1st Battalion, 12th Marines left Saudi Arabia on 13 April 1991, nearly seven and a half months after deploying.

We climbed aboard a 747 with an exceptionally friendly crew and settled in for a long flight to The World. Steve Morgan and I sat in first-class seats and ate the first decent food we'd had in weeks. The food, in fact, was too rich for us—all of us—after months of field chow and MRES. In only a few hours, every head on the plane was out of commission. It didn't matter to most of us, though. We were asleep as soon as we finished eating.

We landed briefly in Brussels, but weren't allowed off the plane. I couldn't have cared less, for I had no intention of leaving the aircraft until I was in the United States.

0511 (EST), 14 Apr 91

En route to San Francisco. Reception in Bangor was unbelievable. A real victory celebration. Got in at 2330; snow on the ground (quite a sight), 36 degrees. Filed in the terminal through a gauntlet of cheering women, handshaking vets, mostly from Vietnam. Funny, after the disgraceful way America treated its Vietnam vets, those men organized our reception. Morgan and I hit the bar, along with nearly every Marine on the plane.

The experience was enough to move one to tears. Shook so many hands. I was literally stunned while walking through the throngs of people, who were sincerely grateful. All I could say was, "You're welcome," to their "thank yous."

Girls asked for my autograph, boys wanted to know what my job was. An indescribable feeling of joy hit me when I realized I was back in the USA. Told many of the younger Marines to soak it up and remember it a long time because they may never see it again. CO made an outstanding off-the-cuff speech, and the crowd loved it.

Our first landfall in the United States was Bangor, Maine, where the locals had made a name for themselves by greeting every plane that brought home Desert Storm veterans.

As we stepped out of the tunnel into the airport, I was completely unprepared for the reception.

First to greet us was a group of graying Vietnam veterans, who stood just inside the tunnel. Most were in their colors, and most had tears in their eyes. I stepped in front of them and looked into those eyes, eyes that had seen more horror than I could imagine, and I wept unashamedly. I was humbled that they should greet me. We should have been honoring them. I shook hands with half a dozen vets, none of whom said a word. They simply nodded, understanding, and nudged me into the gauntlet of humanity awaiting us in the terminal.

Hundreds of people lined the small building, forming a tunnel of human arms touching, patting, and hugging us as we struggled through the bedlam. I was too stunned to react, and I nodded numbly and followed the camouflaged back of the Marine in front of me. Our path wound snake-like to the airport bar, where the bartender worked furiously to set up enough drinks for the thirsty Marines.

After seven and a half months of temperance, we were all cheap drunks. One beer set us wobbling. We careened back onto the plane after a gracious speech by Rivers and several impromptu "thank-yous" from giddy Marines. Before we left, I called Angie from a pay phone and told her what I'd been waiting to tell her for months: "I'll be home in a few hours." I told her to meet me with my wedding band, my Rolex watch, and a cold beer.

And she did.

Hours later, we stepped off the plane on a brilliant Hawaii morning, the scent of the tropics an aphrodisiac to the senses.

We traveled through the somnolent streets of Oahu to the windward side and Marine Corps Air Station Kaneohe Bay, where our families awaited. Oahu residents lined the streets that led over the spine of Oahu. They waved yellow ribbons and American flags. It was a wonderful sight. When we finally pulled up to the battalion headquarters, I stepped off the bus and, at last, into the waiting arms of my wife.

Angie and I held each other for a very long time in the battalion's parking lot, the same spot where I'd left her months ago. When I slipped my wedding ring back on my finger, I felt as if I were marrying Angie all over again. I had made it home to her, and that was all that mattered to me.

· E P I L O G U E ·

I left active duty in 1996, after being passed over twice for promotion to major, a result of the Schofield Barracks firing incident. Angie and I took our two children, Katie and Jake, back to Mississippi.

I chose a career in journalism, the career I had considered on those long nights in Saudi Arabia. I started writing this book several times but always stopped, for various reasons.

Finally I did write it — and in the course of writing, I've learned that I am, in fact, a changed person from the swaggering, invincible young captain who climbed aboard a C-5 back in 1990. In some ways I'm a better person for the experience, and in some ways I'm worse.

It took years for me to fully understand that I came home with a tremendous amount of anger:

Home at last. Angie and I were reunited on a beautiful tropical morning nearly eight months after I departed Hawaii.

anger at losing friends, anger at being separated from my wife for so many months, anger at the military bureaucracy that toyed with our lives, anger at the American public who thought the war was clean and antiseptic and death-free.

And even anger from a feeling that we didn't get it right the first time — or that we weren't allowed to get it right. Saddam is still in power, and American troops still dash to the Gulf at the first sign of trouble. And I still hope my son doesn't have to go finish the job we didn't.

It was only after several interviews about my experience with apparent chemical weapons attacks that I began to understand this anger. It surfaced slowly, over a period of weeks as I relived the memories of those months and reread the entries to my journal. It took months to work the anger out of my system, to purge my soul and start over again. I still have a ways to go.

The Gulf War wasn't the World War II experience. And it wasn't Korea or Vietnam. But it was my experience. And because it's mine, that brief war will always mark me. For better or for worse.

MILITARY HISTORY OF PHILLIP THOMPSON

Phillip Thompson, a native of Columbus, Mississippi, served as an active-duty Marine Corps officer for more than 12 years.

He received his commission as a second lieutenant in May 1984 after graduating from Ole Miss. After training as an artillery officer, he was assigned to 5th Battalion, 11th Marines, in Twentynine Palms, California. During this tour, he served as a forward observer, battery fire direction officer and battery executive officer.

In 1987, Thompson attended Naval Aviation Observer School at Marine Corps Air Station New River, North Carolina, then reported aboard the battleship USS *Missouri* (BB-63) for duties as Marine Detachment Executive Officer. While aboard the *Missouri*, he deployed to the Persian Gulf to participate in Operation Earnest Will, the escorting of re-flagged Kuwaiti tankers through the Straits of Hormuz during the Iran-Iraq war. Thompson also qualified as officer of the deck (inport).

Following sea duty and his promotion to captain in August 1989, Thompson attended the Field Artillery Officers' Advanced Course at Fort Sill, Oklahoma. He then reported to 1st Battalion, 12th Marines, at Marine Corps Air Station Kaneohe Bay, Hawaii. Assigned duties as the battalion operations officer, he deployed with 1/12 in August 1990 at the outset of Operation Desert Shield.

Following the war, Thompson served as the commanding officer of Alpha Battery 1/12. He also served as the aide-de-camp to the commanding general, Fleet Marine Force Pacific; and as the Deputy Force Public Affairs Officer. In this last duty, he planned and helped execute the Marine Corps' participation in the 50th Anniversary of World War II in the Pacific, during which he covered the events as a journalist at Guadalcanal, Tarawa and Kwajalein.

In 1994, Thompson reported to the Marine Corps Air Ground Combat Center in Twentynine Palms, California, for duty as the base public affairs officer, a position he held until he left active duty in 1996. He was promoted to major in the Marine Corps Reserve in 1997, and was honorably discharged in 1999.

His decorations include the Meritorious Service Medal, the Navy-Marine Corps Achievement Medal with two gold stars in lieu of a second and third award, the Combat Action Ribbon, the Navy Unit Commendation, the Meritorious Unit Commendation, the Navy Efficiency "E" Ribbon, the Armed Forces Expeditonary Medal, the National Defense Service Medal, the Southwest Asia Service Medal with three bronze stars, the Kuwait Liberation Medal (Saudi Arabia), the Kuwait Liberation Medal (Kuwait) and the Sea Service Deployment Ribbon with three bronze stars. He is a member of the 1st Marine Division Association.

· I N D E X ·

Abu Hadriyah 35, 37–38, 39, 47, 48, 76, 80, 87
Admire, Col. John 4, 9, 75, 90, 99, 115, 116, 133, 136, 142, 149
Al-Burqan oilfield 150, 168, 172–73, 174
Al-Jaber airfield 150, 168, 172–73, 174
Al-Jubayl 12, 17–18, 21–23, 26, 28, 37, 43, 50, 95, 98, 100, 101, 111, 113, 114, 180
Almanza, SSgt. Michael 23–24, 46
Al-Mishab 66, 87, 91, 97, 98, 99
Al-Qarrah 148
Al-Wafrah oilfield 112, 136, 138, 142
An Nahriyah 26, 46, 28
Aramco 39
Avenetti, GySgt. Quint 138–41, 45

Bahrain 101, 105
Bangor, Maine 181–82
The Basic School 21, 34
Beirut, Lebanon 17, 21
Berlin Wall, collapse of 3, 45
Boomer, Lt. Gen. Walter 49, 65, 139
Bush, President George H.W. 9, 17, 25, 41, 66, 71, 73, 109, 150, 157

Cable News Network (CNN) 13, 22, 110, 129
Camp Lejeune Marine Corps Base, North Carolina 85
Camp Pendleton Marine Corps Base, California 85

Campagna, CWO-2 Tony 164
Caputo, Philip 40
Carlucci, Lt.Col. Nicholas "Nick" 2
Cheney, Secretary of Defense Richard 109
Connor, Sgt. Holly 31
Cook, Maj. Carl (USA) 101–05, 149
Crowe, Cpl. Sam 78, 154, 160

Dean, Maj. Scott 34–35, 42, 43, 50, 51
Dhahran 46, 101
Diego Garcia 18
Draude, Brig. Gen. Tom 77–78, 123–34

Ewing, LCpl. 97
Exercise Imminent Thunder 71–72

Fields of Fire 40–41
Forrest, Lt.Gen. Nathan Bedford (CSA) 66
Fort Irwin, California 80
Fort Sill, Oklahoma 1, 3–4, 14, 21, 34–35, 45, 72, 79, 154, 187

Gates, LCpl. 78, 128, 154
Gray, Gen. Alfred 85–86, 91
Guadalcanal 40, 188
Guadalcanal Diary 40
Gulf War Syndrome 45, 112–113

Haii 3 33–34, 35, 40, 42, 44, 54, 55, 76, 85, 93, 104

Haddad, Capt. Rich 51–52, 53, 57, 66, 67–68, 92

Hardy, Maj. Barry 136, 151, 155, 158, 164

Head, Capt. Dave 56

"Hollywood Marines" 85

Howard, Col. Patrick G. 21, 34, 35, 46, 59, 61, 70–71, 72, 73, 76, 90, 99, 171

Huenfeld, Capt. Rich 50, 53

Jeffcoat, Maj. Mike 132, 140, 141, 149, 153, 157–58, 159, 162–64, 174

Jones, Capt. Mitch 34–35

Kaneohe Bay, Marine Corps Air Station 4, 10–11, 182

Khafji 48, 59, 87, 89, 110, 112, 114, 116, 123, 130, 132–33, 145, 147, 149, 153, 159; battle of 135–44

Kowalski, Capt. Bruce 126

Kuhn, Brig. Gen. Coleman D 84

Kuwait City 22, 26, 99, 150, 166, 171, 172, 174, 176–79, 180

Kwajalein 188

McCarthy, Capt. Pete 15, 143

Manifa Bay 146, 180

Marine Corps Air Ground Combat Center (MCAGCC) 1

Marine Corps Units *see end of Index*

Marshall, 1st Lt. Jack: in combat 138, 141, 145, 151, 157–58, 170; conversations with 100, 108, 111, 147–48, 149, 150; introduced to 4; Khafji "dress rehearsal" 133; MVV files 34; raid planning 125, 131, 134–35; at U-Tapao, Thailand 15

Martin, LCpl. Rob 78, 98, 99, 109, 125, 154, 155, 159, 160, 162–63, 173, 177, 178

Massey, Capt. Tim 125, 126, 127

Matthews, Capt. Richard 12, 97, 111, 132, 171

Miller, GySgt. Robert 78, 80, 86, 92, 93, 108, 111, 124, 125, 126, 127, 128–29, 131, 154, 158, 159, 161, 164, 165, 168

Molofsky, Capt. Joe 15, 17

Morgan, Capt. Steve 65, 76–77, 137, 181

Myatt, Maj.Gen. Mike 68, 69, 70, 71–72, 93–94, 139, 155, 170

Nesbit, CWO-2 Lynn 92, 97–98, 116, 126, 147, 171, 180

Noem, CWO-2 Neal: in combat 126, 130, 139, 160, 162–63, 174; establishment of jump FDC 79–80; leadership abilities of

100, 117, 153–54; relationship with 64, 86, 92, 108, 109–110, 147, 158, 180–81; showers 93, 96

Noem, Stacey 108

Oahu 4, 10–12, 15

Ole Miss 1, 26, 112, 114, 187

Operation Earnest Will, 2, 187

Pack, Cpl. Aaron 162–65, 171

Palm, Lt.Col. Leslie M. 2

Panama, invasion of 3, 51–52

Pennell, Lt. (USN) Grady 90–91

Pohakaloa Training Area (PTA) 4, 57

Powell, Gen. Colin 41, 55, 65

Reed, LCpl. 78, 128, 154

Republican Guard (RGFC) 36, 46, 105, 110, 134, 148, 150, 171, 174

Rivers, Lt.Col. Rob: in combat 109, 111, 126–29, 131, 133, 138, 140–41, 162–64; commanding officer, 1/12 10; debrief of battle of Khafji 145; and 11th Marines 25, 34; establishment of jump FDC 76; and heliborne raid mission 88–89, 91, 97, 98, 99; orders to Saudi Arabia 13; raid planning 125; speech at Bangor, Maine, airport 182; and trip to Bahrain 101

Riyadh 43, 68

Rollings, Col. Wayne 84

rules of engagement 17, 19–20

A Rumor of War 40

Saddam Hussein: combat power against 58, 69–71; during Desert Storm 110, 134, 138, 148, 150, 171, 185; "Howling at the Moon Theory" 24–25; intentions 20–22, 26, 29, 41–42, 46–48, 54, 61, 63–65, 92, 99, 107; invasion of Kuwait 9–10; military capabilities 30; mistress targeted 104; regime of 55, 66; use of "human shields" 17

Sanders, Capt. Bill 20–21, 23, 44

Schneider, PFC Kyle 78, 125, 154, 158, 160, 162–63

Schroeder, Sen. Patricia 29

Schwarzkopf, Gen. Norman H 48–49, 65, 150

7 Armour Division (RA) 76

Soviet Union 10, 45, 47

Speights, Capt. Jeff 24, 26, 30, 114, 153

Speights, Tammy 24, 26

Stuart, Lt.Col. Lynn 21, 34, 35, 54, 59, 76

Tarawa 62, 82, 187

Thompson, Angie: after Gulf War 5; at Fort Sill 2; mail from 39, 53, 56–57, 61, 67, 70, 82–83, 101; New Year's Day 95; phone calls to 42–43, 51, 100; pre–invasion letter to 155; prior to deployment to Saudi Arabia 10, 13; relationship with Speights family 26; religious denomination of 74; reunited with 182–83, 184; separation from, effects of 108–09; TV interview 129; at Twentynine Palms 3

Thompson, Jake 184

Thompson, Katie 184

Thompson, Renee 92

Thorp, Capt. James K. 112–14, 116

Tregaskis, Richard 40

Turqii, Col. 142, 149

Twentynine Palms, California 1, 3, 13, 21, 23, 24, 34, 57, 60, 187, 188

United Nations 41

U.S. Army units: 3rd Armored Cavalry Regiment (3rd ACR) 46; XVIII Airborne Corps 24, 46; 24th Mechanized Division 13, 20, 22, 26, 46, 48; 25th Infantry Division (Light) 101; 82nd Airborne Division 10, 13, 22; 101st Airborne Division 20; 212th Brigade 46

U.S. Central Command (CENTCOM) 49

U.S. Marine Corps Units *see end of Index*

USS *Constellation* 21

USS *Independence* 42

USS *Missouri* 2, 10, 12, 51, 61, 101–04, 108, 109, 110, 187

USS *Wisconsin* 10, 41, 46, 61, 107, 110; during port visit in Bahrain 101–105

University of Mississippi *see* Ole Miss

U-Tapao, Thailand 15–17

Vancouver, Canada 12

Vietnam 5, 31, 40, 55, 78, 181–82

Vontungeln, Maj. Mike 76, 134

Walker, Lt. (USN) Chris 101

Webb, James 40–41

Yuma, Arizona, Marine Corps Air Station 26

U.S. Marine Corps Units are indexed in the order of battle.

Fleet Marine Forces Pacific 47, 187

I Marine Expeditionary Force (MEF) 9, 22, 26, 29, 49, 115, 116, 121–22, 126, 168

    Marine Air Group 16 (MAG 16) 95

        Marine Medium Helicopter Squadron 165 (HMM-165) 95

        Marine Medium Helicopter Squadron 161 (HMM-161) 100

    Task Force Cunningham 76

    Task Force Gecko 89, 98, 145, 148

    Task Force Papa Bear 153, 166, 167, 168, 170, 172

    Task Force Ripper: during Desert Shield 26–27, 28, 75; during ground war 166–68, 170–72, 174

    Task Force Shepherd 58–60, 75, 98, 133 135, 136

    Task Force Taro 75–76, 86, 109,115, 121–22, 148–49, 150, 170, 171

    Task Force Troy 157

    Task Force X-Ray 155

1st Force Service Support Group 30

1st Marine Division: organization for combat 26–27; headquarters, zones during Desert Shield 35, 38, 48, 59; arrival of 2nd Marine Division 85; sandtable 94; Task Force Gecko 98; Gulf War Syndrome investigations 112; artillery raids 124, 129; movements around Khafji 132–33; during battle of Khafji 137–39; movements west 142; preparation for ground offensive 150, 153, 159, 161; during invasion of Kuwait 166; movements in Kuwait 172, 175

    1st Marine Regiment 153

    1st Tank Battalion 136

    3rd Battalion, 9th Marines (3/9) 58, 75; "I" Company 133

    7th Marine Regiment 20, 22, 26

    11th Marine Regiment 21, 23, 24–27, 34, 35, 37–39, 46–48, 51, 52, 55, 57, 63, 76, 83, 92, 45, 133, 135, 150, 154, 155, 168

        1st Battalion (1/11) 153, 155, 168

        3rd Battalion (3/11): 20, 23, 28, 76, 132, 170; "G" Battery 83, 85

5th Battalion, (5/11) 20, 24, 28, 43, 108, 170, 187; "N" Battery 2, 21; "G" Battery, 3rd Battalion, 12th Marines 1; "N" Battery, 5th Battalion, 12th Marines 1, 23, 146; "S" Battery, 5th Battalion, 12th Marines 24, 146

4th Marine Expeditionary Brigade (MEB) 66

5th Marine Expeditionary Brigade (MEB) 157

1st Marine Expeditionary Brigade (MEB) 4, 9, 22, 84

3rd Marine Regiment (*see also* Task Force Taro): during Desert Shield 14, 20, 21, 28, 75–76, 87–88, 90, 99, 101, 111, 112, 114, 116; during Desert Storm 121, 123, 125, 131, 135, 137, 139, 140, 141, 143, 149, 150, 151–52, 157, 158, 160, 171

1st Battalion, 3rd Marines 155

1st Battalion, 12th Marines (1/12): assignment to 4; preparations for deployment 11; attachment to 11th Marines 21, 25–26, 34–35; defense of "The Triangle" 28; suspected infiltrators 42; rotation back to U.S. 63–64; return of Capt. Phillip Thompson 76; establishment of jump FDC 79–80; assignment of heliborne raid mission 87–88, 90, 99–100, 101; movement west 112, 148–49; artillery raids 121, 124–25; departure of Maj. Mike Vontungeln 134; battle of Khafji 136–38, 143, 145; at Manifa Bay 146; movement into Kuwait 150, 151, 153, 161, 163; ground war mission assignments 155; in combat 170–71; return to Hawaii 180–81, 187

"A" Battery: 56–57, 84, 111, 121, 125, 130, 131–32, 133, 136–141, 170, 187

"C" Battery: 65, 115, 121, 125, 130, 133, 136–37, 139–41, 151, 170, 174

"F" Battery: 111, 115–16, 121, 122–23, 125, 126, 128, 129, 130, 131, 133

3rd Battalion, 3rd Marines (3/3) 115, 116, 133, 138, 141, 157

II Marine Expeditionary Force (II MEF) 85

2nd Marine Division 69, 85–86, 150, 166; 10th Marine Regiment 69